RACE, RHETORIC, AND RESEARCH METHODS

PERSPECTIVES ON WRITING

Series Editors, Rich Rice, Heather MacNeill Falconer, and J. Michael Rifenburg
Consulting Editor, Susan H. McLeod | Associate Series Editor, Jonathan P. Hunt

The Perspectives on Writing series addresses writing studies in a broad sense. Consistent with the wide ranging approaches characteristic of teaching and scholarship in writing across the curriculum, the series presents works that take divergent perspectives on working as a writer, teaching writing, administering writing programs, and studying writing in its various forms.

The WAC Clearinghouse, Colorado State University Open Press, and University Press of Colorado are collaborating so that these books will be widely available through free digital distribution and low-cost print editions. The publishers and the Series editors are committed to the principle that knowledge should freely circulate. We see the opportunities that new technologies have for further democratizing knowledge. And we see that to share the power of writing is to share the means for all to articulate their needs, interest, and learning into the great experiment of literacy.

Recent Books in the Series

Kristopher M. Lotier, *Postprocess Postmortem* (2021)

Ryan J. Dippre and Talinn Phillips (Eds.), *Approaches to Lifespan Writing Research: Generating an Actionable Coherence* (2020)

Lesley Erin Bartlett, Sandra L. Tarabochia, Andrea R. Olinger, and Margaret J. Marshall (Eds.), *Diverse Approaches to Teaching, Learning, and Writing Across the Curriculum: IWAC at 25* (2020)

Hannah J. Rule, *Situating Writing Processes* (2019)

Asao B. Inoue, *Labor-Based Grading Contracts: Building Equity and Inclusion in the Compassionate Writing Classroom* (2019)

Mark Sutton and Sally Chandler (Eds.), *The Writing Studio Sampler: Stories About Change* (2018)

Kristine L. Blair and Lee Nickoson (Eds.), *Composing Feminist Interventions: Activism, Engagement, Praxis* (2018)

Mya Poe, Asao B. Inoue, and Norbert Elliot (Eds.), *Writing Assessment, Social Justice, and the Advancement of Opportunity* (2018)

Patricia Portanova, J. Michael Rifenburg, and Duane Roen (Eds.), *Contemporary Perspectives on Cognition and Writing* (2017)

Douglas M. Walls and Stephanie Vie (Eds.), *Social Writing/Social Media: Publics, Presentations, and Pedagogies* (2017)

Laura R. Micciche, *Acknowledging Writing Partners* (2017)

RACE, RHETORIC, AND RESEARCH METHODS

Alexandria L. Lockett, Iris D. Ruiz,
James Chase Sanchez, and Christopher Carter

The WAC Clearinghouse
wac.colostate.edu
Fort Collins, Colorado

University Press of Colorado
upcolorado.com
Louisville, Colorado

The WAC Clearinghouse, Fort Collins, Colorado 80523

University Press of Colorado, Louisville, Colorado 80027

ISBN 978-1-64215-120-6 (PDF) | 978-1-64215-121-3 (ePub) | 978-1-64642-188-6 (pbk.)

DOI: 10.37514/PER-B.2021.1206

Produced in the United States of America

Library of Congress Cataloging-in-Publication Data

Names: Lockett, Alexandria, 1983– author. | Ruiz, Iris D., author. | Sanchez, James Chase, author. | Carter, Christopher, 1974– author.
Title: Race, rhetoric, and research methods / Alexandria Lockett, Iris D. Ruiz, James Chase Sanchez, and Christopher Carter.
Description: Fort Collins, Colorado : The WAC Clearinghouse : Louisville, Colorado : University Press of Colorado, 2021. | Series: Perspectives on writing | Includes bibliographical references and index.
Identifiers: LCCN 2021010553 (print) | LCCN 2021010554 (ebook) | ISBN 9781646421886 (paperback) | ISBN 9781642151206 (pdf) | ISBN 9781642151213 (epub)
Subjects: LCSH: Rhetoric—Social aspects. | Anti-racism. | Mass media. | Culture. | Research—Methodology.
Classification: LCC P301.5.S63 L63 2021 (print) | LCC P301.5.S63 (ebook) | DDC 808—dc23
LC record available at https://lccn.loc.gov/2021010553
LC ebook record available at https://lccn.loc.gov/2021010554

Copyeditor: Meg Vezzu
Designer: Mike Palmquist
Series Editors: Rich Rice, Heather MacNeill Falconer, and J. Michael Rifenburg
Consulting Editor: Susan H. McLeod
Associate Editor: Jonathan P. Hunt
Cover Photos: Spelman College Writing Center. Used with permission.

The WAC Clearinghouse supports teachers of writing across the disciplines. Hosted by Colorado State University, and supported by the Colorado State University Open Press, it brings together scholarly journals and book series as well as resources for teachers who use writing in their courses. This book is available in digital formats for free download at wac.colostate.edu.

Founded in 1965, the University Press of Colorado is a nonprofit cooperative publishing enterprise supported, in part, by Adams State University, Colorado State University, Fort Lewis College, Metropolitan State University of Denver, University of Colorado, University of Northern Colorado, Utah State University, and Western Colorado University. For more information, visit upcolorado.com. The Press partners with the Clearinghouse to make its books available in print.

We dedicate this book to all who have sacrificed their lives through the simple act of speaking publicly against injustice.
We owe a massive debt to their bravery, sacrifice, labor, and instruction.

CONTENTS

ACKNOWLEDGMENTS

As a group, we would like to thank the editors of the Perspectives on Writing series at the WAC Clearinghouse—Rich Rice, Heather MacNeill Falconer, J. Michael Rifenburg, Susan McLeod, and Jonathan Hunt—as well as Mike Palmquist, who coordinates the Clearinghouse, and copy editor Meg Vezzu for their thoughtful suggestions and support throughout this process. Each individual author has provided their acknowledgments, as indicated by the headings below.

ALEXANDRIA LOCKETT

I deeply appreciate my co-authors for their countless hours of labor, creative energy, and overall dedication to this project. Thank you so much for having the patience and willingness to let me lead this project.

First, I am indebted to my ancestors and my parents—Brenda Joyce (Golston) Lockett and Tyrone Respress Lockett (may they honorably rest in power—January 14, 2021, and April 15, 2021)—for my existence. As a first-generation college student, I recognize that the opportunities available to me would not be possible without the fact of them surviving U.S. chattel slavery, segregation, and the aftermath of their legal collapse. I am eternally grateful for their resourcefulness and survival.

Next, many mentors throughout the years offered love, insight, and unwavering support. They are listed in the order of my educational trajectory from high school to present, as follows: Ann (Hoover) Bishop, Shivali Sharma, Abby Edwards, Jennifer Jordan, Colin Ronan, Jeanie Nutter, Kayla Hamilton, Francheska McGary, Tequilla (Myers) Briggs, Linda Seidel, Cole Woodcox, Alanna Preussner, John Ishiyama, Sarah Hass, Crystal Tillman, David Perez, Gabriella Bermudez, Teresa Tassotti, Lesa Edwards, Polly Matteson, David Kinkaid, Jacob Beard, Ivan Ozbolt, Christopher Carter (one of my brilliant co-authors!), Catherine John, Vincent Leitch, Jacqueline Jones Royster, Michele Eodice, Beth Boquet, Annette Vee, Katie Shearer, Ryan Slesinger, Richard Doyle, Lynette (Kvasny) Yarger, Katherine Gines, Shirley Moody-Turner, Elizabeth Jenkins, Robert Bleil, Heather Murray, Nadia DeLane, Mirza Akbar Shah, Seth Evans, Michelle Hite, Michelle Gordon, Opal Moore, Sharan Strange, T. Lang, Aku Kadogo, among countless other amazing scholars, writers, and teachers.

Finally, I want to thank you—the reader! I hope that this book will be an integral part of your philosophical inquiry about race and racism in the humanities.

I also hope that global massive social change will get to the point where racism has been destabilized enough for our book's narratives to be replaced by numerous stories of triumph for the meek and the marginalized. Without this faith in transformation and healing, there can be no possibility of living in a world where antiracism is normalized and we treat each other with cosmic kindness.

Note: Please know that I recognize that expressions of gratitude, due to the spatial-temporal constraints, often fail to fully capture the depth of resources that contributed directly to my ability to produce this work. I sincerely regret if I have left someone out and would appreciate it if you would reach out to me so that I can correct any future omissions in advance.

IRIS RUIZ

I would like to thank the universe, the four corners of the earth, and the four elements for making it possible for the four of us co-authors to meet back in 2015 at the Conference on College Composition and Communication (CCCC). We began a scholarly journey that took us through so many personal and professional challenges, and we endured through this project while experiencing much racial strife taking place in the world around us. I thank my co-authors for dedicating so many hours of their lives to this work. It's amazing how we came together and stayed committed to this work through all we've encountered. I would like to thank my mom, Ida Ruiz; my grandmother, Zulema Treviño; my sister, Angelica Ruiz; my children, Alexandra, Eliana, Jordan, and Lucas; and my colleagues who have been there for me through the many challenges I've endured as a person who identifies as part of the Black and Indigenous People of Color (BIPOC) community in academia—a place that has not always been the most welcoming to me. Transcending those challenges has only been possible through work on projects such as this one with some amazing folks.

JAMES CHASE SANCHEZ

I would first like to thank my co-authors for helping me on the journey that is this book (which began when I was a graduate student) and for their love and patience over the years. We have become family through writing this project. I would also like to thank my other family, especially my mother, father, maternal grandmother, and late-maternal grandfather for the love and support they have provided me along the journey. I also give gratitude to my dissertation committee—Max Krochmal, Charlotte Hogg, and Richard Enos—for helping shape my project and finding ways I could envision it outside of a dissertation. Part of it exists here. To Terry Peterman, Joshua Daniel, and Tyler Branson, you all have supported me in and out of academia over the years, and I am grateful for our friendship and y'all's willingness to look over my drafts. Lastly, I am appreciative of my mentor, Brad Lucas, for his guidance and unwavering support from my time in grad school until this present moment.

CHRISTOPHER CARTER

I am deeply grateful to my co-authors for countless inspiring conversations and for the friendship we have developed since beginning this book in 2015. I also want to thank Lynn Lewis, Composition Director at Oklahoma State University, for bringing me to campus to deliver the talk that became Chapter Four. Thanks finally to Beth, Jonah, and Ben for giving me purpose during troubled times.

RACE, RHETORIC, AND RESEARCH METHODS

CHAPTER 1.

INTRODUCTION—ANTIRACISM AS AN ETHICAL FRAMEWORK FOR RESEARCHING RACE AND RACISM

On June 17, 2015, 21-year-old white supremacist Dylann Storm Roof walked into an African Methodist Episcopal (AME) church and gunned down Cynthia Hurd, Susie Jackson, Ethel Lance, Rev. DePayne Middleton-Doctor, Hon. Rev. Clementa Pinckney, Tywanza Sanders, Rev. Daniel Simmons Sr., Rev. Sharonda Singleton, and Myra Thompson (Scales).[1]

This tragic event resurrected Southern horror, recalling through its specific location what was once a national policy of devaluing Black life.[2] The city of Charleston carries forward the stubborn geopolitics of the American South, which has long been associated with anti-miscegenation, lynching, and other terroristic acts that were intended to maintain stark divisions between Whites, Blacks, and "others." [3] Charleston, in effect, functions as a sign of race relations in America, reminding us that racial (anti-Black) violence is a characteristic of this country. Racism, then, is not a matter of time, but of place.

Both Charleston and Dylan Roof symbolize the drama of racism in America. South Carolina appears to endorse Roof's belief in White supremacy, which is vividly illustrated by the state's refusal to take down the Confederate flag waving over the state Capitol building until after Roof's attack on the AME church.[4]

---

1   See Scales's article at https://fox59.com/news/national-world/charleston-shooting-victims-names-released/.

2   South Carolina has been a location affiliated with several policies leading to southern resistance to equal rights for African Americans. After the Civil War, South Carolina immediately began to implement Black Codes and failed to grant African Americans the right to vote. The Constitution of 1865, passed only a few months after the Civil War, demonstrated a commitment to African American sub-humanity. South Carolina also retained racial qualifications for the legislature, which ensured that African Americans had no power to combat unfair laws. Such laws disenfranchised most African Americans' right to vote through a combination of poll taxes, literacy and comprehension tests, and residency and record-keeping requirements.

3   See Michelle Alexander's *The New Jim Crow* for references to racial hate crimes as acts of terrorism (79).

4   After years of refusal, South Carolina Governor Nikki Haley finally authorized the removal of the confederate flag from the statehouse (Scott, see http://www.cnn.com/2015/07/10/politics/nikki-haley-confederate-flag-removal/), admitting that it "never should have been there" in the first place.

However, the shooting itself did not directly persuade then-governor Nikki Haley to sign that bill. It was, in fact, Brittney "Bree" Newsome,[5] who directly contributed to this intervention when the flag continued to fly in the wake of the eight murdered and three injured Black Christians. Through her thirty-foot climb up the pole, the Black Woman activist boldly articulated national shock and outrage when she removed the flag (Workneh).

At this point, our readers may notice that we capitalize the "B" in the word "Black" and "Brown" throughout this book. We also decided to capitalize "White," but our decision occurs with some ambivalence, which will be explained throughout the next few paragraphs. This citation issue offers a vivid example of how race, racism, and antiracism are currently affecting long-standing debates about how to develop inclusive editorial standards across media knowledge entities. We recognize this social conversation as dynamic, complex, and contextually dependent on how professional organizations' engage their racial politics of editorial standards. AP, for example, recently decided to accept the capitalization of Black, Brown, and Indigenous, but rejected the capitalization of white for several reasons.[6]

First, "White" can be used to signify White supremacy. Next, White people do not share the same history and continuous present of discrimination based solely on their skin color. Third, the term "White," as presented by a global news organization in an international context, could lead to considerable disagreement since discourses on race vary widely based on cultural history and geography. We recognize these reasons as valid and hope that antiracist writers will continue to subvert traditional editorial standards to expose histories of exclusion and a rejection of White supremacy through the lower-case white. However, for now, our position is that we will capitalize "B" to refer to "Black" and "Brown" people and capital "W" to refer to "White" people.

As previously mentioned, this position was difficult to establish. It deserves some further explanation because future debates on this grammar issue will likely persist. In particular, these capitalizations intend to draw attention to the fact of race as a social construct mediated by language, technologies, and communication. We do not use the capital to suggest that race is biologically determined, fixed, or some essence of being that we "naturally" share. Instead, we use this grammatical marker to appropriately recognize a deliberate expression of identity that is claimed by persons whose experiences with skin color stratification are inextricably connected to architectures of White supremacy, capitalism, and patriarchy, which are residual designs of colonialism, feudalism,

---

5   See https://breenewsome.com.

6   See bit.ly/APStyleBlackWhite.

and autocracy. Skin color, among numerous other characteristics, serves as an indicator of our likely relationship to a historically disenfranchised or privileged racial/ethnic group. Therefore, when we capitalize White, we are encouraging all readers to critically reflect on their personal relationship with race and racism—regardless of their identity. Is the capitalization noticeable when applied to all racial groups? Does capitalization encourage White readers to decentralize their whiteness as the default? Does it make all of our readers think about the best ways we should grammatically mark equality?

Meanwhile, we have chosen to resist using a lowercase "b" and will use a capital "B" when spelling Black for the same reason that one (anonymous) author explained in 1878:

> White men being printers long before the black men dared read their works, had power to establish any rule they saw fit. As a mark of disrespect, as a stigma, as a badge of inferiority, they tacitly agreed to spell his name without a capital. The French, German, Irish, Dutch, Japanese, and other nationalities are honored with a capital letter but the poor sons of Ham must bear the burden of a small n. To our journalist brothers we present this as a matter of self-interest. Spell it with a capital. To our Democratic journals we present it as a matter of good grammer [sic]. Spell it with a capital. To Republicans we present it as a matter of right. Spell it with a capital. To all persons who would take from our wearied shoulders a hair's weight of the burden of prejudice and ill will, we present this as a matter of human charity, and beg you to spell it with a capital. (See the following source in our works cited: "Spell it with a Capital"; see also Clark; Gourley; Lanham and Liu; Price; Tharps).

We will also capitalize "B" when referring to "Brown" people and a "W" when referring to "Black Women" for the same purposes of claiming respect and dignity described in these articles, but with two additional critiques.

First, "Brown" identities have emerged as a categorical identity used to refer to indigenous, Asian, and Latinx people as vulnerable populations that are in need of protection against the institutionalization of anti-terrorist and anti-immigrant rhetoric. "Brown" makes a claim about how one's community has responded to being subjected to (White) people's racist attitudes towards them as outsiders, or "others."

Secondly, Black Women occupy an anomalous identity category because both masculine or male is the default association with Black, Brown, and White whereas the feminine or female is typically associated with whiteness, quite literally through veneration. The "ideal" beauty is often assumed to have "fair skin," the literal, symbolic manifestation of whiteness and its assertion of itself as normal, natural, pure, good, and chaste. Black Women, thus, are theoretically erased by the automatic gendering of races as male or masculine, or the racialization of gender as white and female (by default).

The Confederate flag, like the capitalization of racialized cultural identities, is a sign and symbol of the endurance of White supremacist ideologies in contemporary political discourses. Several years after Roof reigned terror upon Mother Emanuel, Haley expressed some regret over her decision to take down the flag. Haley still refuses to acknowledge the flag as a racial or racist symbol. In a December 2019 interview with conservative pundit Glenn Beck, she argued that, "People saw it as service, and sacrifice and heritage—but once he did that, there was no way to overcome it" (Cole). Haley's comments reinforce a strong resistance to associating acts of violence with White supremacy and its iconography. They also reflect a general public uneasiness with talking about race, racism, and their inevitable consequences.

Roof's highly publicized murders were dubbed the *Charleston Massacre*.[7] Since mass shootings tend to be named after locations or shooters only—e.g., Orlando, VA Tech, Columbine, Sandy Hook, the D.C. Sniper—the word "massacre" certainly indicated that something was distinctive about the Charleston event. As a category of murder, the meaning of "massacre" extends beyond the realm of "mass shooting." The term edges into the domain of "terrorism," but mainstream news outlets refrained from referring to Dylan Roof's actions as terrorism or terroristic, despite the many think-pieces that encourage us to rethink those terms (Bump; Gladstone; Friedersdorf). The word "massacre" signifies indiscriminate slaughter, calculated erasure, a method of genocide, and a particularly cruel murder. These characteristics vividly illustrate the practices of terrorism and the inevitable consequences of racism—seen and experienced, but not heard and said. The geographical naming of racist acts constitutes a linguistic cleansing of any racial motivation for the crimes referenced. Therefore, calling the catastrophe a massacre conveniently conceals the motivation for the murder and diminishes the nature of Roof's act as racism or terrorism.

How we name crime affects how race and racism are learned, which in turn affects how Charleston is learned. The relationship between the racially motivated shooting and the presence of a confederate flag flying above a government

---

7   Various news sources referred to Roof's terrorism this way. These outlets include, but are not limited to: BBC (http://bbc.in/2OdYI7s), NBCNews (http://nbcnews.to/3oWyQcM], MSNBC (http://on.msnbc.com/3jxAqAP), New York Times (http://nyti.ms/36M82FW), Huffington Post (http://bit.ly/3cPlLQ0), The Economist (http://econ.st/3oWzjf2)

building in the 21st century clearly demonstrates a continuity between South Carolina's history and present, racism and nationalism, gender and social movements. However, Charleston is hardly the only place where white nationalist mass shooters stake their hunting grounds.

Although racism is often misconstrued as a distinctly Southern phenomenon, Roof's killing spree in Charleston highlighted the fact that white supremacist ideology saturates the architecture of the entire U.S. geography and culture. The Charleston scene unfolded within the context of the proliferation of numerous national and international online and offline antiracist protests against police brutality. In addition to Roof's racially motivated murder, the conditions of his arrest reinforced the grievances of the #BlackLivesMatter movement. Roof stayed alive long enough to be arrested *and* was treated to a meal at Burger King after he was taken into custody, dramatizing nationwide racial inequality. The fact that an armed White mass shooter could be arrested without violence generated outcry, given that the U.S. police have killed hundreds of unarmed Native American, Black, and Latinx men and women in the past several years.[8]

Even as our readers are appalled by the racially motivated mass shooting in Charleston, we recognize that some of our readers might imagine racism as far "worse" before and during the Civil Rights era. Or, perhaps the reader is observing the connections between President Donald J. Trump's racist comments about immigrants, the increase of detention centers, mass deportations and family separations, and mass shootings by young White men whose manifestos resemble Trump's rhetoric. Regardless, we argue that racism exists as a constant, ever-present force that is as destructive now as it has always been. Violent manifestations of racism continue to reverberate from a perverse past, drowning the nation in tidal waves of hate. To clarify this point, Roof's frightening actions illustrate the global spread of white supremacist ideology, which was also enacted in a mosque in Christchurch, New Zealand, another mosque in Québec City, Canada, and a Wal-Mart in El Paso, Texas among several other places.

---

8   1,092 people were killed by the police in 2016; 86 were Native American and 136 were Black, despite the fact that each of these racial groups consists of 1 percent and 13 percent of the population, respectively: Campaign Zero (www.joincampaignzero.org/problem/), The Guardian Counted Project (bit.ly/TheCountedGuardian), and Mapping Police Violence (mappingpolice violence.org/).

We would love to be able to evaluate and cite government reports about this issue. However, the U.S. government does not typically track this information through any of its executive agencies, nor are they required to do so at the state or federal level. In 2014, only "224 of 18,000 law enforcement agencies reported fatal shootings" (Swaine and Laughland). Reports of violence are calculated through citizen-journalists and netizens painstakingly tabulating deaths from news reports and public legal records. As previously cited, these include, but are not limited to: Campaign Zero, PINAC (photographyisnotacrime.com/), Mapping Police Violence (mapping policeviolence.org/), and the Guardian (bit.ly/GarnerRiceMissingFBIRecord).

Given that contemporary media makes America's racial history so painfully visible, one might think, as a nation, we would take immediate action. Racialized discrepancies in police response ought to be a stimulus to mass agitation rather than the accepted norm. The 2016 U.S. presidential election, however, authorized white supremacist political appeals and further entrenched such norms. The victory of Donald J. Trump in the 2016 U.S. presidential election should be interpreted as an ominous sign for race relations nationwide. According to the Southern Poverty Law Center, over 700 instances of "hateful harassment" against vulnerable populations were reported within a week of the election. Their documentation also revealed an increase of hate crimes against Muslim, Jewish, Black, and Latinx people, which were disclosed in the U.S. Department of Justice's 2015 hate crimes report. Former Attorney General Loretta Lynch called the report "sobering" and urged people to report hate crimes (U.S. Department of Justice 2016).

Meanwhile, Trump's administration included David Duke-approved executive appointments[9] such as Steve Bannon, an anti-Semitic[10] founder of the extreme right Breitbart "news," and one-time Chief Strategist. In addition, Jeff Sessions, an Alabama senator, held the position of Attorney General despite the fact that he was denied a federal judge position in 1986 for using the n-word and claiming to be "OK" with the KKK.[11] With such white supremacist-approved administrators, we are seeing an increased reporting of hate crimes, as well as a reduction and/or elimination of crucial protections such as the Civil Rights Act of 1964.[12] These examples demonstrate that racism is being publicly endorsed in the White House, which intensifies the visibility of racism in our everyday lives

---

9   David Duke is a former grand wizard of the Knights of the Ku Klux Klan who unsuccessfully ran for the Louisiana Senate in 2016 and Louisiana governor in 1991 (see http://to.pbs.org/3rxPKjG). Trump claims to disavow Duke, despite receiving praise from Duke on several occasions. Trump also claimed to never know Duke, but video evidence suggested otherwise (see http://wapo.st/3p3pMTm).

10   Steve Bannon's radical right activity has received significant coverage via the SPLC's Hatewatch (see http://bit.ly/3p3qbVS).

11   Joe Biden urged his withdrawal in 1986 (Shenon, http://nyti.ms/3q3woTi). Trump's consideration of Sessions has been praised by White nationalists like Andrew Anglin, who claimed that his nomination (and several others) are "like Christmas" (https://bit.ly/2OlV3EH). However, his potential appointment has been sharply criticized by the NAACP, as follows: "Senator Sessions was denied appointment as a federal judge in 1986 for a slew of racist comments, including calling the work of the NAACP and ACLU 'Un-American.' He has also repeatedly spoken out against the federal Voting Rights Act" (NAACP Statement).

12   According to the SPLC (http://bit.ly/3rAdX9c), over 1,000 hate crimes were reported one month after Trump's election. The most recent (2015) hate crimes statistics can be found at https://ucr.fbi.gov/hate-crime/2015 and the Bureau of Justice Statistics published a report about hate crime statistics from the early 2000s to 2015 (see http://bit.ly/36WaI3V).

(Sanchez). It is within this setting that we, as teachers and researchers, are formulating and expressing our ideas about race and racism. We are very concerned with how researchers assert their commitment to antiracism when studying and making knowledge about race and racism. This ethical problem led us to invent parameters for antiracism *as a methodology,* especially in sociopolitical contexts where the risk of retaliation remains extremely high.

In fact, Roof's attack invites us to consider how academic disciplines and researchers are affected by such intense tragedies. In our field, we must look to "alternative" histories to learn more about the implications of racially violent events. For instance, Felipe Ortega y Gasca, who was among the first Chicano/Latino Compositionists, challenges dominant histories of writing and rhetoric. In Ortega y Gasca's story, the death of Martin Luther King, Jr. directly corresponded to the National Council of Teachers of English's development of antiracist policy statements. He states:

> In 1968 on the death of Martin Luther King, Jr., the National Council of Teachers of English (NCTE) at its national convention in Chicago approved a resolution by the membership to establish a Task Force on Racism and Bias in the Teaching of English as a memorial to the slain civil rights leader. . . . Our charge was to survey high school and college anthologies and readers (collections) of American literature for their content—to ascertain how inclusive they were vis-a-vis the minorities represented by the participating caucuses. Needless to say that inclusiveness was non-existent. The scathing Report of the Task Force published in 1972 entitled *Searching for America* gave all the anthologies F's for inclusiveness. That was 1972. (Ortego y Gasca)

As we evaluate the extent to which humanities scholars practice antiracism in the 21st century, we consider the implications of Ortego y Gasca's memory of the field, which many scholars saw (and still see) as contributing to linguistic imperialism and thus civil unrest. His statement about the NCTE's response to major national crises describes the ways in which its own teachers, scholars, and administrators comply with racist educational and scholarly practices.

How much has changed about the field's inclusivity since 1972? With its many caucuses, committees, and affiliates, many are probably not aware of the numerous task forces and committees for inclusion that have emerged in the NCTE/CCCC over the past 40 years. According to a document composed by a Task Force on Including People of Color on the Council composed in 1996, the following inclusion efforts have arisen:

1. Minority Affairs Advisory Committee wrote reports in 1975–76 to address diversity issues.
2. The Board of Directors approved a Policy on Minority Involvement in 1980 that evolved from these reports.
3. An implementation plan for the Policy on Minority Involvement was developed in 1981.
4. A letter of protest was forwarded to the NCTE President concerning the failure to implement the 1980 policy in 1984.
5. The next year, the Task Force on Minority Involvement submitted a plan to increase the numbers of people of color as participants in all areas of the Council.
6. In 1986, the Task Force on Minority Involvement submitted another report recommending practices and policies for involving people of color.
7. In 1987, the Task Force on Racism and Bias and the Minority Affairs Advisory Committee became actively involved in annual convention planning, developing the Rainbow Strand. During the same year, the Minority Affairs Advisory Committee submitted a report on the involvement of people of color in NCTE committees, and the Minority Affairs Advisory Committee and the Committee on Racism and Bias met with affiliates to discuss involvement of people of color.[13]

How has the field addressed the issue of race, racism, and research in its histories of itself, its pedagogies, and its current methods and methodologies? According to the most current NCTE executive leadership literature on race and racism, the field continues to lack consistent engagement with these issues. One report, composed by the Task Force on Involving People of Color in the Council, argues that despite the inclusivity efforts of various groups who have offered suggestions for procedural changes via policy statements, protest letters, etc., ". . . It is apparent from a review of the history that this making and providing recommendations has become cyclical, resulting in occasional and limited change" (NCTE). In fact, the most updated webpage that summarizes NCTE/ CCCC's attempts to diversify its council reinforces these arguments made well over 20 years ago. Although the Task Force's recommendations were audited in 2001, all of the reports and recommendations that are linked on the page are from 1996.[14]

---

13 Archival researchers may be interested in learning more about the Task Force on Racism and Bias' work from 1968–1980, which is located at the University of Illinois' Archives Research Center (see https://bit.ly/NCTERacismBiasTaskForceFile1968-80).

14 "2001 Audit of Implementation of Recommendations from the 1996 Report on Involving People of Color in the Council" (see https://bit.ly/3eSwB71) and NCTE Position Statements (see http://www.ncte.org/positions/statements/nctediversity).

On the other hand, a significant body of antiracist scholarship has emerged in our discipline that opens up the possibility for researchers to resist academic discourses and education policies that normalize whiteness by excluding knowledge created by diasporic and/or indigenous communities. For decades, teacher-scholars such as Geneva Smitherman, Keith Gilyard, and Victor Villanueva have drawn our attention to racism in the field by mixing personal narrative with sociolinguistic analysis, situating their movement between rhetorical registers within late-twentieth century struggles over language rights in school and out. Damián Baca, Arnetha Ball, Malea Powell, Jacqueline Jones Royster, and Shirley Wilson Logan have grounded similar work in the counter-narratives of marginalized populations—all of whose writing, rhetoric, and media draw our attention to histories of racism in writing instruction and the influence of imperialist ideology on education in general. Adam Banks, Lisa Nakamura, Judy Wajcman, and Barbara Monroe, among several others, pursue similar inquiry while simultaneously tracking the impact of media innovation on cultures of communication, showing how White supremacy, capitalism, gender normativity, and language regulation mutually reinforce each other while coiling their way across national borders.

We build on these scholars' work by examining the ways in which scholars talk about race and anti/racism. Colonial ideology flows through language and language research, placing us in all kinds of ethical conflicts regarding uses of violent literacy, or weaponized speech and communication. Performing and studying the processes of speaking, writing, rhetoric, and computing with little to no historical awareness of empire-in-action will likely reinforce what it ignores. In response, this book showcases how scholarly and public lexicons mediate the ability to perceive, identify, name, evaluate, and analyze racism and its discourses. Each chapter explores various contexts in which we have opportunities to reflect on our personal experiences with race and racism and their dramatic influence on how we produce knowledge—how we learn(ed) about the concepts, how they affect our desire to know, how we connect with other people, how we learn, how we teach, and how we research.

Our approach is partly a Burkean one then, though our politics owe more to work by Royster and Linda Tuhiwai Smith. Their thinking helps us define the exigency of methods that are rooted in antiracist and decolonial thought. In this moment of composing *Race, Rhetoric, and Research Methods*, we are responding to living during a historical present when federal and state governments seem eager to erase concerns about race relations from collective consciousness. Likewise, too many rhetoric, composition, and writing studies (RCWS) teacher-scholars-administrators select and execute forms of investigation that inadvertently, or perhaps all too knowingly, sidestep race in favor of less troubled territory.

RACE, METHODS, AND METHODOLOGY IN RCWS

Within the morbid scene of Roof's racially-driven violence, which occurred as part of a backdrop of historically ongoing racialized instances of police brutality and other white supremacist-inspired mass shootings, RCWS professionals are confronting several race-based dramas via their online professional spaces. During the composition of this book, three recent events—involving a law, an award, and a listserv—have highlighted the critical importance of how we study and talk about race in the field of rhetoric, composition, and writing studies.

THE RACIAL "PROFESSIONAL" SCENE OF RCWS

Four hundred scholars signed an open letter decrying the National Council for Teachers of English's (NCTE) affiliated organization the Conference on College Communication and Composition's (CCCC) decision to host its 2018 conference in Kansas City, Missouri because of the state's passage of SB-43.[15] This controversial law received national attention after the Missouri NAACP issued a travel advisory that explicitly warned Black and Brown visitors to be cautious about coming to its state on account of disproportionate traffic stops and arrests, potential for police brutality, and a lack of recourse—since SB–43 weakens the ability to prove racial "discrimination" if the accused never "intended to cause harm." The problem of SB–43 was made highly visible by our co-author Iris Ruiz, former co-chair of the CCCC Latinx Caucus. She led the composition of the open letter for NCTE/CCCC members, with some assistance from co-author Alexandria Lockett and several other scholars interested in supporting the collective action to refuse to attend the conference and/or pursue other equity demands of NCTE/CCCC.

For Ruiz and her letter's signatories, the decision as to whether to attend the conference was an ethical issue that could serve as a measure of the profession's public commitment to antiracism. However, we should be cautious not to assume that a signature automatically signified solidarity. People's motivations and the extent of their dedication to this particular antiracist effort could be interpreted variously. Certainly, all 400 signers did not refuse to attend. Signing the letter may have enabled a person to offer a simple gesture of their empathy regarding the situation. Others may be opportunistic—seeing the letter as a quick way to represent themselves as progressive. Meanwhile, some people might have decided to go to the conference because they wanted to visit family and friends nearby.

---

15   Open Letter refers to the "Joint Caucus Statement on the NAACP Missouri Travel Advisory" (see http://bit.ly/3tz8GQS). SB–43 refers to "Senate Bill 43" (see http://www.senate.mo .gov/17info/BTS_Web/Bill.aspx?SessionType=R&BillID=57095378, Missouri State Legislature, September 2017).

Many more may have signed the letter but still attended CCCC in Kansas City because they didn't want to risk their tenure and promotion by not going to a major research conference in the field. Some signatories may have been locked into travel plans that could not be canceled because they had already received institutional or organizational financial assistance and/or awards to attend.

Regardless of the outcomes of the open letter and its participants' actions, the drama over SB–43 raised fundamental questions about the way conferences are organized:

- Which criteria should organizations use in order to decide whether to support a particular conference host?
- Do conference organizers recognize that/how certain geographical locations might be more dangerous for its members identifying with marginalized racial/ethnic backgrounds than others?
- How equitable is the governance of our professional organization(s)?
- Who serves on these committees and, ultimately, makes decisions about conferences, membership dues, and benefits for all members?

The same year (2018), a number of scholars belonging to the National Communication Association (NCA) issued a statement criticizing the organization's lack of diversity and inclusion. One of its arguments was that only one of its 70 living distinguished scholars has ever been a (male) person of color since the inception of the award in 1991, despite countless invaluable scholarly contributions from ethnically/racially diverse scholars.[16] Their collective action led to two hashtag campaigns on Twitter: #CommunicationSoWhite and #RhetoricSoWhite. These hashtags were referenced in a petition delivered to the NCA, signed by over a hundred scholars, about the lack of diversity in the field's publication boards (Jackson et. al).

The hashtags gained even more traction in 2019 when Martin J. Medhurst, editor of *Rhetoric and Public Affairs*, defended the organization's distinguished scholar selection's diversity and inclusion.[17] Hundreds of NCA members and

---

16   Since 1992, there have been 104 Distinguished Scholars. 81 (78 percent) are males, 23 (22 percent) are females, and 1 (.96 percent) is a male of color. See this report composed by the NCA president Stan Muir on May 18, 2019 (http://bit.ly/OpenLetterNACDiversity).

17   On June 10, 2019, Medhurst sent an email via the CRTNET listserv (http://bit.ly/3aPJ2yQ), to contest changes to the NCA Distinguished Scholars' selection process, which are outlined in Stan Muir's response (see https://bit.ly/3kT91cB), to the culmination of decades of debate and concern regarding NCA's lack of racial and gender diversity. Notably, Medhurst acknowledges the lack of diversity in the field as a "fact," but repeatedly makes arguments that present diverse representation and merit as oppositional matters. For example, "There is a difference in running an issue of a journal that features two female scholars, a black scholar, and a graduate student, all of whose work has been accepted through the process of blind review versus saying to oneself, 'I

affiliates signed an open letter in the summer 2019 to resist Medhurst's comments and their implication that diversity and inclusion are somehow opposed to "merit," as well as the lack of transparency regarding the awards selection and the overall problem with whiteness and exclusionary racial practices that are normalized in the discipline.

This quasi-public discussion about race and communication studies echoes similar debates going on in RCWS. In particular, both fields (and especially communication studies) are inherently conservative because their teaching and learning advances Standard White English and civility norms that harm minorities. As the NCA petition's authors note,[18] casual rationales like s/he's "too junior" or "too mean" need to be met with critical questions such as:

> What does "junior" mean? How is that determined particularly when we know faculty of color are often not afforded positions of power or always hired and welcomed at Research I universities that afford them high visibility? What does it mean when a white male who is an Associate Professor is not "junior" but a scholar of color at the same level is? How do narratives about "meanness" simply reify assumptions about white middle class civility and discipline faculty of color who speak out against White supremacy, homophobia, classism, ableism, and patriarchy? Does the Publications Council consider issues of power and historical discrepancies in their deliberations and recruitment? (Jackson et al.)

Medhurst's editorial evades this line of reasoning entirely. He instead focuses on color blindness and equality as more "appropriate" values for researchers to uphold in their professional correspondence and exercise in their work. He refuses to consider what it would mean to take the job of increasing diversity seriously as a senior career White male scholar in the field, who repeatedly claims to care about such issues. Even in his apology, which was issued almost a week after he sent the editorial, he will seek advisors to help him "assure full consideration of diversity" and change the mission of the journal to "reflect greater

---

need to publish some female scholars and black scholars and graduate students so everyone will know that I believe in diversity.' Along that pathway lies disaster, for once we substitute identity for scholarly merit as the first consideration, we have lost our reason for being academics." Medhurst's position on diversity is that of equality rather than equity because he fails to present a solution for the problem of representation that doesn't continue to advantage White scholars.

18 See https://www.natcom.org/sites/default/files/NCADistinguishedScholars-Lack_of_ Diversity_Petition8.18.pdf.

commitment to diverse voices."[19] Medhurst does not offer to resign, nor does he offer to be replaced by a reputable scholar representing a historically marginalized background. Instead, he maintains his position of power by relegating "diversity work" to others whose consultations he can freely reject.

Although Medhurst's email was vehemently decried by hundreds of NCA members, some people agreed with his concerns about identity politics. Namely, they don't want to be silenced or change their values regarding "blind review" processes run by predominantly White editorial boards. Medhurst clearly recognizes that increasing the visibility of researcher's cultural backgrounds within the organizational structures would re-mediate publication practices, how the quality of research is evaluated, and the extent of its circulation. Such transformations would present a threat to research traditions that neutralize theoretical investigations about race and methodology. The legitimacy of historical and canonical research in the field is at risk if audiences expect researchers to disclose their own racial identity. In sum, #RhetoricSoWhite and #CommunicationSoWhite contribute a critical perspective of the field's research traditions, which makes it possible to create space for more research that will facilitate inquiry about how race and racism affects the kind of knowledge we make about culture, communication, rhetoric, literacy, and language.

Meanwhile, numerous scholars have been unsubscribing from a major RCWS professional listserv—the Writing Program Administration List (WPA-L)—because of certain users' desire to start a "secret" alternative online community where people could more openly criticize social justice discourse and identity politics in the name of "freedom of speech." The conversation involved heated debate, including what some considered to be racist and sexist remarks. Therefore, when an "anonymous" email from the username GrandScholarWizard@gmail.com showed up on the scene, dozens of users expressed concern about the safety of the online community and questioned the field's commitment to inclusion in general. Ruiz was a major leader in this conversation as well. She co-organized the development of moderation rules that would protect the listserv's members from hateful interactions.

---

19   Almost a week after Medhurst sent his email to the CRTNET listserv, on June 17, 2019, he sent an apology (https://bit.ly/3rO4V8r), to current and former members of the *Rhetoric and Public Affairs* editorial board, diverse constituencies in NCA, his Baylor colleagues, and the field at large. In an effort to clarify that his remarks did not represent the editorial board and that his comments did not accurately represent his "intention," Medhurst states, "I'm sorry this episode has developed in the way it has. My views were inartfully expressed. They have been interpreted exactly opposite of my intention. So that there is no doubt, let me say unequivocally that I do not believe that intellectual merit and diversity are a binary. I will welcome advice and guidance on that point as we together work towards solutions that will make the communication discipline a model for others to follow."

These three events culminated in several resignations from academic journals like *Rhetoric and Public Affairs*, syllabi like #communicationsowhitesyllabus, and press coverage in *The Chronicle* and *Inside Higher Ed*. Each of these cases continue to be passionately discussed on social media, at conferences, and in classrooms. Such deliberation vividly illustrates the problem of how professional organizations and their members strategically and publicly respond to structural oppression. In particular, they sparked dialogues about the cost and location of conferences, the color and gender of the faces of leadership in the field, "appropriate" methods of teaching and learning RCWS, as well as "proper" ways of engaging online communities that represent the discipline. This conversation signifies a pressing need to understand how our scholars, teachers, and students think about race and antiracism, coloniality and decolonialism, as well as how these concepts play out in research practices and representations of scholarly identity.

Our book takes seriously, then, that researchers have an ethical obligation to confront the epistemological, social, and political ramifications of living in a capitalist white supremacist patriarchal society. This obligation means both recognizing and naming racism as an existent, pervasive, deadly problem, as well as analyzing its effect on the work we do, especially in terms of how we choose that work and go about doing it. These critical actions ultimately enact the principles that define an antiracist methodology. After all, we are living in a historical moment when students are searching for the purpose of education in an uncertain and dangerous world. We face problems like hackable elections as U.S. President Donald J. Trump remains in office after being impeached for threatening to cut off aid to the Ukraine unless its president gave him damaging information about his political rival Joe Biden. Through his powerful position, he continues to direct family separations and the unchecked, unsanitary, unsafe detainment of both asylum seekers and citizens. This frightening policy is happening alongside a Congress that has failed to remove Trump or pass legislation that effectively mitigates other major issues like mass shootings, homelessness, hate crimes, climate change, and major disparities of quality of life among the rich and the poor. This intense context is changing how professions operate.

For example, graduate students and their teachers and mentors are no longer communicating in a shadow world of rank and file. Graduate students are assuming positions of leadership and creating their own independent scholarly spaces. For example, vibrant, relatively new organizations like the Council of Writing Program Administration's (CWPA) Writing Program Administration Graduate Organization (WPA-GO), the NextGen listserv, and Digital Black Lit (Literatures & Literacies) and Composition (DBLAC) illustrate powerful shifts in leadership. These groups have emerged alongside active social media conversations in communities like #TeamRhetoric, #AcademicTwitter, and

#CiteBlackWomen, which are all extensions of the broader activist context of #OWS, #BLM, #SayHerName, #YesAllWomen, #TimesUp, and #MeToo. Therefore, it is not uncommon to observe graduate students and early-career teacher-scholars talking publicly about their everyday experiences with racism, sexism, ableism, transphobia, and economic scarcity. Long gone are the days when senior faculty could exert unchecked power in their offices, classrooms, academic journals, and conferences. The possibility of being called out and disgraced has been magnified by grad student organizations and various online communities via major platforms like Twitter and Facebook.

These cases did not directly inspire this book, but they reinforce its purpose. Racism is a fact of our history and present. It affects how we design research, what we claim is the truth about what observe, how we learn, our decision-making, and ultimately who we will communicate with and who we will try to become. In fact, considering the role of racial discourse in our own profession of RCWS led us to develop this co-authored text.[20] RCWS has a somewhat troubled relationship with race and racism. On one hand, the field has produced many texts about how U.S. racial conflict affects our scholarship and pedagogy (Gilyard; Logan; Royster; Villanueva). On the other hand, much of that work responds directly to the ways in which mainstream scholarship in the field marginalizes the issue of race. We will demonstrate how these omissions occur in two ways: 1) how scholars choose to historicize the field of rhetoric and composition studies, and 2) how our research methods and methodologies neglect race and racism. In both cases, knowledge-making reifies colonial perspectives that privilege white hegemony.

TALKING AND WRITING ABOUT RACE IN RCWS SCHOLARSHIP

This subsection examines how our field, RCWS, tends to lack critical engagement with race, racism, and coloniality. It also describes how our research methods and methodologies respond to this absence. Our analysis of some of the field's dominant historical narratives demonstrates their failure to acknowledge the significance of race and coloniality. In their reflections on the teaching of composition and rhetoric during Reconstruction and the Industrial Revolution,

---

20   Throughout this book we refer to the broad, interdisciplinary field of "rhetoric and composition" as RCWS (rhetoric and composition/writing studies). However, we recognize that literacy studies is also a key area of the discipline. We drew on Derek Mueller's justification in his book *Network Sense*. He explains that RCWS ". . . matches with the Classification of Instructional Programs (CIP) designation 23.13, as established by the National Center for Educational Statistics (NCES). This phrasing also underscores ongoing developments in the field with regard to a richer disciplinary history associated with 'rhetoric and composition' and a contemporary relabeling that has taken hold unevenly under the designation 'writing studies.'"

Berlin, Connors, Brereton, and Kitzhaber, among several others, ignore the specific ways that segregation—as a social and legal policy—in American society affected the accessibility of education and rhetorical practices of disenfranchised groups (Ruiz).[21] In addition, histories of rhetorical studies assume a similar tone and character as those histories of composition studies.

For instance, Patricia Bizzell and Bruce Herzberg's widely circulated anthology, *The Rhetorical Tradition: From Classical Times to Present*, normalizes a Western colonial male historiography both in the overwhelming space it affords such voices and in its slender (albeit well-meaning) acknowledgments of difference. Bizzell and Herzberg's large book presents a sequence of scholars and teachers of rhetoric that reinforces a print-centric perspective of Western civilization's intellectual heritage. Aristotle, Isocrates, Cicero, and Quintilian head the pack as readers move through Greece, Rome, Scotland, England, and America—with only a few brief nods to abolitionists like the Grimké sisters and Frederick Douglass. It hasn't been updated in almost 20 years, but its selections and characterizations prevail in similar, more recent anthologies like James A. Herrick's *History and Theory of Rhetoric*.

Published in 2012, Herrick's textbook also treks through Plato and Aristotle's Greece, Quintilian and Cicero's Rome, and Christian Europe before turning its gaze towards philosophical shifts including the Renaissance and the Enlightenment. It sharply moves Rhetoric into a "Contemporary" period, foregrounding twentieth-century theory through critics like Burke, Bakhtin, Booth, and Perelman. Male-centric, Western homogeneity is disrupted in the final chapter of *The Rhetorical Tradition*, which is entitled "Texts, Power, and Alternatives," though Michel Foucault and Jacques Derrida precede the selections representing White feminism. Granted, the counter-cultural contributions of both of these theorists certainly warrants this placement. Foucault was an early exponent of queer theory, and Derrida was an Algerian-Jewish critic of Western logocentrism. Nevertheless, both theorists still signified White male privilege as their translated work flourished enough to become canonized within the same *Anglocentric* discourses they critiqued. Their sections in Bizzell and Herzberg's anthology give way to an inadequate survey of "comparative rhetoric," which is a mélange of African American and Chinese text fragments lumped in the same section. Neither the White feminist nor "ethnic rhetorics" sections feature individual authors, as the previous chapters do.

These survey texts are commonly assigned or encountered during RCWS graduate study. Unfortunately, they omit non-White, non-male authors and

---

21   According to Google Scholar's "most cited" work feature, over 1,000 works cite Berlin, and works that cite him seem to also be most widely circulated.

sufficient attention to structural racism. Consequently, students and faculty lack models for designing research about this very problem. Normalizing representations of disciplinary history that inhibit criticism about the influence of racism and coloniality on canon formation and research traditions makes it difficult to study these issues. Royster and Williams illustrate this point in their article "History in the Spaces Left." They critique the homogeneity of "official" histories of the field, discussing how their universal perspective "sets in motion a struggle between these 'prime' narratives and other narrative views (that for whatever reasons the official narratives exclude) for agency and authenticity and, most of all, the rights of interpretive authority" (580). Furthermore, they argue that, ". . . as existing histories of composition acquire an 'official' status, they participate in the making of metaphors and the symbolic systems of reality by which we draw the lines of the discipline and authenticate what is 'real' and not, significant enough to notice and not, or valuable and not" (580–581). Royster and Williams conclude their article by calling for methodologies that disrupt White and colonial primacy. They claim that this perspective benefits the field because researchers would feel more motivated to develop ways of seeing, and filling, the field's racial knowledge gaps (583). Guided by antiracism, we assume this charge by critically investigating how RCWS researchers write about conducting research.

Before we proceed with our antiracist critique, we must identify "official" definitions of the terms *method* and *methodology*. Lee Nickoson and Mary P. Sheridan, in *Writing Studies Research and Practice*, offer technical definitions for these terms. They associate *method* with researchers' efforts to "identify research topics, design strategies for collecting, managing, and interpreting the collected data, and determine how to represent their findings." Such activities embody "*what* the researchers do and *how* they do it" (2). By contrast, they acknowledge that *methodology* concentrates on the "*whys* of research" as well as "the epistemological and theoretical interests that drive researchers' understanding of their study and of themselves (their roles and responsibilities) within [that] study." Nickoson and Sheridan's definitions guide the major conceptual pathways that we will explicitly discuss throughout our book.

However, even as we drew on Nickoson and Sheridan's working definitions of methods and methodologies, we discovered that their own agenda for knowledge production seemed contained within a discourse that privileged "prime" narratives over the "others." For example, the vast majority of their collection does not engage how race and racism impact research practices. Out of 20 essays that describe the interplay of what, how, and why in RCWS, only one chapter focuses explicitly on race and racism. In this chapter (and in his own single-authored book *Antiracist Writing Assessment Ecologies*), Asao Inoue performs a powerful critique of writing assessment's inattention to race in its investigative protocols. He also specifies its failure to understand race as a rhetorical phenomenon that infuses historical ways of educating and communicating (128–29). In this book, we extend Inoue's critique beyond the parameters of writing assessment to the larger interdisciplinary domains in which it unfolds.

Inoue encourages researchers not to layer considerations of race into existing research protocols, but to attend to race and racism in the very formulation of our queries. We take Inoue's cue by moving from critique to praxis, offering numerous, interlocking ways to think about race and its relationship to the processes and performances of communication, writing, rhetoric, media, and literacy. For example, we don't merely acknowledge the need for antiracism to neatly conclude chapters, articles, and books that ignore race in their theorizing of teaching and learning research, writing, rhetoric, and communication. In this book, antiracism fundamentally shapes the whys of our research. Consequently, critical race theory (CRT) frames our book's structure and its featured research methods, which are designed to serve the purpose of destabilizing the kind of dominant research writing traditions that derive their authority from exempting White researchers from disclosing the politics of their identity and its potential impact on their research's subject matter, design, and analytical approaches.

Since we believe that RCWS research subjects and practices are variously affected by race and racism, we have selected a research methodology—antiracism—to guide our research design and methods. This critical framework enables us to focus on two interrelated processes: 1) how we make knowledge about these phenomena and 2) how we ought to pay careful attention, and resist, the ways in which knowledge production structurally involves violence against marginalized people. CRT informs our methodology because it informs our ability to question the centrality of race in interdisciplinary methods and applications that claim "neutrality" while hiding their Eurocentric philosophical foundations and ordering mechanisms of society such as the law, education, and literacy (Bell; Crenshaw; Delgado and Stefancic; Dixson and Rousseau; Freeman; Ladson-Billings; Montoya; Omi and Winant; Prendergast; Romm; P. Williams; Yamamoto). Stifled racial progress, an exigence of CRT, drives our work and the purpose of a CRT methodology "[which] focus[es] on 'race' and racism and its intersections and a commitment to challenge racialised power relations" (Hylton 27). We are especially interested in how these relations work through language. Since a CRT methodology holds researchers responsible for contributing to the eradication of racism, we argue that antiracism operationalizes research as an ethical action capable of showing what Hylton describes as a "commitment to challenge [racism]." Our praxis of antiracism, then, means "forms of thought and/or practice that seek to confront, eradicate and/or ameliorate racism" (Bonnet 3).

To further illustrate antiracism as methodology, we examine how this framework is informed by other critical theoretical positions that constitute CRT. For example, we have attempted to demonstrate the relationship between antiracism and decolonialism. Ruiz's chapter, "Critiquing the Critical: The Politics of Race and Coloniality in Rhetoric, Composition, and Writing Studies (RCWS) Research Traditions," critiques the field's citation practices, as well as its methods of producing histories. By reclaiming the work of colonized populations, Ruiz shows how they are embedded in unequal race relations that marginalize their knowledge and cultures. This decolonial approach to historiography illustrates the use of CRT as an antiracist methodological framework for epistemic justice.[22]

Indeed, racism is a complex rhetorical object. It is categorically a fact, a fiction, a consequence, and a physical and metaphysical influence on human interactions. Furthermore, White supremacy is systematically ordered and maintained by multiple discourses of exclusion that are embedded in racialized technological, linguistic, and legal codes. We take these issues into consideration when observing human experience, reflecting on it, and giving words to what we see and how we remember it. This intensive process demands a futile attempt to "tell the truth" about what happened. The problem of truth looms large in research. Many conflicts about whether some knowledge production is credible are structured as a drama over "objectivity," "neutrality," and "bias." These debates still go on in the social sciences and education. Indeed, at the core of the ethical conflict that characterizes the drama of research lies the decision to disclose or conceal what one knows about race and racism.

Although this is not a textbook, we recognize that the relationship between race and research methods and methodologies needs to be explicitly taught as a part of the core under/graduate curriculum. There are few published examples of how this is being formally learned. CRT theorist Thandeka K. Chapman offers one notable exception of antiracism being taught as a methodology in her graduate course that introduces students to qualitative research. In her chapter in *Researching Race in Education,* Chapman reflectively analyzes her use of race-based approaches, considering how "Language is a key element for demonstrating bias and reframing research" (237).

---

22   In her book, *Decolonizing Rhetoric and Composition: New Latinx Keywords for Theory and Pedagogy,* Ruiz features a chapter on "Race." This chapter discusses "the use of CRT as a decolonial methodology, which Mignolo describes as questioning an allegedly objective body of knowledge" (13). Similar to Royster and Williams, Ruiz attempts to disrupt the field's tendency to present its own histories as universal prime narratives. She argues that canonized knowledge in RCWS unethically ignores the intensely violent consequences of colonialism and racism—the continuous erasure of diasporic and displaced populations.

One of the biggest challenges for Chapman is building learning environments that enable students to actually talk about race (242–43). To resolve this issue, she argues that "Race-based research makes visible explanations of distress and misinterpretation that people of color fear from white researchers and academics of color" (237). According to Chapman, her most impactful teaching moments occurred when her students discussed how they noticed race and racism operating in their everyday lives, via family, friends, etc. Chapman observes that such interactions helped them learn to ". . . embrace and challenge their epistemological understandings of difference as a means to cultivate ethical research practices" (243). We, too, are committed to opening up space for our field's professionals to contemplate their relationship to communicating about race.

Unfortunately, the structural power of racism is carefully controlled through stylistic conventions of research writing and communication. Race is political. It affects what people, places, and things mean, yet it is not "polite" to talk about race in public—a cultural norm that affects "professional" spaces. Research, then, is political because the researchers' writing performance will reinforce certain attitudes towards language and, thus, ideologies of race. Narrative and textual inquiry does not attempt to evade this particular problem of "bias," but rather to investigate it by exploring what kinds of stories we make. Indeed, a researcher's racial awareness affects their epistemology and how they construct identity narratives. Sanchez's chapter, "Towards Reconciliation: Composing Racial Literacy with Autoethnography," offers a useful model for instructors and students seeking ways to start difficult conversations about race and racism. In particular, Sanchez showcases how autoethnography can be used as a method for composing a racial literacy narrative. Throughout his reflection about what led to his desire to be antiracist, he grapples with the possibilities for reconciliation and the extent to which this process meaningfully contributes to the goal and/ or philosophy of antiracism.

We hope that this book will be useful to researchers like Chapman, who are tasked with teaching research methods courses to aspiring professionals in humanistic fields. We also crafted the book with graduate students in mind. By focusing each chapter explicitly on how race and racism affect ways of thinking and the processes of claim making, we demonstrate and actualize antiracism *as a methodology* in four single-author chapters of this book that utilize the following research methods (respectively): critical historiography, autoethnography, visual rhetorical analysis, and critical technocultural discourse analysis.

Each of us authors explicitly discusses how considering race and racism affects our analysis and communication of research findings, as well as the implications of our research to publics inside and outside the field. Through this kind of reflection, we seek to increase the epistemological and rhetorical value of recalling and articulating personal experience, which helps us ground our theory in real-life substance (Malagon, Huber, and Velez). Thus, narrative is embedded in our methods because storytelling, as a form of argumentation, subverts the idea of a "neutral," aracial point of view. By grounding our theoretical observations in lived experience, we take a metacognitive approach to the mechanisms of race and racism operating in our everyday lives and the cultures, scenes, texts, and media of society.

We also converse with each other's work in between chapters. These interchapters showcase each co-author further discussing concepts in their work, current events, among several issues. Each one clarifies, through reflective dialogue, what understandings our distinct subject positions afford and what they might obscure. In that way, we follow cues offered by Meredith J. Green and Christopher C. Sonn in "Problematising the Discourses of the Dominant: Whiteness and Reconciliation," wherein they address how unacknowledged power relations within diverse political groups can derail activist programs and dilute antiracist methods. Overall, the interchapter dialogues are intended to give our audiences additional access to our work, as well as an opportunity to experience our voices in an alternative format. Through the interchapter dialogues, we aim to create a more integrated, nuanced conversation about race and research.

In addition, our book's postscript also discusses collaboration as antiracist action. It specifically describes how the authors collaborated, as well as the challenges they faced and the critical and creative insights they discovered throughout the process. In the postscript, we discuss major contemporary issues that unfolded during the final stages of the book's production. We draw on these events to further elaborate on our book's significance and applications.

ANTIRACIST PRAXIS: THE ROLE OF DISCLOSURE IN RACE-BASED RESEARCH

Why did a Black woman, White man, Latinx woman, and Chicanx man—all scholars under age 50—choose to write this book? How did our cross-cultural contact enable us to leverage our interracial contact and varying professional ranks and backgrounds to develop this book?

We felt compelled to make a substantive contribution to the field, in regards to defining and operationalizing antiracism. We resist living in a culture in which violent scenes like the massacre at Mother Emanuel and numerous recorded incidents of police brutality are historically consistent with anti-Black racism. We know that these aren't sporadic events, and we recognize that they reverberate in our personal lives. In Christopher Carter's chapter, "Taser Trouble: Race, Visuality, and the Mediation of Police Brutality in Public Discourse," he demonstrates how the ongoing saga of police violence against unarmed (mostly Black, Indigenous and people of color, or BIPOC) persons exposes the necessity of citizen surveillance because "official" police accounts frequently differ dramatically from mobile phone video footage of these events. Any of us could bear witness to wrongdoing and be put in a position to have to decide to record.

More troubling still, the footage we capture may end up inadmissible and disregarded while we are subject to retaliation, intimidation, and even imprisonment. Without accountability, police testimony is more persuasive than what appears on a citizen's film, which diminishes the public's hope that telling the truth offers pathways to justice. This crushes our faith in democracy and the justice system. Facing the possibility of a fatal police encounter, or being regularly confronted with visual evidence of unnecessary murders, harms everyone—albeit disproportionately. We, the authors, feel these (and other) consequences of racism deep in our hearts, at the forefront of our minds, and in the marrow of our bones. They directly affect the fear we feel when we leave our homes, our loved ones' concern for our lives, the empathy we have for our students, and the anxiety we have about the purpose, cost, and responsibilities of post-millennium education.

Too often, predominantly White rhetoric and composition researchers carefully acknowledge the importance of taking race and racism into account when teaching and researching while concealing their specific relationship to racial identification. From a decolonial antiracist perspective, their self-image illustrates normative whiteness. They are almost always strategically naive, appearing before their audiences as benevolent, well-meaning colonizers who generously utilize their social status and privilege to study subaltern populations such as our composition students, or other downtrodden "barely literate" or "aspiring-to-become-literate" populations—including their historically marginalized colleagues (Heath; Sternglass). However, such posturing raises questions about how racial dynamics affect exchanges of power between researcher and the researched.

For example, what motivates a White researcher to study "people of color" without disclosing what's at stake for them to be writing about difference, race, equity, diversity, etc.? What kinds of risks are White researchers willing to take in their work that match the intensity of the life/death urgency of eradicating racial, gender, and economic inequality?

Furthermore, how is it possible for a White feminist to theorize about Mexican female rhetors of the late 19th century when she is not a historian, is not Mexican, is not Latinx, does not speak Spanish, and does not show interest in that same community which inhabits her profession? Such researchers produce "knowledge" about ethnic/racial communities without having any real contact with the people that identify with them (Yancey). Despite ongoing controversy about White researchers increasingly occupying disciplinary spaces such as

Africana/Black studies, Native/Chicana studies, and Mexican and Latinx studies, the "authenticity" questions seem to have been laid to rest.

When researchers seek to make "exotic" cultures and language practices familiar, they may unknowingly (or deliberately) assimilate, consume, and appropriate the epistemological traditions of the "other." Their subject selection reveals that whiteness increases scholarly authority, or the ability to make claims about cultural groups, regardless of one's degree of participation or history of contact with said groups. Yet, as we will show throughout the book, this is a problem when researchers representing historically marginalized identities—whose selves and communities are affected by their work—remain invisible in their efforts to identify structures of oppression that prevent them from being seen. Iris Ruiz addresses these issues in her chapter, "Critiquing the Critical: The Politics of Race and Coloniality in Rhetoric, Composition, and Writing Studies (RCWS) Research Traditions," which analyzes the racial and colonial politics of citation in RCWS scholarship. Specifically, Ruiz argues that scholarly publications in RCWS privilege White scholars advancing racial discourses that reinforce racially neutral histories of the field and a relatively racially homogenous canon. In addition, the demographics of published RCWS researchers fail to accurately reflect the culturally diverse participation that constitutes the profession (although racial/ethnic diversity among professionals in the field remains very limited).

When researching race and racism, one's relationship to these concepts should be explicitly identified. This act, for us, is one of the primary characteristics of antiracism. Taking whiteness for granted as the assumed—or default—subject position of a researcher, or the audience, contributes to the idea that only White people can be considered intelligent and/or (culturally) literate. Thus, these racially biased misconceptions persistently reproduce racism in the processes of knowledge production. Hence, we argue that supposedly aracial or non-racial feminist methodologies that call out bias, such as many White RCWS feminist scholars who conduct studies about social injustices, fail to be critical of their own privileged position because they are often given the space and opportunity to perform research and publish findings on individuals who occupy linguistic minority spaces—despite the lack of authorship representation from the very groups they make knowledge about. They maintain their dominance by failing to expose their colonial gaze, which justifies their research about historically disadvantaged racial and ethnic groups to "increase awareness," as if they are doing that group a favor.

We recognize that researching this subject is deeply emotional work. Therefore, we carefully established parameters for antiracism as a methodology while pondering the broader significance of being a researcher in this historical moment. Of course, we believe that excellent research about any subject can be produced by anyone who engages the subject with care, comprehension, and commitment. This standard of attempting to practice antiracism would be upheld by any researcher who claims to challenge White hetero-normative epistemologies if they acknowledge their identity and privilege. Next, they should be able to articulate the continuity between historical practices of exclusion and their contemporary relationship to structures of power and oppression. Furthermore, RCWS researchers should concede the limitations of their cultural knowledge as an outsider, recognizing that their vantage point will not be as rich as those intimately tied to the traditions of literacy and rhetorical prowess under discussion.

Alexandria Lockett's chapter, "What is Black Twitter? A Rhetorical Criticism of Race, Dis/information, and Social Media," explores various ways these issues could play out when researchers examine a complex racial, technological, textual, and rhetorical object like Black Twitter. Her research analyzes the cultural impact of "Black Twitter" and the performativity of online Blackness. With careful attention to the issue of embodiment, Lockett argues that Black Twitter enacts dramas about the ownership of Black creativity and culture, given the challenges of attributing authority to a global distributed information network comprised of a mixture of human and non-human (bot) agents. Indeed, Black Twitter affects what we know about the preservation of Black culture and opens space to think about the economics of digital labor and cultural production. For instance, how should we study and talk about networked communication? What kind of language should we use to describe linguistic acts of collective intelligence? How should individual authors be recognized for their eloquence amid the crowd and the hive? In other words, researchers must not separate issues of race and technology when deciding to study "public" writing and communication. Any source has authors, even if the author must be referred to by a username and their social media profiles. When obtaining knowledge about "others," researchers should always credit the source—even if it is digital, public, and hard to trace back to its authors—and articulate meanings they do not make as if they are invented from one's own thoughts. Finally, one should explicitly state how their experiences relate to their work, as well as how their research benefits the subject(s) and communities that they study.

Since we exist in an uncivil political terrain, our awareness of the current hostile racial climate directly affects how we research and teach. Disclosing cultural identity changes the narrative about the possibility for researchers to be unbiased and "objective" when studying race and racism. In this context, such disclosure enables the audience to determine what's at stake for the researcher when doing this kind of work. Any absence of this utterance in scholarship about human performance says to the interlocutor that the subject is beyond race, and thus, beyond the influence of networked information systems operating across geographies and technologies.

Furthermore, the refusal to participate in "racialized" communication further contributes to misinformation and an inability to recognize the aesthetic nature of information access and production. In our professional experience, "academic writing" tends to be defined by an author's ability to present arguments without overtly discussing how their personal experience plays a role in the research and writing process. Some fields like anthropology, psychology, and education regularly confront this issue because their researchers struggle to gain trust from the communities they study. When researchers make their conclusions about the value of human beings and their social activity transparent, it opens up the possibility to more deeply engage the limitations and potentials of what we think we know.

Therefore, we work in different, but related, ways to reveal our positionalities throughout this book. A researcher's gaze, as we have previously argued, constitutes an important consideration in qualitative studies in RCWS (see *Ethics and Representation in Qualitative Studies of Literacy*, edited by Peter Mortensen and Gesa Kirsch). It also applies to our work's theoretical exploration of language, epistemology, and race. Race and racism as lived, symbolic phenomena inspired us to conceive of this project as a co-authored book. Since this work is the product of four researchers representing different backgrounds, identities, and locations, designing this book demanded the use of synchronous and asynchronous communication technologies for collaborative composition.

We paid very close attention to how we negotiated our various areas of expertise to discover and invent—not simply document—how race and racism affect our identities as researchers, teachers, and citizens. We deliberated intensively about what our research was *doing* and whether the ability to observe its generative potential would lie in the mutually supportive character of our stories, as well as the instructive places where they diverge. As we previously discussed, RCWS professionals must function within a "hostile racial climate" that requires them to engage in uneasy contemporary public discourse about discrimination and inequality. We highlight some of the ethical stakes involved in researching and talking about race through a critical discussion about key intersections between the racial violence in Charleston and our digital disciplinary scene, in which heated debates about how race affects our disciplinary identity are leading to resignations, public letters, generational factions, and transformations in social justice branding.

This is not another book that assumes White scholars are the only audience, that people need to be better "rhetorical listeners," nor does it attempt to persuade our audiences that "diversity and inclusion" matter. Instead, this book is a meditation on how race and racism operate in multiple sites of knowledge production about language and communication. As authors coming from different cultural backgrounds, we wanted to experiment with composing a collective, integrated text that could draw on our diverse subject positions in society and explicitly consider how our identities affect the kind of research we are able to do about race.

More specifically, our book foregrounds three ethical challenges of studying race and racism in RCWS. These include, but are not limited to

1. Disclosing our cultural identities and their direct relationship to our research about race and racism;
2. Identifying how the discipline of RCWS has failed to comprehensively theorize and discuss race and racism in ways that amplify their intellectual and social complexity; and
3. Acknowledging antiracism as a necessary but experimental concept that needs to be explicitly developed responding to how living in a racist society affects our ability to truthfully and accurately observe reality as it exists vs. how people desire to imagine and invent it.

Towards this end, the book showcases three distinctive features that we will elaborate near the end of this introduction:

1. Single-author chapters that illustrate how we each individually constructed research with the issue of race at the center of our investigations
2. Interchapter dialogues that offer more in-depth coverage of the authors' ideas and motivations regarding how we learned to invent, analyze, and claim knowledge about race, racism, and antiracism
3. An afterword that explicitly discusses the rationale for our book's title, as well as some of the challenges and insights offered by antiracism as a research methodology, and collaborative writing across race and gender

Our primary purpose, then, is to identify and utilize research methods that enable researchers to focus on how race and racism affect epistemologies of place, self, and society. We also examine how the collaborative authorship process itself might support researchers interested in creating and participating in structured communication contexts that facilitate inquiry about meaningful ways to communicate about race in scholarship.

OVERVIEW OF CHAPTERS: OUR METHODS AND METHODOLOGICAL APPROACHES

Overall, we do not believe that any researcher stands outside of race and racism because we reject the notion that a researcher—especially of language, communication, society, technology, information, and/or writing—is capable of researching these concepts as phenomena external to the making of knowledge. Antiracism is the goal of our research. This purpose informs our methods and methodologies because we believe that racial stratification is constructed and reproduced in all kinds of professional communications contexts. We attempt to demonstrate that our work is "antiracist" by interrogating how race affects the ways in which we see, talk, write, and attempt to produce institutionally recognized scholarship about human beings, their arrangements, how they learn, and how they communicate. Moreover, we do not underestimate the ways in which research may inaccurately and negatively represent historically disenfranchised individuals, cultures of resistance, and sites of knowledge production that are located outside of "formal" educational institutions.

The first single-author chapter of the book (Chapter 2) builds on the narratives of this introduction and examines rhetoric, composition, and writing studies' imperialist politics of citation, which have been practiced within the field since at least 1949. Iris Ruiz focuses on how certain disciplinary textual and citation practices, rituals, values and beliefs construct the field's limited cultural literacy, as well as how that literacy enables certain historiographies to assert and maintain White scholastic hegemony and disciplinary power. Inventing a decolonial gaze from a curandera methodology, Ruiz critiques three critical RCWS methodologies by calling attention to how they engage in imperial scholarship practices, cultural and historical erasure, and "white-washing." Such methods, Ruiz claims, affect how race appears and disappears in "critical" research practices, especially in terms of who is permitted to write, research, and circulate stories about race and racism.

This methodology allows for historical recovery, or historical curanderisma, as well as personal and disciplinary healing. This kind of historical recovery, which builds upon her earlier scholarship featured in *Reclaiming Composition for Chicano/as and other Ethnic Minorities: A Critical History and Pedagogy*, seeks to make silenced voices and histories of rhetorical education and engagement more audible. Ultimately, Ruiz—like her co-authors Sanchez, Carter, and Lockett—argues for the necessity of research methods that are capable of mapping race to specific geographies, communities, and forms of textual production.

In the next chapter (Chapter 3), James Chase Sanchez enacts autoethnography, or self-critically researching one's own cultural identity, as a research method that contributes towards the process of racial reconciliation. Specifically, Sanchez investigates his own upbringing as a Chicanx individual in a rural Texas town known for a history of racism, while claiming that autoethnography provides a lens for better understanding how race is epistemic and can help reconcile injustices against one's body. For Sanchez, it began with feeling outside of two communities: the minority Brown kids who spoke Spanish (which he didn't) and the White-majority kids who were, well, White. These differences and the feeling of not having a community emphasized whiteness as normalized in his hometown. Therefore, class, language differences, space, interactions between peers and elders, and Sanchez's own response to these issues all were variables in producing Sanchez's racial awareness, or his racial literacy. Throughout his chapter, Sanchez analyzes the purpose of autoethnography as a scholarly and pedagogical exercise, suggesting that the study of race via autoethnography can elicit transformation of attitudes and memories that inhibit reconciliation. In other words, the desire to resolve the problem of racism depends on a person's willingness to learn about the limitations of prejudice and bias, admit their own participation in systems of exclusion, believe that one's survival depends on the well-being of other people, as well as care about the livelihood and subjectivity of all human beings.

In Chapter 4, Christopher Carter expands current methods of investigating civic dialogue by concentrating on the visual mediation of violent arrests of unarmed Black men in South Carolina and Oklahoma, placing particular emphasis on rhetorics of citizen videography and police camera footage. As a White man from Kentucky, he is familiar with narratives of White victimhood and brotherhood that give power to the arguments that police use to defend their use of violence. Carter finds that although arresting officers generally provide oral defenses of their actions in shooting cases, video reveals details that differ from or are not acknowledged by the official narrative, as follows: 1) suspects under investigation do not pose an immediate threat to their pursuers; 2) police begin to construct a rationale for the gunfire almost immediately after it occurs; and 3) attending officers continue to mistreat the subjects as they are dying or after they are dead.

Similar to Sanchez and Lockett, Carter investigates the dynamic relationships between geography, race, and citizenship. Like Ruiz, he critically examines how authority mediates truth-telling in regards to whose testimonies of knowledge (about injustice) are likely to be believed. However, Carter's focus on visuality and networked publics introduces key methodological challenges such as how to assess "evidence" within a technological context where anyone with access to a mobile phone and the internet can record and share footage. These processes include tracking the virality and accessibility of both "official accounts" and those that come from activist counter-surveillance. Visual rhetorical analysis provides a method of critiquing the role of race and its relationship to the persuasiveness of images in public debate.

In Chapter 5, the final single-author chapter, Alexandria Lockett examines the complexity of studying the discourses of racial online publics. Through her critical technological discourse analysis of several instances of the rhetorical activity of "Black Twitter," Lockett identifies some of the ways in which Black Twitter reveals opportunities for developing more nuanced methodologies for studying the intersections between race, digital technology, and culture. Although Black Twitter has powerfully responded to the police brutality discussed by Carter, it evades traditional definitions of "community" and "culture" that are named and located in the physical spaces interrogated by Sanchez. In this chapter, Lockett reflects on her relationship to Black Twitter—as a (Black) Twitter user—to consider how racial identities are mediated on social media. She asks, "What is Black Twitter?" Noting that Black Twitter is virtually absent from academic studies in RCWS even though it is widely acknowledged by many mainstream media outlets, Lockett reviews some key intersections between academia, journalism, and Black Twitter.

According to Lockett, Black Twitter is subject to misinterpretation and even data warfare. The "blackness" of Black Twitter is recognized through racially coded language practices that can be improperly performed by outsiders such as Russian hackers seeking to disrupt the U.S. political process. Some researchers will acknowledge the power of Black Twitter while simultaneously overlooking its relationship to Black English. Lockett analyzes the rhetorical and political significance of Black English, especially the persuasive value of public expressions of Black English (BE) and/or African-American Vernacular English (AAVE). Twitter's complex technical mechanisms (e.g., algorithms, archiving, and "trending" functions) also intensify the challenge of studying cultural expression through ethnographic and linguistic methods.

As we previously discussed, this book's primary purpose is to establish research methods that enable researchers to focus on how race and racism affect epistemologies of place, self, and society. We also examine how the collaborative authorship process itself might support researchers interested in creating and participating in structured communication contexts that facilitate inquiry about meaningful ways to communicate about race in scholarship. In some ways, our book is similar to *Critical Rhetorics of Race*. We appreciate that its editors, Lacy and Ono, offer one of the few more recent books in the field that is exclusively dedicated to critically analyzing race and racism from a transdisciplinary orientation. However, their edited collection "aims for broad knowledge about how race and racism emerge and function in their various guises and conditions" (3), whereas we are far more interested in how race and racism affect scholars during the process of composing research for our field. While locating and describing race and racism constitute necessary steps towards awareness of their manifestations in everyday life, we do not believe that understanding racism enables one to "navigate such a world [and] ultimately change it" (3–4).

Indeed, we take for granted that the audience of this book does not need for us to exhaustively document and describe racism in its everyday forms. We also take for granted that the audience rejects the idea of a "post-racial" U.S. society. However, we are writing for researchers in the field who want to learn additional strategies for cultivating creative, reflective responses to matters of race and racism. In our case, we are writing for researchers interested in figuring out what antiracism looks and feels like as part of our research traditions and as a methodology that is capable of influencing our methods.

Thus, we decided to write this book collaboratively, not as an edited collection, but as a representation of four individuals contemplating their experiences as citizens, researchers, teachers, scholars, artists, friends, daughters, sons, mothers, fathers, brothers, and sisters. We chose this method of composition to make visible some of the ways in which we are self-consciously and artistically describing and modeling antiracist research. We understand our research approach as a deliberate, political act that illustrates how we feel, not just what we think, about experiencing race and racism in the work we are doing and the kind of society we want to work in.

WORKS CITED

Alexander, Michelle. *The New Jim Crow: Mass Incarceration in the Age of Colorblindness*. The New Press, 2020.

Anglin, Andrew. "It's Like Christmas: Sessions for AG, Gen Flynn as National Security Advisor." *Daily Stormer*, 18 Nov. 2016, dailystormer.su/its-like-christmas-sessions -for-ag-gen-flynn-as-national-security-advisor/.

Baca, Damián. *Mestiz@ Scripts, Digital Migrations, and the Territories of Writing*. Springer, 2008.

———. "Rethinking Composition, Five Hundred Years Later." *JAC*, 2009, pp. 229–42.

Ball, Arnetha F. "Teaching Writing in Culturally Diverse Classrooms." *Handbook of Writing Research*, edited by Charles A MacArthur, Steve Graham, and Jill Fitzgerald, The Guilford Press, 2008, pp. 293–310.

Banks, Adam. *Digital Griots: African American Rhetoric in a Multimedia Age*. Southern Illinois UP, 2011.

———. *Race, Rhetoric, and Technology*. Routledge, 2005.

Bell, Derrick A. "Who's Afraid of Critical Race Theory." *University of Illinois Law Review*, no. 4, 1995, pp. 893.

Berlin, James. A. *Rhetoric and reality: Writing Instruction in American Colleges, 1900– 1985*. Southern Illinois UP, 1987.

Bizzell, Patricia, and Bruce Herzberg. *The Rhetorical Tradition: From Classical Times to Present*. 2nd ed., Bedford, 1990.

Bonnett, Alastair. *Anti-Racism*. Routledge, 2000.

Brereton, John. *The Origins of Composition Studies in the American College, 1875–1925.* U of Pittsburgh P, 1996.

Bump, Phillip. "Why We Shouldn't Call Dylann Roof a Terrorist." *Washington Post*, 19 Jun. 2015, www.washingtonpost.com/news/the-fix/wp/2015/06/19/why-we -shouldnt-call-dylann-roof-a-terrorist/.

Burke, Kenneth. *The Philosophy of Literary Form.* Vintage Books, 1957.

Calafell, Bernadette Marie. "An Open Letter on Diversity in the Communication Discipline." *Bernadette Marie Calafell*, 28 Jun. 2019.

Campaign Zero. "The Problem." *Join Campaign Zero,* 2020, www.joincampaignzero .org/problem/.

Chapman, Thandeka K. "Teaching Race and Qualitative Research." *Researching Race in Education*, edited by Adrienne D. Dixon, Information Age Publishing, 2014, pp. 233–45.

Clark, Meredith. "Making the Case for Black with a Capital B. Again." *Poynter*, 23 Aug. 2015, www.poynter.org/reporting-editing/2015/making-the-case-for-black -with-a-capital-b-again/.

Cole, Devan. "Haley: Dylann Roof 'Hijacked' Confederate Flag from People Who Saw It as Symbolizing 'Service, and Sacrifice and Heritage'." *CNN*, Cable News Network, 6 Dec. 2019, www.cnn.com/2019/12/06/politics/nikki-haley-confeder-ate-flag/index.html.

Connors, Robert. *Composition-Rhetoric: Backgrounds, Theory, and Pedagogy.* U of Pitts-burgh P, 1997.

Crenshaw, Kimberlé W. *Critical Race Theory: The Key Writings that Formed the Move-ment.* New Press, 1995.

———. "Demarginalizing the Intersection of Race and Sex: A Black Feminist Critique of Antidiscrimination Doctrine, Feminist Theory and Antiracist Politics." *University of Chicago Legal Forum*, vol. 129, 1989, pp. 139–67.

———. "Twenty Years of Critical Race Theory: Looking Back to Move Forward." *Connecticut Law Review*, vol. 43, 2010, pp. 1253–1354.

"The Counted: Tracking People Killed by Police in the United States | US News." *The Guardian*, Guardian News and Media, 2017, (2015–2017), www.theguardian.com /us-news/series/counted-us-police-killings.

Delgado, Richard, and Jean Stefancic. *Critical Race Theory: An Introduction.* NYUP, 2017.

Dixon, Adrienne D., and Celia K. Rousseau. "And We Are Still Not Saved: Critical Race Theory in Education Ten Years Later." *Race, Ethnicity, and Education*, vol. 8, no. 1, 2005, pp. 7–27.

The Diversity Subcommittee of the NCTE Executive Committee. "2001 Audit of Implementation of Recommendations from the 1996 Report on Involving People of Color in the Council." Chaired by Leila Christenbury. NCTE, Champagne -Urbana, IL, 2001, cdn.ncte.org/nctefiles/involved/volunteer/elections/audit_of _the_report_on_involving_people_of_color_in_the_council.pdf.

"Explaining AP Style on Black and White." *AP NEWS*, Associated Press, 20 July 2020, apnews.com/article/9105661462.

FBI. "About Hate Crime Statistics, 2015." *FBI UCR*, 2016, ucr.fbi.gov/hate-crime /2015.

Freeman, Alan David. "Legitimizing Racial Discrimination Through Antidiscrimination Law: A Critical Review of Supreme Court Doctrine." *Minnesota Law Review*, vol. 62, 1978, pp. 1049–119.

Friedersdorf, Conor. "Why It Matters That the Charleston Attack was Terrorism." *The Atlantic*, 22 Jun. 2015, www.theatlantic.com/politics/archive/2015/06/was-the -charleston-attack-terrorism/396329/.

Frinzi, Samantha. "Black Lives Matter: Remember Their Names." *Odyssey*, 12 Jul. 2016, www.theodysseyonline.com/black-lives-matter-remember-their-names.

Gilyard, Keith. *Voices of the Self*. Wayne State UP, 1991.

Gladstone, Rick. "Many Ask, Why Not Call Church Shooting Terrorism." *The New York Times*, 18 Jun. 2015, www.nytimes.com/2015/06/19/us/charleston-shooting-terrorism-or-hate-crime.html.

Gourley, Lenore E. "Capital B for Black." *American Psychologist*, vol. 30, no. 2, 1975, pp. 181, doi:10.1037/h0078439.

Green, Meredith J., and Christopher C. Sonn. "Problematising the Discourses of the Dominant: Whiteness and Reconciliation." *Journal of Community and Applied Social Psychology*, vol. 16, no. 5, 2006, pp. 379–95.

The Guardian. "The Counted." *The Guardian*, 2016, www.theguardian.com/us-news /ng-interactive/2015/jun/01/the-counted-police-killings-us-database.

Hatewatch Staff. "Update: Incidents of Hateful Harassment Since Election Day Now Number 701." *SPLC*, 18 Nov. 2016, www.splcenter.org/hatewatch/2016/11/18 /update-incidents-hateful-harassment-election-day-now-number-701.

Heath, Shirley Brice. "Protean Shapes in Literacy Events: Ever-Shifting Oral and Literate Traditions." *Spoken and Written Language: Exploring Orality and Literacy*, edited by Deborah Tannen, ABLEX Publishing Corporation, 1982, pp. 91–117.

———. "The Sense of Being Literate: Historical and Cross-Cultural." *Handbook of Reading Research 2.3*, 1991, pp. 3–25.

Herrick, James. *The History and Theory of Rhetoric*. 5th ed., Pearson, 2012.

Hylton, Kevin. "Talk the Talk, Walk the Walk: Defining Critical Race Theory in Research." *Race Ethnicity and Education*, vol. 15, no. 1, 2012, pp. 23–41.

Inoue, Asao, B. *Antiracist Writing Assessment Ecologies: Teaching and Assessing Writing for a Socially Just Future*. The WAC Clearinghouse; Parlor Press, 2015, doi:10.37514 /PER-B.2015.0698.

———. "Racial Methodologies for Composition Studies: Reflecting on Theories of Race in Writing Assessment Research." *Writing Studies Research in Practice: Methods and Methodologies*, edited by Nickoson and Sheridan, Southern Illinois UP, 2012, pp. 125–139.

Jackson, Ronald E., et al. "Lack of Diversity in NCA's Journal Editorships and Editorial Boards." Letter/Petition. June 23, 2018, bit.ly/3kPd4qa.

Kessler, Glenn. "Donald Trump and David Duke: For the Record." *Washington Post*, 1 Mar. 2016, www.washingtonpost.com/news/fact-checker/wp/2016/03/01 /donald-trump-and-david-duke-for-the-record/.

Kitzhaber, Albert Raymond. *Rhetoric in American Colleges, 1850–1900.* Southern Methodist UP, 1990.

Lacy, Michael G., and Kent A. Ono. *Critical Rhetorics of Race.* NYUP, 2011.

Ladson-Billings, Gloria. "Just What is Critical Race Theory and What's it Doing in a Nice Field Like Education?" *International Journal of Qualitative Studies in Education,* vol. 11, no.1, 1998, pp. 7–24.

Lanham, David, and Amy Liu. "Not Just a Typographical Change: Why Brookings Is Capitalizing Black." *Brookings,* 23 Sept. 2019, www.brookings.edu/research/brookingscapitalizesblack/.

Logan, Shirley Wilson. "Changing Missions, Shifting Positions, and Breaking Silences." *College Composition and Communication,* vol. 55, no. 2, 2003, pp. 330–42.

———. "'When and Where I Enter': Race, Gender, and Composition Studies." *Feminism and Composition Studies: In Other Words,* edited by Susan Jarrat and Lynn Worsham, The Modern Language Association, 1998, pp. 45–57.

Malagon, Maria C., Lindsay Perez Huber, and Veronica N. Velez. "Our Experiences, Our Methods: Using Grounded Theory to Inform a Critical Race Theory Methodology." *Seattle Journal for Social Justice,* vol. 8, 2009, pp. 253–72.

Mapping Police Violence. *Mapping Police Violence,* 27 Sep. 2020, mappingpolice violence.org/.

Medhurst, Martin J. "Apology." *Communication Research and Theory Network,* 17200, National Communication Association/Penn State University, 17 June 2019, bit.ly /3rO4V8r.

———. "Editorial." *Communication Research and Theory Network,* 17193, National Communication Association/Penn State University, 12 June 2019. bit.ly/3aPJ2yQ.

Missouri State, Legislature. Senate Bill 43. *Missouri State Legislature,* September 2017, www.senate.mo.gov/17info/BTS_Web/Bill.aspx?SessionType=R&BillID =57095378.

Monroe, Barbara Jean. *Crossing the Digital Divide: Race, Writing, and Technology in the Classroom.* Teachers College Press, 2004.

Montoya, Margaret E. "Mapping Intellectual/Political Foundations and Future Self Critical Directions-Introduction: LatCrit Theory: Mapping Its Intellectual and Political Foundations and Future Self-Critical Directions." *U of Miami Law Review,* vol. 53, 1998, p. 1119.

Mortensen, Peter, and Gesa E. Kirsch, editors. *Ethics and Representation in Qualitative Studies of Literacy.* National Council of Teachers of English, 1996.

Mueller, Derek N. *Network Sense: Methods for Visualizing a Discipline.* The WAC Clearinghouse; UP of Colorado, 2017. doi:10.37514/WRI-B.2017.0124.

Muir, Star. "Distinguished Scholars of NCA." *National Communication,* Aug. 2019, www.natcom.org/sites/default/files/NCADistinguishedScholars-Letter_from_ Muir-EC5.8.19.pdf.

NAACP. "Travel Advisory for the State of Missouri." *NAACP,* 2 Aug. 2017, www .naacp.org/latest/travel-advisory-state-missouri/.

Nakamura, Lisa. "Cyberrace." *PMLA,* vol. 123, no. 5, 2008, pp. 1673–82. *JSTOR,* www.jstor.org/stable/25501969.

National Council for Teachers of English Task Force on Involving People of Color. "1996 Report from the Task Force on Involving People of Color in the Council." NCTE, 1996, bit.ly/3aZO1NB.

Nickoson, Lee, and Mary P. Sheridan. *Writing Studies Research in Practice.* Southern Illinois UP, 2012.

Office of Justice Programs. "Hate Crime Victimization, 2004–2015." *Bureau of Justice Statistics,* 29 Jun. 2017, www.bjs.gov/index.cfm?ty=pbdetail&iid=5967.

Omi, Michael, and Howard Winant. *Racial Formation in the United States.* Routledge, 2014.

Ono, Kent A., and Michael G. Lacy, editors. *Critical Rhetorics of Race.* NYU P, 2011.

Ortego y Gasca, Felipe. "La Leyenda Negra/The Black Legend: Historical Distortion, Defamation, Slander, Libel, and Stereotyping of Hispanics." *Somos Primos,* no. 141, 2011. www.somosprimos.com/sp2011/spaug11/spaug11.htm.

Piggott, Stephen. "White Nationalists Rejoice at Trump's Appointment of Breitbart's Stephen Bannon." *SPLC,* 14 Nov. 2016, www.splcenter.org/hatewatch/2016/11/14/white-nationalists-rejoice-trumps-appointment-breitbarts-stephen-bannon.

Powell, Malea. "Rhetorics of Survivance: How American Indians use Writing." *College Composition and Communication,* vol. 53, no. 3, 2002, pp. 396–434.

Prendergast, Catherine. *Literacy and Racial Justice: The Politics of Learning after Brown v. Board of Education.* Southern Illinois UP, 2003.

———. "Race: The Absent Presence in Composition Studies." *College Composition and Communication,* vol. 50, no. 1, 1998, pp. 36–53.

Price, Anne. "Spell It with a Capital 'B.'" *Medium,* Medium/Insight Center for Community Economic Development, 1 Oct. 2019, medium.com/@InsightCCED/spell-it-with-a-capital-b-9eab112d759a.

Romm, Norma. *New Racism: Revisiting Researcher Accountabilities.* Springer Science & Business Media, 2010.

Royster, Jacqueline Jones. *Traces of a Stream: Literacy and Social Change Among African American Women.* U of Pittsburgh P, 2000.

Royster, Jacqueline Jones, and Jean C. Williams. "History in the Spaces Left: African American Presence and Narratives of Composition Studies." *College Composition and Communication,* vol. 50, no. 4, 1999, pp. 563–84.

Ruiz, Iris D. *Reclaiming Composition for Chicano/as and Other Ethnic Minorities: A Critical History and Pedagogy.* Palgrave Macmillan, 2016.

Ruiz, Iris D., and Raúl Sánchez, eds. *Decolonizing Rhetoric and Composition Studies: New Latinx Keywords for Theory and Pedagogy.* Springer, 2016.

Sanchez, James Chase. "Trump, the KKK, and the Versatility of White Supremacy Rhetoric." *Journal of Contemporary Rhetoric,* vol. 8, no. ½, 2018, pp. 44–56.

Scales, Kylee. "Charleston Shooting Victims' Names Released." *Fox59,* 18 Jun. 2015, fox59.com/2015/06/18/charleston-shooting-victims-names-released/.

Scott, Eugene. "Nikki Haley: Confederate Flag 'Should Have Never Been There.'" *CNN,* 10 Jul. 2015, www.cnn.com/2015/07/10/politics/nikki-haley-confederate-flag-removal.

Smith, Linda Tuhiwai. *Decolonizing Methodologies.* Zed Books, 2012.

"Spell It With A Capital." *Weekly Louisianian*, 7 Dec. 1878, p. 2. *Readex: African American Newspapers*, bit.ly/2NgFHAX.

Sternglass, Marilyn S. *Time to Know Them: A Longitudinal Study of Writing and Learning at the College Level*. Routledge, 1997.

Swaine, Jon, and Oliver Laughland. "Eric Garner and Tamir Rice among Those Missing from FBI Record of Police Killings." *The Guardian: The Counted*, Guardian News and Media, 15 Oct. 2015, www.theguardian.com/us-news/2015/oct/15/fbi-record-police-killings-tamir-rice-eric-garner.

Tharps, Lori L. "The Case for Black With a Capital B." *The New York Times*, 18 Nov. 2014, www.nytimes.com/2014/11/19/opinion/the-case-for-black-with-a-capital-b.html.

United States Department of Justice. Attorney General Lynch's Video Statement on Hate Crimes in America. November 18, 2016. www.justice.gov/opa/video/attorney-general-lynch-s-video-statement-hate-crimes-america.

Villanueva, Victor. *Bootstraps: From an American Academic of Color*. National Council of Teachers of English, 1993.

———. "On the Rhetoric and Precedents of Racism." *College Composition and Communication*, vol. 50, no. 4, 1999, pp. 645–61.

———. "The Rhetorics of the New Racism or the Master's Four Tropes." *FYHC: First-Year Honors Composition*, vol.1, 2006, pp. 1–21.

Wajcman, Judy. "Feminist Theories of Technology." *Cambridge Journal of Economics*, vol. 34, no. 1, 2010, pp. 143–52.

———. "Gender and Work: A Technofeminist Analysis." *Handbook of Gender, Work and Organization*, edited by Emma Jeanes, David Knights, and Patricia Yancey Martin, Wiley, 2011, pp. 263–75.

Williams, Patricia J. *The Alchemy of Race and Rights*. Harvard UP, 1991.

Williams, Stereo. "The Power of Black Twitter." *Daily Beast,* 14 Apr. 2017, www.thedailybeast.com/the-power-of-black-twitter.

Workneh, Lilly. "Bree Newsome, Activist Who Took Down Confederate Flag, Says She Refuses 'To Be Ruled by Fear.'" *Huffington Post*, 6 Dec. 2017, www.huffpost.com/entry/bree-newsome-speaks-out_n_7698598.

Yamamoto, Eric K. "Critical Race Praxis: Race Theory and Political Lawyering Practice in Post-Civil Rights America." *Michigan Law Review*, vol. 95, no. 4,1997, pp. 821–900.

Yancey, George. "Colonial Gazing: The Production of the Body as 'Other'" *The Western Journal of Black Studies*, vol. 32, no.1, 2008, search.proquest.com/openview/f26b4f1ed2fcadad05a2d9157a10f39e/1?pq-origsite=gscholar&cbl=47709.

CHAPTER 2.

CRITIQUING THE CRITICAL: THE POLITICS OF RACE AND COLONIALITY IN RHETORIC, COMPOSITION, AND WRITING STUDIES RESEARCH TRADITIONS

Iris D. Ruiz

University of California-Merced

Key Terms and Concepts: Critique, Decoloniality, Delinking, Historiography, Curanderisma, Nahui Ollin

In most disciplines, a body of scholarship defines what can be regarded as traditional and "critical" of that tradition. However, when that scholarship has been predicated on White, heteronormative, patriarchal, settler-colonial discourse, even the "critical" can be exclusionary. This colonial disciplinary solipsism is the problem that this chapter seeks to explore. Here, I argue that although certain rhetoric, composition, and writing studies (RCWS) methods claim to be "critical," when filtered through an epistemic act of decoloniality—epistemic disobedience—it becomes clear that current critical methods are embedded in traditions of Whiteness and Western oriented epistemologies. If one understands epistemological racism as continuing to uncritically support exclusionary research and publication practices, even when claimed to be critical, then RCWS is implicated in racist epistemological acts.

RCWS is a relatively new discipline. Written documentation of its disciplinary origins is tied to the second half of the twentieth century, a conservative and racially tense moment in history when the Conference on College Composition and Communication and its accompanying journal, *CCC,* were initiated. (Ruiz, "Creating a 'New History'"). The 1950's are well known for their conservative academic movements, such as New Criticism and Project English (Strain). In this same moment, the "southern strategy," enduring Jim Crow Laws, and anti-Mexican sentiment in the Southwest characterized the U.S. political-racial climate.¹ In addition, RCWS is historically and epistemologically situated in dominant disciplinary references, rituals, values, conventions, and beliefs that construct its unique disciplinary cultural literacy (Brodkey; Hirsch). This cultural literacy enables certain historiographies to assert and maintain scholastic hegemony and disciplinary power (Aronowitz and Giroux; Ruiz, "Race") and, therefore, by default, marginalizes counter histories. This context is provided while considering that RCWS is also known as an interdisciplinary field because it borrows from and incorporates other disciplines and scholarly fields. It is, however, still characterized as most disciplines are—resting upon a static body of foundational epistemological traditions credited to the pioneers of the professionalization of a field largely tied to the first-year composition course (Ruiz, "Race"). Most of these pioneers have been White European males. Following the trajectory of a well-established, White-dominated historical pattern of RCWS, one can discern that its cultural literacy is one that is characterized as a form of cultural capital (Bourdieu) for certain cultural habits and shared norms. Creating disciplinary cultural capital also ensures a type of epistemic exclusivity in that the highest reward will go to those that best fit within Eurocentric epistemic trajectories of the discipline.

In this chapter, it will be important to understand that, positionally speaking, when BIPOC (Black and Indigenous People of Color) perform their academic identities through standard conventions, disciplinary legitimacy, and other actions that ensure professional access, they are immersed in a colonizing practice that results from the historical colonization of intellectual space in which BIPOC often find themselves. For example, in RCWS, BIPOC often must acknowledge Greco-Roman historical and epistemological traditions to give a nod toward scholarly "credibility" and gain a badge of "academic rigor" from their peers (Ruiz and Baca; Sánchez). Further, as I demonstrate below, the "politics of citation" in RCWS still struggles with scholarly recognition and meaningful inclusion of its BIPOC scholars with histories of both/and colonization and displacement (African Americans and other ethnic minorities). Here, we've come to the point where we need to call out the White-supremacist origins of RCWS through antiracist methodologies.

Practicing antiracist methodologies within RCWS has various connotations, but it denotes the act of countering racist methodological practices and performing anti-racist epistemic acts, one of which is to examine the institutional politics of RCWS and their affiliate research methodologies that often claim to be "critical" "liberatory" and even "counter-hegemonic" while still practicing racist citation practices by excluding BIPOC works from research engagement.

---

1   Examples include the Zoot Suit Riots and Mendez v. Westminster.

Unlike many of our white counterparts in RCWS, when BIPOC perform acts of intellectual critique and claim to be "critical," they engage in several practices that perform a systematic analysis of structures of power and privilege operating in some socially constructed disciplinary context. The politics of citation is one of these systemic critical analyses. What is often ignored, however, is that BIPOC scholars must often contend with race and racism within the act of "critique," by being side-stepped in disciplinary citations practices in works that claim to be "critical."

For example, let us consider Karl Marx's critique of social class inequality or Foucault's critique of the relationship between people, power, and institutions, while exposing the boundedness of human subjects to discursive structures and habits that cannot be easily shed or performed as an "outsider looking in" (Butler). Where is the mention of race in both Marx's and Foucault's methods? Often, in both Francophone and German philosophical traditions, the mention of race is subtly embedded by implication in the margins of their most notable contributions or indicated in some obscure lecture notes that end up on some wiki somewhere. In this sense, one might ask, "What does it mean to be critical of what has already been claimed to be "critical" through an antiracist lens?" If one agrees with Foucault, for example, and sees no possibilities for true critique outside the bounds of discourse, what, then, can one make of claims to performing critique of long-standing traditions such as patriarchy, White supremacy, or capitalism? For my purposes here, I'm more inclined to consider critique of the "critical" as a necessity that occurs when disciplines reach a point of "epistemic rupture"—a disciplinary paradigm shift (Kuhn)—in this case the rupture of unquestionable White supremacist origins for both critique and disciplinary validity at the expense of a discipline's BIPOC members.

RCWS has reached a point where the field's discourses have become incommensurable with the realities they initially sought to theorize and explain—realities embedded in revolutionary events such as the civil rights movement, the City University of New York (CUNY) and open-admissions, desegregation mandates, challenges to de facto and de jure segregation, and the growth of basic writing, writing centers, and writing programs. Today, we see this incommensurability of White-dominated disciplinary discourses growing even wider through numerous digital movements—#CommunicationSoWhite, #BlackLivesMatter, #MeToo, #CiteBlackWomen, and #DefundthePolice. These movements are again asking the nation to take a long, hard look at race relations and the role of education in responding to these movements. Writing programs are not immune to this critical examination due to their centrality within higher education.

In such moments, a scholar-researcher might consider the point at which "[o]ne asks about the limits of ways of knowing because one has already run up against a crisis within the epistemological field in which one lives" (Butler 215). In this moment, I argue that critiquing the "critical" is a necessary response to epistemic ruptures. It is a way that critique can challenge long-held traditions and beliefs [and] expose the hidden, silenced, ignored, and "other" (Spencer). In the case of this chapter, the "other" can be both/and bodily and/or epistemological, but they are referred to as "other" because they suffer from a lack of representation in either their bodily and/or material presence and/or through exclusive and exclusionary scholarship. Therefore, I seek to explore ways that both traditional and "critical" methods are in a state of epistemic rupture as decolonial options have provided mechanisms to disrupt both traditional and "critical" RCWS methods, two of which are the decolonial act of delinking and an accompanied performance of a series of engagements with epistemic disobedience.

In order to begin this delinking journey in a moment where colonialism has become pejorative instead of coveted, one should ask, "What does it mean to be "critical" when our current disciplinary paradigm shift calls for pushing race and racism to the center of our philosophical inquiry and epistemological practices?" To begin, consider that current "critical" RCWS methodologies continue to practice racist citation practices, aka "the politics of citation." White scholars get cited more so than scholars of color, and therefore, their ways of knowing become privileged. In *Reclaiming Composition*, I examined citation practices within *College Composition and Communication* (*CCC*), and I found that the same White scholars were cited repeatedly from 1950–1993. In 1993, *CCC* had not yet had a female editor—it was exclusively a White and male epistemological enterprise. Further, there were virtually no authors of color that were most cited (Figure 2.1).

Although 1993 does not seem like that long ago, it is only due to the presence of digitized venues today that more scholars of color are being published. This technological shift, however, does not mean that scholars of color are being cited more. In a study that is currently being performed by Steven Parks in partnership with Literacy in Composition Studies (LiCS), he mentioned that the whiteness of the field is quite evident in the field's major flagship journals. He referenced 17,000 data points, and this is going to be unsurprising in many respects because most disciplines in the United States have operated similarly.

Academia is a White-majority profession (Figure 2.2). Within disciplines marked by whiteness, "critical" topics such as race, class, gender, critical historiography, feminism, social justice, and embodiment challenge normative,

1950–1964	1965–1979	1980–May 1993
H. Allen (4)	R. Larson (8)	R. Connors (6)
D. Lloyd	R. Lloyd-Jones (6)	A. Lunsford
R. Braddock (3)	F. D'Angelo	M. Rose
B. Kogan	R. de Beaugrande (5)	L. Faigley (5)
P. Wikelund	T. M. Sawyer (4)	L. Flower
H. Wilson	R. Gorrell (3)	M. Hairston
E. Steinberg (2)	E. Corbett	C. Berkenkotter (4)
V. Rivenbaugh	E. Suderman	D. Stewart
S. Radner	G. Sloan	S. Stotsky
	J. Lauer	S. Witte
	L. Odell	C. Anson (3)
	R. Hoover	L. Bridwell-Bowles
	R. Gebhardt	G. Brossell
	W. Ross Winterowd	E. Corbett
	W. Marqhardt	F. D'Angelo
	W. Pixton	R. Fulkerson
	G. Cannon	J. Hayes
	S. Crowley	J. Hoetker
	M. Sternglass	D. Murray
	A. M. Tibbetts	L. Peterson
	F. Christensen	L. Podis
		G. Sloan
		N. Sommers
		E. M. White

Figure 2.1. Most frequently published authors of major articles.
Source: Phillips, Greenberg, and Gibson.

objective, or uncritical research agendas that otherwise sustain White heteronormative and patriarchal agendas. Furthermore, these topics are often written about by scholars of color, which was made apparent through my work on writing program administration and race, and this work further reveals why anti-racist methods are few (Garcia de Mueller and Ruiz). To make matters worse, racism in citation practices, aka "the politics of citation," occurs through excluding citations of minoritized voices and academics of color, and it also happens through citing White authors who do "race work" (see Clary-Lemon; Ruiz and Garcia de Mueller; Prendergast, Villanueva, and Phillips et al.). All of this makes for a racist and colonial discipline in many respects.

In practicing epistemic disobedience, one can disrupt BIPOC invisibility and reclaim research that is performed through, for example, a Chicana perspective. Although I write as a Chicana, anyone can perform antiracist and decolonial methods. As a Chicana within RCWS, I have done research on race from a decolonial lens (Ruiz, "Race"). However, I have not yet been able to articulate the ways that racism is embedded in research and knowledge production and legitimated in RCWS. In an act of reclamation, I turn to decolonial theory to problematize RCWS's dominant disciplinary trends. This is an act of decoloniality. I am not "decolonizing RCWS." More pointedly, I carry out a decolonial antiracist methodology through applying a reciprocal, decolonial gaze (Mignolo) toward three of the field's common "critical" methodologies, aka "commonplaces" in research practices. These methodologies are historiography, embodiment, and feminism. Looking at them through a decolonial lens is more than "an outsider looking in." It is a "looking back" at as in a reflection of the antithesis. Doing so reveals RCWS being strongly implicated in what critical race theorist Richard Delgado calls "imperial scholarship" (Chang 28), a citation practicve which stems from critical race legal studies scholarship and demonstrates how sanctioned disciplinary knowledge controls both how race appears in research as well as who is permitted to create this knowledge through sanctioned methods— ultimately determining what counts as "making knowledge" and who gets to make it (North). Recovery of oversights in this context becomes an important response to what one does NOT see when looking back.

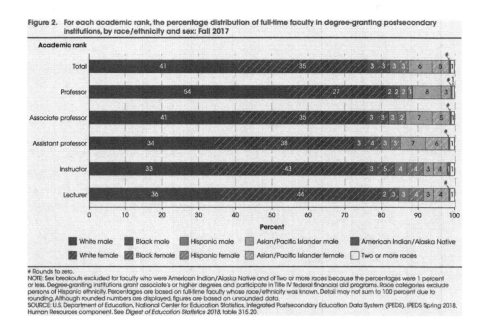

Figure 2.2. Characteristics of postsecondary faculty. Source: McFarland et al.

Walter Mignolo's decolonial option of "delinking" is key to this decolonial application because it allows for a specific type of historical recovery: what I call "historical curanderisma."[2] Mignolo claims that "de-colonial thinking presupposes de-linking (epistemically and politically) from the web of imperial knowledge (theo- and ego-politically grounded) from disciplinary management" (20). Historical curanderisma is what I've named my practice of delinking from dominant disciplinary discourses of whiteness associated with RCWS. I chose the figure of the Curandera to perform this option because it is a healing epistemic practice. Curanderisma refers to an act of indigenous healing performed by one who has dedicated themselves to the arts of holistic medicine and natural homeopathy. A Curandera is akin to a medicine doctor who has also studied the alchemy of botanicals and biological organisms and can function as a horticulturist, life coach, and medicinal and spiritual healer. This person is desired by an individual or group that has fallen under the unfortunate circumstance of a physical sickness or demonic possession, as in the scene in the recent movie *La Llorona* and in many real-life instances (I was once healed from an illness by my great-grandmother, a Curandera). Being that many Mexicans and Mexican Americans practice Catholicism, the idea of demonic possession is not uncommon, and the ability of prayer and healing through religious rituals has deep roots within indigenous cultural histories. The acts of Curanderas are still present today in Latin America and the United States. In line with such spiritual beliefs and practices, there is an element of the metaphysical that is associated with the practice, as is with my "methodological" approach in this chapter. Through words that come from a committed critical historian interested in returning a decolonial gaze with an intent to delink from and relink to a story that empowers rather than negates her existence and for others who have for too long occupied marginal positions in this field, I engage in an alchemy of remaking, recovery, and engaging the politics of race and coloniality in RCWS research traditions.

This type of decolonial work is timely and imperative in the age of Trump, the 45th president of the United States, known for his support of White supremacy, hate speech, and xenophobia toward Latinxs, made clear through

---

2   Curanderismo is a type of holistic medicinal practice and system associated with Latin America, but more commonly with the indigenous populations of Latin America. The way in which Curanderisma is practiced varies by region (Guatemala, Nicaragua, Honduras, Argentina, Mexico, the southwestern region of the United States, etc.). It is a blend of indigenous spiritual practices, religious beliefs, faith, and prayer with the use of herbs, massage, and other traditional methods of healing. Curanderismo can be used holistically to cure or address various physical, spiritual, psychological, and social needs of the people who use it. The Spanish verb *curar* means to heal. It is a method of healing. It refers to healing. Practicing rituals associated with Curanderismo serves to create a balance between the patient and his or her environment and contributes to sustaining one's health. I'm interested in the branch of Curanderismo that is practiced in Mexico and is based on Aztec, Mayan, and Spanish influences.

his inactions toward many deaths and abuses of detained immigrants as well as his inaction toward many highly visible traumatic separations of Latinx families. Due to these inactions, his presidency has negated the idea of a post-racial society. These recent traumas of racism make practicing historical curanderisma an opportunity to present more accurate representations of multicultural knowledge production and, by consequence, provide an ethical engagement with the field's tendency towards racist epistemological exclusion. Healing, as I will showcase in this chapter, involves resisting academia's celebration of self-destruction through toxic practices of depreciation (WOC Faculty; Yancy, "Dear White," *Look, A White!*, and "The Ugly Truth"). This method rejects the normalization of trauma inflicted on scholars of color by both implication and exclusion and by pretending that this epistemological exclusionary practice does not create trauma. Recognizing and legitimating the healing potential of such practices will enable scholars, regardless of color, gender, and dis/ability, to counter imposter syndrome, and, instead, will rightfully stigmatize those who deny others' experiences as racist.

Furthermore, historical curanderisma is a historical methodological practice that promotes personal and disciplinary healing and can result in what we understand as praxis because of the proposed humanizing impact upon the researcher and the reader. Through decolonial historical recovery, which builds upon my earlier scholarship featured in *Reclaiming Composition for Chicano/as and other Ethnic Minorities: A Critical History and Pedagogy*, RCWS is called upon to further consider its deep involvement with and perpetuation of colonial methods through continuous legitimation of colonial epistemologies even while claiming to be "diverse," "inclusive," and "critical." Ultimately, I call upon RCWS to rethink its Eurocentric and White disciplinary center that dominates its research methods. I recenter and reclaim minoritized ways of knowing and provide nuanced antiracist ways of being in the world and of conducting research. Doing so allows for a re-mapping of specific geographies, communities, and textual productions for the purpose of healing and sustaining the well-being of professional and personal lives of marginalized scholars who have trouble seeing themselves as legitimate knowledge makers in RCWS.

RCWS' PROBLEMATIC HISTORY WITH RACE AND RACISM

RCWS, like most other disciplinary fields, is diverse but still has marginalized populations that are non-White (Kynard). RCWS also relies upon Eurocentric histories to legitimize its disciplinary status, which is colonial and marginalizes certain groups. The knowledge that is produced by marginalized groups through their publications is minoritized and, I argue, can be clearly seen when one takes a close look at how race has functioned throughout our disciplinary history. One way to look at this history is through archival research practices, which provide opportunities to see what was taking place behind the scenes of disciplinary creation both racially and politically. Another way to look at this marginalization is to look at what was happening ON the scenes at the front lines of the discipline. These scenes would be cast and directed by the dominant scholarship of RCWS since its inception as a field in 1949, when the Conference on College Composition and Communication (CCCC) was founded (Ruiz, Reclaiming 103). However, OFF the scenes of disciplinary textual representations were important responses to civil rights movements for minoritized populations evidenced with the formation of the National Council of Teachers of English (NCTE) Task Force on Racism and Bias in 1969 and the formation of the Black and the Latinx Caucuses (known as the Chicano Teachers of English at this time) the same year. The 1960s marked a historical imperative when NCTE took a much more active role in racial matters, yet the folks who were doing the work of creating these social justice groups were often marginal scholars who have remained marginalized in the present.

In 1964, the NCTE Board of Directors mandated that the "Council and its affiliates be open to all races and ethnicities" (Hook 232). The goal of the task force on racism and bias was to help "to continually bring attention to issues concerning minorities and their representation" (National Council). If one looks at NCTE's webpage titled "Advocacy for Minority Groups," there are references to efforts throughout the years that reflect the field's attempt to be inclusive of marginal populations. For example, there is a commitment to opening the Council to all races and ethnicities and a commitment to hold conferences in places where no racial discrimination exists: "Throughout its life, [NCTE] had attempted to treat all groups—all students, all teachers, all its members—alike. It had, for instance, been one of the first professional organizations to insist that its conventions be housed only in places where there would be no racial discrimination" (Hook 232).

For CCCC, however, one has only to look at the organization's most recent position statements to see substantial progress toward racial inclusivity to the same extent as NCTE. NCTE's attempts to show its social justice commitments are enacted by making diversity part of its mission, narratives about its history, and position statements, in which they have a specific category, unlike CCCC. The way the field has not paid enough attention to race and minoritized ways of making knowledge through research methods, partially evidenced by CCCC's scarce consideration of race in its position statements, has been problematic from the start. Catherine Prendergast's article "Race: The Absent Presence in Composition Studies" is still considered to be quite relevant 20 years later. In her article, she admits that

> It has always been my experience when reading Shirley Brice
> Heath's *Ways With Words* that I have to exert a little extra
> effort to keep straight which of the focal communities Heath
> studies—Roadville or Trackton—is the working-class black
> town and which is the working-class white town; I find myself
> often flipping back to the introduction where this racial
> distinction is initially made and then almost immediately dis-
> missed as irrelevant. I have come to think of this extra effort
> I have to go through to locate race in the first part of *Ways
> With Words* as emblematic of my experience reading much
> of the scholarship in composition studies where race seems
> to function as an absent presence. For while it is often called
> upon as a category to delineate cultural groups that will be the
> focal subjects of research studies, the relationship of race to
> the composing process is seldom fully explored. Instead race
> becomes subsumed into the powerful tropes of "basic writer,"
> "stranger" to the academy, or the trope of the generalized,
> marginalized "other." (36)

She further argues that race remains undertheorized, unproblematized, and under-investigated in composition research, leaving us with no means to confront the "racialized atmosphere of the university and no way to account for the impact of the persistence of prejudice on writers and texts" (36).

Furthermore, when academics of color do decide to represent their experiences and worldviews through revealing their positionalities which draw upon the notion, the "personal" as "political" (Lorde 4), their work is dismissed as anti-intellectual and non-empirical (Prendergast 42). bell hooks also writes about her experiences at Stanford University, where she struggled to find herself at an Ivy League institution where there are not many Black women, and her desire to keep herself "close to home" in her academics by keeping the average working-class Black woman in mind as her audience keeps her in the realm of skepticism by other mainstream academics who question her resistance to dense theoretical language and academic jargon. hooks demonstrates the challenge of being an academic of color from a working-class background as manifold: there is pressure from the top to sound like them and there is pressure from the bottom to sound like them too. Compounding this tension of feeling both insider and outsider at all times while negotiating academic communal belonging and staying connected to home, Prendergast adds an extra dimension to consider for those committed to antiracist practice that avoids further marginalization of people of color (POC): "[t]he present challenge for compositionists is to develop theorizations of race that do not reinscribe people of color as either foreign or invisible, nor leave whiteness uninvestigated; only through such work can composition begin to counteract the denial of racism that is part of the classroom, the courts, and a shared colonial inheritance" (51). What might this look like on paper? How can POC reclaim their space while challenging always being placed in the margins as invisible and foreign? One might answer with, "legitimize their stories."

However, when POC decide to engage the personal as political (Victor Villanueva comes to mind) in RCWS, the field tends to relegate these works to "exceptions to the rule," "alternative genres," or "cultural rhetorics," or reject them altogether and suggest publishing personal works in "creative writing" publication venues that do not have the scholarly parameters that present themselves as objective assessment tools for reviewers to make decisions—aka as "rigorous." One does not stop to consider how these editorial practices are also racially biased because they fail to represent both the POC author while simultaneously neglecting how this author might engage with the subject matter in ways that demonstrate the journal's commitment to antiracism. One must only look at the past seven issues of *College English* or *College Composition and Communication* to see this phenomenon in current action. The field is hegemonic, and it is very much invested in maintaining its "scholastic White hegemony."

In our article "Race, Silence, and Writing Program Administration," Genevieve Garcia de Mueller and I discuss how scholars have critiqued the problem of how the field talks about race in its scholarly texts. For example,

> In "The Racialization of Composition Studies: Scholarly Rhetoric of Race since 1990," Jennifer Clary Lemon "examines the discourses of the journals *College Composition and Communication* and *College English* since 1990. Her study reveals that the majority of race-related works published in these journals rarely use the actual words "race or racism." Instead, authors utilize euphemistic language such as "diversity, inclusion, and social justice" when alluding to racialized phenomena (Clary-Lemon W6). (23)

Such language has caused much needed disciplinary discussions about "race" to lose their transformative potential. Later, I discuss how the term can become distanced from its origin of intent, but here, with the word "race" in mind, one thinks of biology, categories of inferiority/superiority, histories of racism, and ethnicity, or should I say that the telos of "race" more often than not becomes muddled when contentious discussions arise about definitions of diversity and inclusion? The goals of antiracism are understood partially through the terms we employ and agreed upon definitions. In Steve Lamos's book *Interests and Opportunities: Race, Racism, and University Writing Instruction in the Post-Civil Rights Era*, he traces the history of racism in basic writing. Victor Villanueva notices in "The Rhetorics of New Racism" that racism often disguises itself, stating, "the new racism embeds racism within a set of other categories—language, religion, culture, civilizations pluralized and writ large, a set of master tropes (or the master's tropes)" (16). New racism functions differently than simply replacing words with other words to effectively elide their significance and power, as Clary-Lemon's critique notes.

While the former operates at the level of language, the latter, new racism, functions at the level of discourse referred to as "master tropes" in Villanueva's analysis. In short, discussions of race have become further invisible due to the disappearing acts of "race" caused by metaphor, metonymy, and blind discourses of neutrality resulting in a "new racism."

This metaphorical/metonymic problem can be counteracted by scholarship that pays direct attention to race and writing programs. Daniel Barlow, for instance, looks at the "productive potential" of racial inquiry in composition scholarship and pedagogy in "Composing Post-Multiculturalism." He claims that "celebratory multiculturalism" does not provide sufficient opportunities for critical inquiry into race and racism. He agrees with Clary-Lemon, stating that the field looks at "race" as a discursive problem, and while this is a productive point of critique, it still does not move the field forward in a way that gets beyond either celebratory multiculturalism or discursive polemics. Race still seems to be a problem that is complex, context dependent, and avoided as a point of departure, with exceptions such as composition scholars who have focused on rhetorics of race that challenge outdated, celebratory multicultural rhetorics, and provide writing pedagogies with critical race dimensions (Smitherman; Gilyard; Kennedy, Ratcliffe, and Middleton; Martinez; Prendergast; Jones Royster; Parks). Such critical expansions are the addition of critical race theory, whiteness studies, and critical historical research, which look to add the missing voices of those considered absent from composition pedagogy and scholarship (Prendergast qtd. in Ruiz). (23)

If RCWS scholarly practices continue to marginalize the work of POC scholars, it continues to be imperialist because it is and continues to be dominated by Whites. One recent example of this type of scholastic imperialism is noted in Doug Hesse's recent article "Journals in Composition Studies, Thirty-Five Years After." Its bibliography contains one person of color. It is important then to question the implications of this scholarship for other racial populations that are also part of those bodies of knowledge (Ruiz, *Reclaiming* 36). Another example of marginalization is how I recently had to "call out" CompPile, a notable resource for works related to the RCWS scholarship, for not including two of my recently published books and for not properly cataloguing the NCTE/CCCC Latinx Caucus bibliography. It was not until late February, 2020 that the Latinx Caucus bibliography was listed on the CompPile bibliography.

Continuing with the official documentation of a negligent field of scholarship when it comes to the inclusion of POC and their topics of research interest, in the article "Chronicling a Discipline's Genesis," from *College Composition and Communication* (*CCC*), mentioned above, Phillips et al. claim that RCWS mainstream scholarship works "towards its support, its enlargement, or its overthrow" (454). This article takes inventory of who is cited, what subjects are most prominent, and the implications of this exclusivity in publishing. In short, *CCC* was exclusive in the way many scholarly journals were at this time. The minority voice was the exception and not the rule, and I argue that this is still the case.

One does not have to look far to locate voices of scholars of color mostly concentrated in special issue sections of mainstream RCWS journals such as *College English* and the *Journal of Advanced Composition* (now out of print). I could go on and on about how one of my manuscripts was outright rejected without having been read by the *CCC* editor or reviewers, or how my colleague's proposal on a special issue of race in writing program administration (WPA) was admittedly ignored because the editors were not "well-equipped" to carry out such a contentious full-blown publication on "race," but the point is, as I have just alluded to, there are real gatekeepers at work doing real gatekeeping in popular RCWS journals that are said to be unbiased and "diverse."

I recently wrote about the multiple rejections of Felipe de Ortego y Gasca's work by two *College English* editors at different moments in history because his work did not fit the mission of the journal or there was already one White man being published on a Latinx research question ("Huevos con Chorizo"). Also, the recent National Communications Association upheaval concerning the *Rhetoric of Public Affairs* editor's statement about rigor being at odds with identity-politics or diversity lucidly demonstrates how journals are invested in keeping a certain type of scholastic identity: in this case that meant White and male. For more information about this controversy, see our discussion about Medhurst in Chapter 1, as well as Collen Flaherty's *Inside Higher Ed* article, "When White Scholars Pick White Scholars," in which it is noted that, due to Medhurst's implied racism, the journal should be boycotted, and he should resign.

At CCCC 2017, a prestigious member sitting on a roundtable I attended about editorship composed of top scholars in the field stated that they wanted to open the gates to more women and more diversity of scholarship. However, not once did they mention the diversity of scholars. Diversity in this case meant diversity of subject matter. Only recently, as of summer 2018, has it been mentioned by this prestigious member's mentor that the politics of citation needs to be attended to (Chang). It can be deduced, then, that the politics of citation have very much to contribute to the ideas of imperial and colonial scholarship as well as to the conventions that are set forth by the discipline that result in a White majority being in control of idea dissemination and legitimacy. By default, this marginalizes important works by scholars of color who may be working to disrupt a White hegemonic epistemological tradition or may be trying to articulate something very notable about how to bring alternative and diverse pedagogies into our institutions that are continuously becoming more and more diverse and whose students occupy our classrooms. One cannot simply claim that people of color are not producing work. The Latinx Caucus bibliography, for example, has over 500 citations and is only recently being taken on as a project to add to legitimized bibliographies such as those found in CompPile. Such legitimized textual and digital locations have long operated as hegemonic and textual places and can be regarded as colonial in that they sanction what methods can be used to convey official practices of the field while marginalizing "alternative" methods, which are regarded as non-official and "undocumented." Whether this is done intentionally or not is beyond consideration of the mere fact that, currently, certain groups are virtually invisible and delegitimized and by default de-legitimized.

THEORETICAL FRAMEWORK: DECOLONIAL DELINKING AND EPISTEMIC DISOBEDIENCE AS ANTIRACIST METHODOLOGY

Through recognizing these limited epistemological spaces, I now engage the concept of epistemic disobedience, drawn from Walter Mignolo's theory of decolonial options, in order to problematize the colonial epistemologies that legitimize traditional research methods in RCWS. It is directly related to the practice of historical curanderisma. Epistemic disobedience operates by the "unveiling of epistemic silences of Western epistemology and affirming the epistemic rights of the racially devalued and considering de-colonial options to allow the silences to build arguments to confront those who take 'originality' as the ultimate criterion for the final judgment" (4). What this decolonial heuristic asks of its practitioners is to understand the primacy and provincialism of Western epistemology as a veil that has effectively hidden other forms of making knowledge and living in the world. Those trying to reclaim their colonized identities, for example, are given the support and space to do so with an openness to bring Western epistemology into a crisis or rupture that allows for a sincere decolonial reclamation to occur. When this rupture takes place, points of origin can be called into question, and the very concept of origins is exposed as a colonial narrative mired in multiple silences and multifarious meanings. In engaging this task of reclamation, I assert a decolonial emergence of looking at the ways our field currently does research in order to cause a similar rupture in the origin and function of research methods that are claimed to be objective, as in the case of historiography, and "critical," as in feminist methodologies.

Through a decolonial lens, I see how RCWS traditions are deeply steeped in empirical and objective methodologies that are founded upon the pursuits and gains of colonialist actions—read: White supremacy, Manifest Destiny, and genocide and destruction of civilizations intimately tied to the histories of many compositionists of color, who have had their voices silenced, particularly African Americans and Latinxs. Scholars in positions of power in RCWS have been guilty of perpetuating a deafening silence of minoritized voices and experiences that do not align with traditional Western values. Although the field has grown and expanded to be more inclusive of minoritized voices, approaches, and research areas, there is much work to be done in aligning what we say we value and what we demonstrate to value through positions of power, policy, engagement with community, and even values expressed in prominent spaces of the field.[3]

In his article "Epistemic Disobedience, Independent Thought and De-Colonial Freedom," Mignolo claims that Western epistemology has hidden self-serving interests and that the work of de-colonial thinking is to reveal such epistemic silences in order to affirm "the epistemic rights of the racially devalued" (4). In other words, Western ways of creating knowledge have been established as the norm by those whom they serve. Decolonial thinking advocates for marginalized groups to not only make visible this self-serving norm, but also to challenge it to value other ways of knowing. Mignolo points to two paths, de-westernization and de-colonial options, and the main point of departure is that the former does not question what is eliminated for the sake of modernization, while the latter "starts from the principle that the regeneration

---

3   What I refer to here is the professed need for more minoritized people as editors of prominent journals, as chairs of departments, and as heads of professional organizations; policies such as tenure and promotion that value community work and nontraditional and collaborative research; resources that allow academics to engage with their communities to benefit the communities, not just to provide research for the academic; and atrocious discussions on listservs and in executive committees that present a complete disregard for minoritized people's voices and ways of creating knowledge.

of life shall prevail over primacy of the production and reproduction of goods at the cost of life" (3).

Equipped with a Chicana mindset, it is my intent to perform a healing of the trauma of being silenced as a colonized woman of color. It is important to note that I am building from decolonial options and not de-westernization, and it is important to point out the nuance of decoloniality in consideration of colonial wounds. Mignolo claims that those engaging in a decolonial option have one commonality: colonial wounds, which are the effects of groups of people historically "classified as underdeveloped economically and mentally" (3). If I start from a point of colonial wounds, then the decolonial option is based upon a reaction to a colonial legacy. It seeks to heal wounds and reclaim wellness and well-roundedness. Therefore, colonial wounds are the remnant effects of a colonial legacy, and these wounds provide a commonality for those engaging in a decolonial option. As a decolonial option assumes a delinking from imperial knowledge, I can see that the work of decolonial options and delinking is in reaction to colonial legacies. Therefore, delinking and decolonial options can also be construed as methodologies that do not aim to completely remove the colonial legacy, but instead acknowledge and challenge its effects on colonial subjects in colonial spaces, which include colonial epistemological hegemony and maintenance in RCWS. They are both options within the methodological framework of historical curanderisma.

Decolonial epistemologies, then, ask those who suffer from colonial wounds to challenge normalized Eurocentric ways of knowing and to value other ways of knowing. Within RCWS, claims to knowledge have been directly connected to histories of colonialism and continue to colonize alternative perspectives by relegating them to the margins of illegitimacy (Baca; Connal; Prendergast; Ramirez; Royster and Williams; Ruiz). However, as Mignolo suggests, it is not enough to change the conversation, but to change the terms of the conversation, and in order to do that, I must call into question the control of knowledge (4). And in order to do that, Mignolo claims I must shift the focus onto the knower and, therefore, the "assumptions that sustain locus enunciations" (4), also known as commonplaces. Presented below then is a decolonial focus on three different commonplace "critical" methods that are commonly used and written about within RCWS. The three methodological critiques that I provide below question who controls knowledge in the field and suggest other ways of producing knowledge.

In order to assist myself and my reader in the process of decolonial delinking, this "Historical Curanderisma toolkit" informs my practice to better confront the epistemic trauma often expressed by "colonized scholars," who do not see themselves in claimed critical methodologies. These scholars should:

1. Understand that canonical notions of Western epistemology are in service to those whom they benefit because they derive from colonial actions and relations.
2. Encourage scholars to practice shifting the center of understanding knowledge creation from the West to the East, which involves an unwavering commitment to cultural and epistemological research and reclamation.
3. Be willing to continually shatter and delink from colonial scholarship practices through critical self-reflection from old notions of the colonial self with a profound commitment to constant ontological renewal and spiritual recovery.
4. Be willing to constantly return the gaze, as I do with Jessica Enoch's work, from colonized to the colonizer.
5. Consider and recognize whose colonial stories are being told or examined and by whom.
6. Embrace critical self-reflection.
7. Contemplate their place (e.g., how they are impacted and implicated) within the research question they are attempting to answer.

CRITICAL HISTORIOGRAPHY'S METHODOLOGICAL LIMITATIONS IN RCWS

While I critique Critical Historiography in RCWS here, I want to be clear that historical curanderisma serves as my method of choice to effectively delink from commonplace and critical methodologies. Furthermore, I acknowledge the rich and vast tradition of both quantitative and qualitative research methods, which create epistemologies of RCWS (Banks; Glenn and Ratcliffe; Heath; Kirsch; Moss; Sternglass). However, here, I want to look at "critical" historical methodologies common in the field, particularly those that critique traditional histories written by John Brereton, Robert Connors, Albert Kitzhaber and "critiqued" by Lynn Z. Bloom, Richard Ohmann, Wallace Douglas, Lester Faigley, and Sharon Crowley, as well as by those who have challenged an exclusive history of rhetorical studies within the US, namely Cheryl Glenn, Krista Ratcliffe, and Melissa Ianetta.

In RCWS, scholars have discussed the history of the field for a long time and continue to revise this history to be more inclusive. Although the field addresses some "critical" and "alternative' historical studies and has worked to critically reclaim stories of those who have been erased by dominant histories and narratives, it still has distance and epistemological space to transverse before it can claim to understand the colonial worldviews it purports and maintains through its imperialistic scholarship traditions discussed above.

As we noted in the introduction, many scholars have dedicated their scholarship to writing histories of composition studies (John Brereton, Albert Kitzhaber, Robert Connors, Richard Ohmann, Wallace Douglass, Sharon Crowley, Lynn Bloom, and Susan Miller). When this Western elite trajectory is presented as the *only* history of composition, "other" histories are effectively erased. I have worked to recover them in *Reclaiming Composition*. However, while there has been reclamation work of histories that are non-elitist, such as those associated with the Normal schools or those that take place in alternative geographical landscapes, the existing methodological work has not yet acted on behalf of methodologies that work to reclaim lost/erased knowledges and rhetorical traditions. Marie Louise Pratt, Susan Romano, and Victor Villanueva stand out as some of the only exceptions, in that their work focuses on alternative knowledges associated with indigenous epistemologies.

Villanueva, for example, acknowledges colonial history when he recounts the indigenous Inca people's history associated with Peru and the Aztecs of Tenochtitlan or ancient Mexico in his article "On the Rhetoric and Precedence of Racism." Furthermore, works by Damián Baca, Ellen Cushman, Raúl Sánchez, and myself explore histories of reclamation focusing upon Latinx and indigenous rhetorical contributions. These works have attempted to challenge colonial definitions used in the field's scholarship, and, while some histories have been critical in noting absences with regard to location, gender, and class (Bloom; Douglass; Faigley; Gold; Miller; Ohmann), few address the absence of race in these histories (Garcia de Mueller and Ruiz; Ruiz, *Reclaiming*). Still, these "critical" histories of class and pedagogical variety are regarded as providing "critical" and unofficial perspectives to the elitist "Harvard history" because they have worked to recover silences. However, I contend that they still do not question the extent of their "critiques" or the types of knowledge production they are complacent to. Ultimately, current histories of RCWS are limited in scope and adhere to the Western tradition or elitist locations and do so at the expense of ceding the fact that histories of rhetoric and composition studies existed "elsewhere and otherwise" (Baca; Sánchez).

Western, elitist traditions of knowledge making can be ideologically ruptured if one engages in the decolonial option to shift the geopolitical center of "epistemological" discoveries and practices away from the Western Hemisphere and the Eastern United States. *However, I caution against an identity politics approach to epistemological recentering.* In other words, I am not suggesting a method that makes broad generalizations about groups of people based on superficial, prescriptive identity categories, nor am I arguing for replacing one way of knowing with another because it is superior. However, I suggest that decentering the currently valued way of knowing in our field and in academia and re-centering other ways of knowing will glean nuanced understandings of the world that may facilitate knowledge production in positive ways for racially minoritized people.

Historical curanderisma allows for this knowledge to come to the fore when, as a researcher, I intentionally delink from a normative Western center from which to gaze using a historical method that privileges Aztec consciousness and belief systems. This delinking exercise is the "medicine" in the decolonial practice of performing decolonial, epistemic disobedience and engaging the healing method of "curandera" historiography. Medicinal history is a decolonial method that allows for the practice of historical reclamation and healing by recentering knowledge production of the indigenous Nahua, the Aztec, or the East (Morales). For example, historical curanderisma as an act of decolonial delinking and reclaiming history allows for a comparison between Western and non-Western understandings of the human relationship to the universe and particularly to human existence here on earth.

Many indigenous of the Americas conceived of the human relationship to the earth quite differently than Europeans. For example, Rene Descartes, famous for his contributions to rational thought and to The Enlightenment, as well as the quote "I think, therefore, I am," or "cogito ergo sum," or "je pense, donc je suis," exemplifies what is known as the Cartesian split. There is no equivalent for this type of split in Aztec thought and philosophy. The smoky mirror, for example, which is associated with Tezcatlipoca, signifies introspection and reflection, but it does so holistically, as it is one of the four aspects of Nahui Ollin, which means "harmony" in Nahuatl, the Aztec indigenous language. This comparison is classified as "medicinal" because it also heals that which was severed through colonial relations and colonial renditions of human relationships to the earth. When Christians imposed their belief systems on the Americas to facilitate colonial projects, Aztec belief systems were undermined and demonized: they were said to have worshipped many gods and practiced the most heinous and inhuman crimes (Casas; León-Portilla; Sahagún).

Historical curanderisma allows these biased, ill-informed renditions of Aztec religious practices to lose legitimacy when their colonial motives are exposed, and further allows one to heal and regain the symbiotic Aztec worldview and philosophy, which are characterized by cosmological conceptions of the human relationship to the land and to the heavens rather than an egocentric, Western view of the autonomous individual. Unlike Westernized individuals who are said to be only good or bad or light or dark in modern human philosophy, Aztecs embraced duality. For example, duality, also known as "both/and," was a much privileged and natural concept for the Aztec goddess Coatlicue (later named Tonantsi) and other female goddesses; however, through colonization, binary opposites such as good and evil were the only concepts available. It can be argued then that for Latinx researchers in RCWS, both Aztec philosophies and the Aztec spirit died through colonization, when the human became objectified as an object, aka "thingafied" (Yancy, "Colonial Gazing"), to be enslaved and de-legitimized so as to not get in the way and assist in colonial pursuits of land, bodies, and natural resources such as gold.

It's hard to perform this task of deep self-reflection while delinking, so before moving on to limiting Western notions of embodiment methodology, it is useful to invoke Gloria Anzaldúa's refusal of dichotomies and her promotion of both/and approaches to the world. As a Chicana, Mestiza, Anzaldúa is able to transverse borders as a bicultural, tricultural, pluriversal queer women. She states that Mestizos are the best suited to occupy several worldviews at once because the Chicanx community is composed of individuals who occupy the many spaces of the colonized, colonizer, indigenous, European, documented, undocumented, straight, queer, etc., and are, therefore, accustomed to crossing multiple borders through their corporeal experience of occupying a body that is characterized by these many identities and experiences.[4] Therefore, I look at Chicanxs as an example of a population that has been forcefully removed and displaced from not only their land and their history, but also from their humanity; they are a colonized population who are direct descendants of the colonized indigenous of the Americas to various extents and generational status. As mentioned above, the Chicanx's relationship to the earth and the way they view their relationship to the earth is not the same as a Cartesian mind and body split or a postmodern understanding of a conglomeration of meaningless subject positions.

Although subjected to many stereotypes and essentialist notions of identity and mannerisms such as language, dress, documented status, and range of intellectual interests and abilities, the bottom line is that Chicanxs in the US have been forcibly removed from their intimate ties to the land in the name of capitalism, which views land as a resource in which to extract goods and resources for profit. This forced removal, both physical and spiritual, has caused a double displacement for Chicanxs who are intimately tied to the history and lands of the Americas. Therefore, the reclaiming of history through indigenous methods is very much a spiritual practice as it is an intellectual practice because it draws upon indigenous ways of knowing and of making knowledge, also known as methods and methodologies. It is akin to the practice of Curanderisma because

---

4   Drawing upon Ruben Salazar's definition of Chicano/a, the term Chicanx brings an added element to the word Chicano. According to Salazar, a Chicano/a is a Mexican- American with a non-Anglo view of him/herself. When the "x" replaces the o/a, it removes the gender binary and recognizes the European imposition of gender codes brought upon the indigenous by Spanish colonizers.

it invites the practice of healing and serves as a type of "medicinal" practice that cures and revives while it reclaims the practices which were already in existence before colonization. Next, I discuss the "critical" method and theory of embodiment, and while I discuss each of the methods singularly, I am fully aware of the connections between the mind, body, and spirit that I have just briefly touched upon so far, and that will continue to be problematized with each proceeding method below. Also, while I've just explained medicinal history as a way to decolonize and delink from RCWS critical historiographic methodologies, I continue to use this same medicinal decolonial methodology to delink from both embodiment and feminist methodological critiques.

WHOSE BODY? THEORIES AND METHODS OF EMBODIMENT AND THE CARTESIAN MIND/BODY SPLIT

Frida Khalo is, in my opinion, the best example of an embodied, BIWOC (BIWOC: Black and/or Indigenous Woman of Color) and third-world, feminist colonial trauma. She embodies interdisciplinary methodology. Period.

In this section, I would like to consider three commonplaces of embodiment theory as discussed in the field of RCWS. According to Abby Knoblauch, scholars in RCWS talk about and access theories of embodiment in three ways: embodied language, embodied knowledge, and embodied rhetoric. Each of these serves the purpose of critical inquiry and knowledge production that seeks to bring the previously ignored body into the realm of objectified knowledge that can be valued for its own sake, possibly by being completely divorced from corporeal considerations as in the case of embodied language. As a matter of fact, many RCWS scholars claim these practices as non-traditional and departing rationalist notions of knowledge making because as Cartesian logic goes, the body cannot be conceived of except for the existence of the mind. As the common adage goes, "I think, therefore I am"; through such conception, the body itself becomes objectified and has little relevance in claiming space toward the pursuit of learning and knowledge making. Theories and practices of embodiment then seek to reclaim that which is lost through such divisive thinking which leads to divisive as opposed to holistic methodologies.

Knowledge from a Cartesian perspective, then, is disembodied in rationalist circles and Western scientific epistemic traditions. Knoblauch notes however, that "[s]cholars such as Foucault and Butler would of course remind me that bodies are constructed, that social positionalities are performed, and that there is no unified body that needs to or could stand in for another" (60). Foucault would call these types of distinctions biopolitics in that bodies are divided the way they are in service to broader power structures that benefit some bodies and denigrate others. "When he first employed the term 'biopolitics' in the mid–1970s, he meant to identify a new kind of power which is carried forward by technologies and discourses of security that take the life of populations as their object and play a central role in the emergence of modern racism and eugenics" (Lemm and Vetter 40). An in-depth consideration of the history of biopolitics is beyond the scope of this chapter, but I suggest that there are connections between the discursive manipulation of bodies and the embodied rhetoric that Knoblauch advocates for at the end of her article. Interestingly, she alludes to biopolitics as she quotes bell hooks who points out that "'the person who is most powerful has the privilege of denying their body' ([hooks] 137). Who is asked to deny the body and who is asked to reveal it is a question I believe we must continually ask ourselves" (59)?

In a more dated book (2003), *The Teacher's Body: Embodiment, Authority, and Identity in the Academy*, Freedman and Holmes provide a list of considerations of embodiment that have been written and researched about relating specifically to the college teacher, which most professionals who are members of CCCC can relate to because, as Knoblauch notes, the concept of embodiment has an established history in RCWS. As far as bodily reality considerations, the list includes: "cancer, and/or cartwheels and body-piercing [tattoos], ED, pregnancy miscarriage, aging, youth, beauty, arthritis, depression, AIDS, heart disease, physical intimidation, diabetes, infertility, sleep deprivation, mobility impairment, paralysis, deafness, blindness, post-traumatic stress, rape, anorexia—many situations seen and unseen and many situations beyond those described in this volume [race, sexual orientation]" (6). I included what I felt was a glaring absence in this list in brackets, and in this book, there are eighteen chapters; however, only one chapter is specifically focused upon the racialized Caribbean female body. Race is mentioned several times throughout the book, but the close analysis only occurs in this chapter. Part of this oversight has to do with imperial scholarship practices (Ruiz, *Reclaiming* 170–72); however, that only serves as a partial explanation. The other reason for the lack of embodiment rhetoric as it specifically relates to the racialized body has to do with the three commonplaces that get accessed when embodiment theory is the framework used for epistemological discovery, otherwise known as methodology: embodied language, embodied knowledge, and embodied rhetoric.

Embodied rhetoric seems to be the most in-line with the practice of reclaiming the body's contribution to knowledge making. Knoblauch defines embodied rhetorical practice as

> [L]ocating a text in the body (understanding the importance
> of embodied knowledge) and . . . locating the body in the text

[;] writers utilizing an embodied rhetoric work against what might be seen as the potential hegemony of (some) academic discourse, thereby beginning to enact [Adrienne] Rich's politics of location, [which] must 'challenge our conception of *who* we are in our work,' and must be 'accompanied by a rigorously reflexive examination of ourselves as researchers.' (142)

Here, one begins to see connections between the colonial influence on the ideological and spiritual denigration of indigenous populations such as the Aztecs, who believed in more holistic notions of the human species. For example, Aztecs thought of human life as part of a cycle that was a magical and miraculous cosmological conglomeration of mind, body, and spirit—all three intimately tied to the land and the cosmos.

One only has to look so far as the Aztec sunstone to see the ways in which all three of these elements are interconnected and dare to not be separated out of fear of cosmological discord and resultant existential and bodily imbalance. Centuries have passed since colonialism has witnessed the ways this discord and separation of mind and body have been detrimental, not only to the survival of indigenous populations, but also to the modern world that is constantly in crisis-mode due to capitalism's colonial influence. Colonial pursuit destroyed and delegitimized indigenous knowledge, philosophy, and people native to this land relying on rhetorical constructs such as "religious salvation" that eventually became discredited with the reign of science, which had the effect of separating the mind, the spirit, and the body. However, while these connections are absent in current considerations of theories of embodiment, there have been a small number of studies that have come forward which acknowledge the connection between colonialism and the body, claiming that colonialism created the idea of disease that grew directly out of the role of disease dissemination during colonial pursuits (Ramirez).

While this discussion is also beyond the scope of this chapter, a book titled *Romanticism and Colonial Disease* by Alan Bewell is worth a brief mention. As one studies the "success" of colonialism, it is common knowledge that disease played an instrumental role in genocide of indigenous bodies in mass numbers. Bewell notes that smallpox embodies an experience that was repeated in different places at different times throughout the colonial period. To a degree that historical and literary critics have not adequately recognized, colonial experience was profoundly structured by disease, both as metaphor and as reality. For different people at different times, it was an age of epidemiological crisis. In the legend, one glimpses what it meant for a people to undergo total social collapse, the destruction of children, wives, and warriors.

Bewell further personifies smallpox as a colonial disease as being able to state that "no people who have looked on me [smallpox disease] will never be the same" (2). As the field continues in its development of theories of embodiment, medical humanities, and the decoloniality of science, such studies seem to be further warranted as we continue to discuss rhetorics of science that are part and parcel of embodied rhetoric and biopolitics in general. However, in an effort to reclaim the holistic human aspect of indigenous epistemologies that account for the connection between the Aztec philosophical view of the cosmos to the mind, body, and spirit, I turn to Sean Arce's powerful piece, "Xicana/o Indigenous Epistemologies: Toward a Decolonizing and Liberatory Education for Xicana/o Youth."

In this article, Sean Arce explores the power of "recognition and embracing of the Xicano/Xicana connection to the land of this continent, that which reifies their existence and humanity as Indigenous."[5] (25) For Chicanxs, it can be detrimental to their conception of their humanity if they are not allowed to reclaim their native connection to this land we call the United States cosmologically, spirituality and physically. As a matter of fact, Arce argues that provided the ability to reclaim indigenous notions of the spirit, Chicanxs can challenge an educational system that he claims is based on the dehumanization of those with colonial bodies and histories.

This type of historical reclamation calls upon both Chicanx educators and non-Chicanx educators to realize that the connection of the Chicanx body to the land is an act of reclamation that is essential for Chicanxs who have lost their way in a dehumanizing, colonial educational system. In his article, Arce quotes Berta-Avila, who says that spiritual and material manipulation is what causes educational oppression: "The experiences of oppression in the United States can be described as a mental/spiritual and social/material domination that is fueled by manipulation and alienation" (Berta-Avila 2). The erasure of native beliefs and traditions in the name of both nation and state building has been detrimental for Chicanxs who seek to decolonize and reclaim their identities.

This reclamation process is especially difficult within educational institutions that do not recognize Chicanxs as Native Americans who are native to this land. It is disempowering when one group's worldview is discounted and outright ignored, and when their "methodologies" for understanding their humanity are shunned, and when the world around them and their place within it are delegitimized. Arce expands this notion:

> Xicanas/os are indigenous to this land on which they live. The
> land is the connection to their identity and the understanding

5   "Xicano/Xicana" is more decolonial way to identify as Chicano/Chicana.

of life. This connection is a threat to the growth of capitalism in the United States, thus making it necessary to impose on Xicanas/Xicanos a dehumanizing cultural hegemony. When Xicana/Xicanos enter the schooling system, they come with a sense of displacement. Xicana/Xicanos are not sure how to view themselves. (25)

An embodied rhetorical practice that recognizes the ways Chicanxs are forced to deny the histories of their own bodies could be one step toward encouraging a decolonial theory of embodiment that looks at the body of the indigenous as one that has been colonized, traumatized, divorced from their own land, and de-legitimized in the name of both capitalism and a democracy that values profit over people and schooling systems that support a neoliberal political agenda. An embodied rhetorical practice is a praxis that acknowledges this reality for minoritized populations. It is one step closer to performing an antiracist method that relies on decolonial options, such as epistemic delinking, to achieve the goal of antiracist scholarship. It is an engagement with Curandera praxis as healing praxis.

FEMINISM'S CLAIMED CRITICAL PRACTICE AND THE COLONIZATION OF INTERSECTIONALITY

In order to effectively decolonize, we need to collectively decolonize. To support that point, I want to briefly touch upon the increasingly popular concept of intersectional feminism (a term invented by attorney, scholar, and activist Kimberle Crenshaw in the 1980s) before I go back to make a connection with embodied rhetoric and feminist theory and scholarship within RCWS. Women of color do not often see themselves in White-dominated feminist movements, and this is the power of intersectionality: it allows women of color to account for their particular feminisms. However, the term "intersectionality" is suffering from appropriation and dilution, which leads to a kind of delusion about its practical applicability, purpose, and function. While it is not unheard of that academics borrow concepts in order to metaphorically apply them to practices not initially connected to the concept, such as the concept of "diversity," for example, when one is committed to performing antiracist research methods, this type of borrowing, also known as appropriation, cannot occur without racist consequences. Intersectional feminism is inseparable from race because its reason for existing was to be able to account for Black Woman experience with workplace discrimination in the 1980s. Creating and defining intersectionality was a specific attempt to counter "single-axis" analyses that overlook multiple forms of oppression that Black Women face, especially when they are from a middle-to lower social class. In her groundbreaking essay, "Demarginalizing the Intersection of Race and Sex: A Black Feminist Critique of Antidiscrimination Doctrine, Feminist Theory and Antiracist Politics" published in *The University of Chicago Legal Forum*, Crenshaw points to the analytical limitation of a single categorical axis, or the opposite of an intersectional analysis:

> With Black women as the starting point, it becomes more
> apparent how dominant conceptions of discrimination
> condition us to think about subordination as disadvantage
> occurring along a single categorical axis. I want to suggest
> further that this single-axis framework erases Black women in
> the conceptualization, identification and remediation of race
> and sex discrimination by limiting inquiry to the experiences
> of otherwise-privileged members of the group. (140)

In the end, Crenshaw advocates embracing the intersection of sources of marginalization. More specifically, she points to the need for an intersectional feminism and the need for racial subordination to be analyzed along with sexism and patriarchy: "If any real efforts are to be made to free Black people of the constraints and conditions that characterize racial subordination, then theories and strategies purporting to reflect the Black community's needs must include an analysis of sexism and patriarchy. Similarly, feminism must include an analysis of race if it hopes to express the aspirations of non-white women" (166). I provide these two quotes at length because I have noticed trends in feminist circles that tend to use this term in ways that claim to be critical-feminist practice and point to the exclusion of women, queer, and trans populations in prominent understandings of both first-wave (19th century to mid–20th century) and second-wave (1960 and beyond) feminism.

This trend has also been documented by Elisa Lopez in "The Colonization of Intersectionality," in which she claims that "intersectionality has been taken from its originator- a Black Woman- and has been re-appropriated in order to serve the interests of white people." Divorcing the term "intersectionality" from its focus upon women of color takes away its power and that in itself is an act of colonization by appropriation of the term for White feminist purposes. Sirma Blige also wrote about how, in addition to foregoing the plight of Black Women invisibility, current feminist movements overlook important historical realities for women of color by coining new feminist movements that lack critical self-reflection by focusing on all women being subjected to the same experience regardless of race. In "Intersectionality Undone: Saving Intersectionality from Feminist Intersectionality Studies," published in the Du Bois Review, she explores political feminist movements such as Slutwalk and the Occupy movement, both of which she claims that "[d]espite their best intentions and claims of inclusiveness and solidarity . . . have fallen short of intersectional reflexivity and accountability, and prompted their own kinds of silencing, exclusion or misrepresentation of subordinated groups'" (406). She claims that these movements have been divorced from an intersectional analysis because they overlook the racial elements of being a "slut" or of what it means to already "occupy" a space of resistance, as many women of color have done since before and after first and second wave feminism.

While I turn to these examples to note a trend in social justice movements that claim to be critical and intersectional, I also briefly note my reflection for how I've seen this phenomenon occur in my own field. For example, in my interactions with other feminists in the field who have claimed an interest in intersections between medical rhetorics, feminism, and writing, the term "intersectionality" was used to discuss the intersections of medical procedures and processes that pertain to White women's bodies without ever exploring dimensions of race within their analyses, which has the effect of universalizing their findings by not accounting for the racial dimensions of their stories/studies. If their approaches were intersectional as in considering both White and non-White bodies, they might have considered that in *Medicalizing Blackness: Making Racial Difference in the Atlantic World, 1780–1840*, Rana A. Hogarth claims that "whether by design or by chance, physicians' objectification of black people's bodies in slave societies became an essential component to the development of the medical profession in the Americas" (1–2).

In *Medical Imagery and Fragmentation: Modernism, Scientific Discourse, and the Mexican/Indigenous Body, 1870–1940s*, Dora Ramirez claims that between the years of 1870–1940, Mexican writers saw themselves as "transnational authors" attempting to grasp the impact of imperial expansion on both Mexico and the United States. With such a goal in mind, "Mexican women writers focused on the modernist construction of the body and brought in aspects of how the soul (through racial, gendered, national, political, and socioeconomic lenses) was (re)constructed as a way to manage the health and space of Mexican/Indigenous populations and as a way for modernization to progress into an industrial era" (1). Those claiming to be feminists in the field then are overlooking possibilities for antiracist dimensions of the initial definition of intersectional feminism as specifically referring to Black Women and acknowledging the inseparable analytic of race and gender as necessary overlapping identity characteristics in need of mutual and complementary analyses for a more accurate representation of their interdependency. This type of appropriation of the term has been called the "colonization of intersectionality" (Lopez; Utt) and the "depoliticization" of intersectionality (Bilge).

The appropriation of this term creates a distance from Crenshaw's reason for creating the analytical possibilities of intersectionality as an antiracist method. Although many feminists are behaving as if the concept of intersectionality can be both generalizable and widely applied as a mere metacognitive task in many disciplinary circles, that's not really the point of applying an intersectional framework. Those who use the term are tasked with actively working to dismantle and transform intersectional oppressions that are specific to women of color because, currently, there are no frames of reference with which to account for the invisibility of women of color created by the failure of identity politics to account for gender and race.

In RCWS, the use of intersectional analyses has been used in this way. See "The Queer Turn in Composition Studies: Reviewing and Assessing an Emerging Scholarship," for example (Alexander and Wallace). When the term is colonized in this way, it can become diluted, and those who use it for other purposes can become delusional, thinking that they are practicing another sort of "critical" scholarship that is "critical" because it claims to be "intersectional." As such, looking back at the reasons for the creation of this term would demonstrate that it was created out of a dire necessity to recognize the female of color, particularly the female of color that has suffered discrimination and racism, or, more recently, the embodied representation of the "female of color who has suffered police brutality" (Ersula Ore comes to mind as a participant in the Coalition of Feminist Scholars in the History of Rhetoric and Composition (CFSHRC) 2017 workshop "Intersectionality within Writing Programs and Practices").[6]

I wanted to cover this danger of appropriation briefly because it is one that threatens the potential of decolonial options that aims to epistemically delink from Western notions of official knowledge, and I would carry this official label so far as to implicate Western feminism, also known as "White feminism" or "mainstream feminism."

Commenting upon the ways that White feminism diminishes the experience of women of color, Crenshaw states that White women share many of the same social characteristics as White men, except for gender, and White women participate in the silencing of other women who don't share their social status:

> The value of feminist theory to Black women is diminished
> because it evolves from a white racial context that is seldom
> acknowledged. Not only are women of color in fact over-
> looked, but their exclusion is reinforced when white women
> speak for and as women. The authoritative universal voice—
> usually white male subjectivity masquerading as non-racial,

---

6   This workshop review confirms Ore's participation (see http://bit.ly/3jK9m1f).

non-gendered objectivity—is merely transferred to those who, but for gender, share many of the same cultural, economic and social characteristics. (154)

Given that Crenshaw's essay dates back three decades, one must wonder how far feminism has traversed to account for its limited application and who have been the women who have fought for their recognition in a limited feminist tradition.

Like Crenshaw asked then, RCWS scholars need to ask the question, "If this is so, how can the claims that 'women are,' 'women believe' and 'women need' be made when such claims are inapplicable or unresponsive to the needs, interests and experiences of Black women?" (154). It is beyond the scope of this chapter to give a complete survey of the range of feminist scholarship that is practiced within RCWS; however, I hope it will suffice to say that most feminist scholarship in the field is complicit in contributing to this problem of universal applicability to RCWS scholars who identify as women of color. They are complicit because they continue to contribute to the current rampant problem of inclusive "politics of citation," also known as imperial scholarship, regardless of the "types" of feminist scholarship referred to in the introduction that claim to be inclusive and critical. When one examines the field's most popular scholarly venues, one cannot miss glaring absences of a genuine intersectional approach that considers not only the female but the minoritized female who practices a minoritized, intersectional feminism. In the pursuit of antiracist research methods, this is an abomination to the many historically marginalized women who are RCWS scholars, such as myself and fellow co-author Alexandria Lockett. The result of this oversight has been a blatant neglect of many women who occupy histories tied to colonialism, and the effect of this exclusivity in the field currently is a type of continued colonization and imposed silence (Enoch; Ramirez; Royster; Ruiz, Reclaiming).

I want to briefly turn back to the notion of an embodied rhetoric before going on to examine one example of a White feminist's "critical" attempt to introduce the voice of Mexican female rhetors into the field. (As a decolonial scholar, I give myself permission to play with structure a bit.) Aside from embodied rhetoric, there are other ways one could discuss the role of positionality as a method of triangulation and a way to avoid appropriation and unethical research, but I choose to talk about positionality through Knoblauch's call for embodied rhetoric because it postulates that the body of the researcher is a very important part of the research process and resultant findings. She states that "[w]hile not appropriate for all purposes, an embodied rhetoric that draws attention to embodied knowledge—specific material conditions, lived experiences, positionalities, and/or standpoints—can highlight difference instead of erasing it in favor of an assumed privileged discourse" (62). In short, when one fails to divulge their particular relationship to the "bodies" of their research, they also divorce their body from the research analysis and they, therefore, erroneously make claims about the research that, although they are meant to be widely generalizable, are only a partial examination in that the researcher is situated in their own form of embodied rhetoric, which encompasses their upbringing, their social class, their privilege, and their education; not to mention, such an embodied rhetor is contributing to a body of knowledge that they have the most familiarity with.

Knoblauch confirms the need to acknowledge these intersectional connections: "The writer's positionality within the academy and her social positionality are not necessarily mutually exclusive. In fact, social positionality often affects standing within the academy, and standing within the academy often affects the ways in which one is 'allowed' or sanctioned to write . . ." (61). In the case of RCWS, its "body of knowledge" has often gained legitimacy from a Western hegemonic Greco-Roman rhetorical tradition. However, as Knoblauch notes, "Embodied rhetoric, when functioning *as* rhetoric, connects the personal to the larger social realm, and makes more visible the sources of *all* of our knowledge" (62).

When one fails to account for their own positionality, which is often expected to be a part of the triangulation of ethical research,

> [t]he disembodied view from nowhere further assumes that, because bodies do not matter, 'any *body* can stand in for another' (Banks 38). In some ways, this is a comforting thought. As members of minority groups struggle for recognition within the academy, the lack of embodiment in prose might lead one to believe that we're all on a level playing field. To be able to erase or ignore markers of difference, at least in written texts, might imply a sort of race/gender/sexuality blindness. (Knoblauch 58–59)

I am sometimes seduced by the thought of erasing the body, my body, in my texts because some of the markers of my identity are less valued than others. However, this is not possible, for my name as author reveals my position as a colonized female with a history of genocide, dispossession, cultural annihilation, trauma, and oppression.

My embodiment is always different than a White woman's embodiment, and the ability to acknowledge this openly in my research gives me more credibility than someone who pretends that they can stand in for another without revealing their social standing and limited view. If one cannot admit that their research methods, no matter how scientific or objective, are hindered by their own terministic screen, one is not performing research that is antiracist or intersectional. Positively seen as a mirror of one's mind, terministic screens are epistemically situated and sanctioned by Western notions of the rational mind without the body: they are not value-free and they reside within the body of the researcher. The aim in decolonial research, then, is to depart from any division of the two (body and mind) in order to delink from accepted norms of research and to perform embodied rhetoric that is reflective, intersectional, and decolonial.

Such self-reflection has been difficult for White feminists to demonstrate in their scholarship as noted earlier by Prendergast regarding the work of Shirley Brice Heath. However, for women of color who are working toward decolonizing research methods, self-reflection is a survival mechanism for the colonized mind, body, and spirit that is rendered invisible in academia more often than not. As a woman of color seeking to practice decoloniality, I would like to raise one of the philosophical indigenous symbols of the Aztec quadrant, which is visible in the Aztec sunstone, also known as Mexica Sun Stone (Arce 32–36): Tezcatlipoca, which is also known as the "smoky mirror." The smoky obsidian mirror is materially imagined to be a hard, dark, glass-like volcanic rock formed by the rapid solidification of lava without crystallization. However, the significance of this mirror reaches beyond its material appearance.

The significance of the mirror and reflection, in this case, is accompanied by a constant flux or movement that serves to shatter any static image rendered by glass mirrors. This kind of movement is what characterizes the "nahui ollin" or movement, of which the action of Tezcatlipoca is one action of four. If one looks at the symbol for movement in Aztec pictographic language, it resembles a mirror that is in constant movement, and this is the same of critical self-reflection in which one is called upon to see themselves as not only a body, but also a mind and a spirit that is in constant flux, always growing, always learning, and not only acting but also being acted upon. This type of self-reflection embraces duality and provides perceptual, spiritual, and cognitive options that are dynamic and closely associated with the cosmos. The mirror can be said to be the cosmos staring back at us; it is considered a powerful tool toward the continuing development of consciousness. It calms while it confronts the inner self-war; it allows one to conquer the limitations of oneself and therefore embraces multiplicity in making meaning of one's experience. It governs both what we know and do not know. It allows us to see and to be seen.

The Ollin symbol represents generational change and congregation and a coming together as a cycle that both attracts and repels like protons, electrons, and neutrons constantly rotating around a nucleus (Figure 2.3). In the symbol, one can discern both direction and displacement as a type of self-reflection that allows one to grow, expand, contract, disappear, reappear, and transform in a symbiotic manner much like the cosmos. As the cosmos influence the seasons and the motion of the ocean, so do they govern our bodily functions, our present moment, and the resulting memory that leaves subconscious marks upon our psyche, never leaving one the same as before they met the mirror of self-reflection: Tezcatlipoca, the smoking obsidian mirror. In it, dual forces meet together; its dual essence forces a natural integration of two intertwined, inseparable forces such as mother and father, bodily cell unification and division, or resistance and free movement, similar to the Taoist Chinese concept of Yin and Yang.

Figure 2.3. "Ollin" Plate 10 of the Codex Borbonicus.
Source: Wikimedia Commons.

Moving along with this critique of "critical" feminism, I want to mention why both methodological practices associated with ethical feminist research practice, namely, intersectionality and self-reflection, are not altogether new for twenty-first century RCWS practitioners; therefore, both of these methods should already be a part of the mores of feminist research and practice. However, when looking at the inclusion of Mexican women in the field, it is evident that Mexican women have yet to be recognized as contributing to the rhetorical traditions recognized in RCWS. Given this absent presence, as one can deduce that Mexican women rhetors existed on both sides of the Mexican-American border, it seems that the researcher would have an obvious ethical responsibility to perform such research with intersectional and self-reflective practices that are textually represented in any research endeavor that is contributing to this neglected area of study.

Given this context, I want to briefly consider Jessica Enoch's article, "Para la Mujer," published in 2004. The stated goal of this article is to demonstrate how three women, Renterfa, Ramirez, and Astrea, argued for new opportunities for themselves and their readers. It proceeds through definitional arguments, common in current-traditional frameworks. It also aims at defining a new Chicana feminist rhetoric. However, when analyzed for intersectional and self-reflective practices, the article proves to be lacking in both areas. Furthermore, this piece colonizes the analysis of these women by situating their challenge to define themselves for themselves within a Greco-Roman tradition. Specifically, this type of colonial framing and legitimating occurred like this:

> Of course, to pinpoint definition as a method of argumenta-
> tion is not new. Aristotle and Cicero both cite definition as one
> of the koinoi topoi (common topics)-one of the seats of argu-
> ment or "the 'regions,' as it were, from which arguments are
> drawn" (Cicero, Topica 1:5–11). Aristotle teaches that when
> one defines, one explains or argues the essence of something;
> one signifies "the what-it-is-to-be". . . Instead, my interests lie
> in the ways Renteria, Ramirez, and Astrea's definitional claims
> illustrate a Chicana feminist rhetoric-a rhetoric that infuses
> rhetorics of/from color with concerns of gender and class (21).

It is notable that Enoch brings up the concerns of gender and class to be included with rhetorics of color in order to define a Chicana feminist rhetoric (21). However, when thinking about the role of self-reflection as critical feminist practice, the intersectional approach falls short in that Enoch does not address her own privileged position in being published in a journal that has a history of being complicit in colonial and imperial scholarship practices discussed at the start of this chapter whilst the subject matter is about Mexican women's rhetoric. For a specific example of these practices, see an "unofficial" account offered by the father of Chicano literature, Felipe Ortego y Gasca's "Huevos con Chorizo: A Letter to Richard Ohmann."

Unfortunately, without knowledge of previous Chicanos who have been rejected when writing about topics pertinent to Chicano literary representation, Enoch provides very little knowledge of Chicano history to provide a grounded connection between Chicana feminist rhetoric and the rhetoric that she ana-lyzes, which occurred in the early 1900s, at least 60 years before the popularity of the term Chicano and the resultant creation of a Chicana feminist. This is an oversight that, for most Chicanx studies scholars, is unacceptable. As a matter of fact, whenever a Chicanx writes about the concept of Chicanismo or Chicanx history, due to scholarly convention in this field, they must clarify in which sense they are using the concept. They are expected to acknowledge the creation of the term as an identity that was forged at least 50 years after the Mexican American War, although the fragmented Mexican experience occurred after the Treaty of Guadalupe Hidalgo in 1848, as Enoch notes that

> even though I continue to call these women "Mexican," because
> that is how they designate themselves in their writings, I see that
> their work in 1910 and 1911 fortifies and elucidates a Chicana
> feminist rhetorical tradition . . . These Mexican women lived
> more than fifty years before the term "Chicana" was formulated
> as a result of both the Chicano student movement and the femi-
> nist movement of the late 1960s and 1970s. (21)

The reader never gets a sense of how Enoch is using the political term Chicana, and the focus seems to be more so upon restating the classed position of
those Mexican women able to write and publish at this time. The historical context around this privilege is also absent. However, the word "Chicana" appears
in the title and is used 56 times in the article.

Further, she claims that the three women focused upon use definitional arguments to redefine what it means to be Mexican but does so from an Aristote-
lian point of view even while saying that they are creating their own rhetorical
tradition: that of a Chicana rhetorical tradition. She compares these women to
Anzaldúa because they embrace contradictions and are challenging traditional
roles while also facing criticism for doing so, yet she still grounds these women
within traditional feminist legitimation when she admits that Mexican women
have not learned all they know from White women or White feminism. In the
end, this publication is problematic because Enoch claims that the three "Chicana rhetoricians" are creating their own tradition, yet she states that her goal is
not to merely enter them into the existing rhetorical cannon. However, this is
what actually ends up happening in this case while Enoch does not question the
authority from which she grounds them in.

With these reasons in mind, Enoch's treatment of "pre-Chicanas" is not a
critical decolonial treatment of Chicanas, though she cites Emma Pérez's *The
Decolonial Imaginary: Writing Chicanas into History* in a footnote:

> Emma Pérez notes that the word feminista appeared in
> Mexico at the beginning of the century. Perez also makes it
> clear that Mexican women "did not become aware of gender-
> specific issues only through their contact with European
> feminists. Mexican feminism has always taken its own cultural
> forms." (footnote 6, 35)

She also misses the colonial point altogether, recolonizing these women and
keeping them inscribed in a colonial matrix of power. She is trying to be critical
but, instead, she maintains hegemonic legitimacy within a Greco-Roman rhetorical tradition and the current-traditional heuristic of definitional arguments.

Her positionality is basically that of a researcher turning their White feminist gaze upon an exoticized marginal community.

In *Imperial Leather*, McClintock addresses the common oversight that occurs in colonial societies where White feminists claim to be critical but cannot escape their position as "complicit both as colonizers and colonized, privileged and restricted, acted upon and acting" (7). I also wonder why Enoch did not discuss Anzaldúa's claim to dualistic thinking and her discussion of Nepantla and La Facultad. Discussing these terms would show a better-grounded attempt and employ both feminist practices of intersectionality and self-reflection more closely associated with a more well-rounded, grounded, and critically and historically informed analysis that would work toward decolonial ends and an antiracist methodological practice. This type of oversight touched upon in this chapter can occur in critical historiographic, embodiment, and feminist methodologies when

1. White supremacist spaces of academia ignore and routinely reject publications by scholars of color.
2. White scholars are given the green light on researching communities with which they are not a part of while scholars of color are silenced and discredited.
3. White heteronormative research practices are continuously repeated at the expense of considering alternative research practices.
4. One only seeks out the advice of scholars of color for translation purposes.
5. No one calls out all of these racist practices within academia.
6. A researcher fails to be truly self-reflexive in their research.
7. Editorial boards don't have diverse enough representation to be able to call out these oversights.
8. Scholars are not historically conscious of their limited ways of knowing and making knowledge in settler-colonial environments.
9. Books like this one don't get published.

The decolonial option of historical curanderisma, an act of epistemic disobedience, functions as a decolonial response to colonial methods in RCWS, and as such, performs both healing and reclamation practices of colonized people's ways of making knowledge and ways of being in the world. In addition, performing decolonial epistemic disobedience is an alternative way to critically engage in reclamation. I offer these options as possible methods because they contribute to a growing body of sustainable decolonial methodologies, and they contribute to more equitable and inclusive research and citation practices for BIPOC. They also increase ethos in RCWS, a discipline that has always claimed to be inclusive, antiracist, and accommodating.

In the next chapter, James Sanchez models systematic approaches to connecting personal experience with research, which effectively disrupts the notion that we can somehow do research without focusing intently on how race and racism affects the way we make knowledge in the world. In Chapter 4, Christopher Carter discusses the politics around surveillance and race to prompt an awareness of how antiracism might combat disinformation. As Carter shows, truth-telling about racially charged incidents of police brutality involves a conflict between "official" interpretations of events vs. citizen-recorded events that show what "really" happened. This conflict clearly illustrates that control over data is what's at stake in an almost ubiquitously surveilled reality. In other words, researchers can ask, "Can data be neutral?" and "Can data be presented from a neutral position?" According to Alexandria Lockett's analysis of Black Twitter as a counter-response to mainstream journalistic reporting in Chapter 5, the answer would be "no" (see also "Scaling Black Feminisms" and "I am Not a Computer Programmer").

The political nature of information is multidimensional and increasingly complex. While some users of technology are claiming to have become a part of a consciously "woke" society, prompted by the web's massive and free archive of knowledge to be consumed, they continue to elude the ways in which becoming "woke" through digital means comes with a cost: being surveilled. It is the driving force of our current information economy: an information economy that is heavily entrenched in political processes—political debates, political positions, and political motives. While data is often claimed to be neutral and serves as an empirical mirror, critical researchers often ask if information can be presented apolitically. Whether one would like to think of digital spaces as neutral conveyors of information (both critical and objective), or as digitized spaces that function like the Wild Wild West, both Lockett and Carter further remind us in Chapters 4 and 5, that we live in a digital information society that is riddled with cultural codes when engaged by both human and non-human participants, which are deeply embedded and implicated in political and racialized discourses. #BlackLivesMatter, #SayHerName, #BlackintheIvory, and #ShutdownSTEM are just a few examples of resistance responses to current political and racialized realities. However, I wonder, as Lockett does in Chapter 5, who is participating in these movements? How can we be sure? Are they even human?

WORKS CITED

Alexander, Jonathan, and David Wallace. "The Queer Turn in Composition Studies: Reviewing and Assessing an Emerging Scholarship." *College Composition and Communication*, vol. 61, no. 1, Sep. 2009, pp. 300–320.

Anzaldúa, Gloria. *Borderlands/La Frontera: The New Mestiza*. Aunt Lute, 1987.

Arce, Sean Martin. "Xicana/o Indigenous Epistemologies: Toward A Decolonizing and Liberatory Education for Xicana/o Youth." *White Washing American Education: The New Culture Wars in Ethnic Studies*, edited by Denise M. Sandoval, Anthony J. Ratcliff, Tracy Lachica Buenavista, and James R. Marín. Praeger, 2016, pp. 11–42.

Aronowitz, Stanley, and Henry Giroux. *Postmodern Education: Politics, Culture, and Social Criticism*. U of Minnesota P, 1991.

Associated Press. "White Supremacist David Duke Runs for U.S. Senate." *PBS*, 22 Jul. 2016, www.pbs.org/newshour/politics/white-supremacist-david-duke-runs-u-s -senate-says-time-come.

Baca, Damián. *Mestiza@ Scripts, Digital Migrations, and the Territories of Writing*. Palgrave Macmillan, 2008.

———. "Rethinking Composition, Five Hundred Years Later." *JAC*, vol. 29, no. 1/2, 2009, pp. 229–42.

Banks, Adam J. *Race, Rhetoric, and Technology: Searching for Higher Ground*. Lawrence Erlbaum, 2006.

Berta-Avila, Margie. "The Process of Conscientization: Xicanas(os) Experience in Claiming Authentic Voice." Annual Meeting of the American Educational Research Association, Apr. 2002, New Orleans, LA.

Bewell, Alan. *Romanticism and Colonial Disease*. Johns Hopkins UP, 2003.

Bilge, Sirma. "Intersectionality Undone: Saving Intersectionality from Feminist Intersectionality Studies." *Du Bois Review*, vol. 10, no. 2, 2013, pp. 405–24.

Bloom, Lynn Z. "Freshman Composition as a Middle-Class Enterprise." *College English*, vol. 58, no. 6, 1996, pp. 654–75.

Bourdieu, Pierre. *Distinction*. Routledge, 1986.

Brereton, John. *The Origins of Composition Studies in the American College, 1875–1925*. U of Pittsburgh P, 1996.

Brodkey, Linda. *Academic Writing as Social Practice*. Temple UP, 1987.

Butler, Judith. "What is Critique? An Essay on Foucault's Virtue." *The Political*, edited by David Ingram, Blackwell, 2002, pp. 212–28.

Casas, Bartolomé de las. *In Defense of the Indians: The Defense of the Most Reverend Lord, Don Fray Bartolomé De Las Casas, of the Order of Preachers, Late Bishop of Chiapa, Against the Persecutors and Slanderers of the Peoples of the New World Discovered Across the Seas*. Northern Illinois UP, 1974.

Chang, Robert S. "Richard Delgado and the Politics of Citation." *Berkeley Journal of African-American Law and Policy*, vol. 11, no. 1, 2009, pp. 28–35, digitalcommons. law.seattleu.edu/faculty/268.

Clary-Lemon, Jennifer. "The Racialization of Composition Studies: Scholarly Rhetoric of Race since 1990." *College Composition and Communication*, vol. 61 no. 2, 2009, pp. 1–17.

Coalition of Feminist Scholars in the History of Rhetoric and Composition. Review of CCCC Feminist Workshop 2017: Intersectionality within Writing Programs and Practices. 26 April 2017. cfshrc.org/review-of-cccc-feminist-workshop-2017 -intersectionality-within-writing-programs-and-practices.

Connal, L. R. "Hybridity: A Lens for Understanding Mestizo/a Writers." *Crossing Borderlands: Composition and Postcolonial Studies,* edited by Andrea Lunsford and Lahoucine Ouzgane, U of Pittsburgh P, 2004, pp. 199–217.

Connors, Robert. *Composition-Rhetoric: Backgrounds, Theory, and Pedagogy.* U of Pittsburgh P, 1997.

Crenshaw, Kimberlé. "Demarginalizing the Intersection of Race and Sex: A Black Feminist Critique of Antidiscrimination Doctrine, Feminist Theory, and Antiracist Politics." *The University of Chicago Legal Forum,* Article 8, 1989, pp. 136–67.

Crowley, Sharon. *Composition in the University: Historical and Polemical Essays.* U of Pittsburgh P, 1998.

Cushman, Ellen. *The Cherokee Syllabary: Writing the People's Perseverance.* U of Oklahoma P, 2011.

Delgado, Richard. "The Imperial Scholar: Reflections on a Review of Civil Rights Literature." *U Pennsylvania Law Review,* vol. 132, 1984, pp. 561–78.

Douglas, Wallace. "Rhetoric for the Meritocracy." *English in America: A Radical View of the Profession.* Richard Ohmann. New York: Oxford UP, 1976. 97–132.

Enoch, Jessica. "Para la Mujer: Defining a Chicana Feminist rhetoric at the Turn of the Century." College English, vol. 67, no. 1, Sep. 2004, pp. 20–37.

Faigley, Lester. *Fragments of Rationality: Postmodernity and the Subject of Composition.* U of Pittsburgh P, 1992.

Flaherty, Colleen. "When White Scholars Pick White Scholars." *Inside Higher Ed,* 13 June 2019, bit.ly/3pdM2Kt.

Freedman, Diane P., and Martha Stoddard Holmes, editors. *The Teacher's Body: Embodiment, Authority, and Identity in the Academy.* State U of New York P, 2003.

Garcia de Mueller, Genevieve and Iris Ruiz. "Race, Silence, and Writing Program Administration: A Qualitative Study of U.S. College Writing Programs." *WPA: Writing Program Administration,* vol. 40, no. 3, 2017, pp. 19–39.

Glenn, Cheryl, and Krista Ratcliffe, editors. *Silence and Listening as Rhetorical Arts.* Southern Illinois UP, 2013.

Gold, David. *Rhetoric at the Margins: Revising the History of Writing Instruction in American Colleges.* Southern Illinois UP, 2008.

Heath, Shirley Brice. *Ways with Words: Language, Life, and Work in Communities and Classrooms.* Cambridge UP, 1983.

Hesse, Doug. "Journals in Composition Studies, Thirty-Five Years After." *College English,* vol. 81, no. 4, Mar. 2019, pp. 367–396.

Hirsch, E. D. *Cultural Literacy: What Every American Needs to Know.* Vintage, 1988.

Hogarth, Rana A. *Medicalizing Blackness: Making Racial Difference in the Atlantic World, 1780–1840.* U of North Carolina P, 2017.

Hook, J. N. *A Long Way Together: A Personal View of NCTE's First Sixty-Seven Years.* National Council of Teachers of English, 1979.

hooks, bell. *Where We Stand: Class Matters.* Routledge, 2000.

Kirsch, Gesa and Patricia A. Sullivan. *Methods and Methodology in Composition Research.* Southern Illinois UP, 1992.

Kitzhaber, Albert R. *Rhetoric in American Colleges, 1850–1900*. Southern Methodist UP, 1990.

Knoblauch, A. Abby. "Bodies of Knowledge: Definitions, Delineations, and Implications of Embodied Writing in the Academy." *Composition Studies*, vol. 40, no. 2, 2012, pp. 50–65.

Kuhn, Thomas S. *The Structure of Scientific Revolutions*. 1962. U Chicago P, 2012.

Kynard, Carmen. "The 'White Turn' in Composition Studies." *Education, Liberation & Black Radical Traditions for the 21st Century*, 19 June 2020, carmenkynard.org/the-white-turn/.

Lamos, Steve. *Interests and Opportunities: Race, Racism, and University Writing Instruction in the Post-Civil Rights Era*. U of Pittsburgh P, 2011.

Lemm, Vanessa, and Miguel Vetter. "Michel Foucault's Perspective on Biopolitics." *Handbook of Biology and Politics*, edited by Steven A. Patterson and Albert Somit. Edward Elgar, 2017, pp. 40–55.

León-Portilla, Miguel. *The Broken Spears: The Aztec Account of the Conquest of Mexico*. Beacon Press, 1962.

Lockett, Alexandria. "I am Not a Computer Programmer." "Introduction to 'The Role of Computational Literacy in Computers and Writing.,'" edited by Mark Sample and Annette Vee, *Enculturation*, vol.14, 2012. enculturation.net/node/5270.

———. "Scaling Black Feminisms: A Critical Discussion About the Digital Labor of Representation." *Humans at Work in the Digital Age*, Routledge, 2019, pp. 250–66.

Lopez, Elisa. "The Colonization of Intersectionality." *Medium*, 4 Oct. 2018, medium.com/gender-theory/the-colonization-of-intersectionality–91ddafe9ee90.

Lorde, Audre. *A Burst of Light: and Other Essays*. Ixia P, 2017.

Martinez, Aja. "A Plea for Critical Race Theory Counterstory: Stock Story vs. Counter-story Dialogues Concerning Alejandra's 'Fit' in the Academy." *Composition Studies*, vol. 42, no. 2, Fall 2014, pp. 33–55.

McClintock, Anne. *Imperial Leather: Race, Gender, and Sexuality in the Colonial Contest*. Routledge, 1995.

McFarland, J., et al. *The Condition of Education 2019 (NCES 2019–144)*. National Center for Education Statistics, 2019, nces.ed.gov/ pubsearch/pubsinfo.asp?pubid=2019144.

Mignolo, Walter D. "Epistemic Disobedience, Independent Thought, and De-Colonial Freedom." *Theory, Culture, and Society*, vol. 26, no. 7–8, 2009, pp. 1–23.

Miller, Susan. *Textual Carnivals: The Politics of Composition*. Southern Illinois UP, 1991.

Morales, Aurora Levins. "The Historian as Curandera." JSRI Working Paper #40, The Julian Samara Research Institute/Michigan State University, 1997.

Moss, Beverly. "Ethnography and Composition: Studying Language at Home." *Methods and Methodology in Composition Research*, edited by Gesa Kirsch and Patricia A. Sullivan, Southern Illinois UP, 1992, pp. 153–171. archives.library.illinois.edu/ncte/about/october.php.

National Council for Teachers of English Task Force on Involving People of Color. "1996 Report from the Task Force on Involving People of Color in the Council." *National Council of Teachers of English*, 1996. bit.ly/3aZO1NB.

North, Stephen M. *The Making of Knowledge in Composition: Portrait of an Emerging Field*. Heineman, 1987.

Ohmann, Richard. *English in America: A Radical View of the Profession*. Oxford UP, 1976.

———. *Politics of Letters*. Wesleyan UP, 1987.

"Ollin" Plate 10 of the Codex Borbonicus. *Wikimedia Commons*. commons.wikimedia .org/wiki/File:Ollin_17.JPG.

Ortego y Gasca, Felipe de. "Huevos con Chorizo: A Letter to Richard Ohmann." *Nosotros: Newsletter of the Chicano Caucus of NCTE*, June 1970. bit.ly/2NnKBvE.

Pérez, Emma. *The Decolonial Imaginary: Writing Chicanas into History*. Indiana UP, 1999.

Phillips, Donna Burns, et al. "College Composition and Communication: Chronicling a Discipline's Genesis." *College Composition and Communication*, vol. 44, no. 4, Dec. 1993, pp. 443–65, www.jstor.com/stable/358381.

Pratt, Marie Louise. *Imperial Eyes: Travel Writing and Transculturation*. 2nd ed., Routledge, 2007.

Prendergast, Catherine. *Literacy and Racial Justice: The Politics of Learning after Brown v. Board of Education*. Southern Illinois UP, 2003.

———. "Race: The Absent Presence in Composition Studies." *College Composition and Communication*, vol. 50, no. 1, Sep. 1998, pp. 36–53.

Ramirez, Dora. *Medical Imagery and Fragmentation: Modernism, Scientific Discourse, and the Mexican/Indigenous Body, 1870–1940s*. Lexington Books, 2017.

Rich, Adrienne. *Arts of the Possible: Essays and Conversations*. W. W. Norton, 2001.

Romano, Susan. "The Historical Catalina Hernández: Inhabiting the Topoi of Feminist Historiography." *Rhetoric Society Quarterly*, vol. 37, no. 4, Fall 2007, pp. 453–80.

Royster, Jacqueline Jones. *Traces of a Stream: Literacy and Social Change Among African American Women*. U of Pittsburgh P, 1994.

Royster, Jacqueline Jones, and Jean C. Williams. "History in the Spaces Left: African American Presence and Narratives of Composition Studies." *College Composition and Communication*, vol. 50, no. 4, 1999, pp. 563–85.

Ruiz, Iris D. "Race." *Decolonizing Rhetoric and Composition Studies: New Latinx Keywords for Theory and Pedagogy*, Palgrave Macmillan, 2016.

———. *Reclaiming Composition for Chicano/as and Other Ethnic Minorities*. Palgrave Macmillan, 2016.

———. "Creating a 'New History' within NCTE/CCCC: Civil Rights, The Chicano Movement, and Honoring Felipe de Ortego y Gasca." *Viva Nuestro Caucus: Rewriting the Forgotten Pages of Our Caucus*, edited by Romeo García, Iris D. Ruiz, Anita Hernández and María Paz Carvajal Regidor. Parlor, 2019.

Ruiz, Iris D., and Damián Baca. "Decolonial Options and Writing Studies." *Composition Studies*, vol. 45, no. 2, 2017, pp. 226–29.

Sahagún, Bernardino de. *General History of the Things of New Spain: Florentine Codex*. School of American Research, 1970.

Salazar, Ruben. "Who Is a Chicano? And What Is It the Chicanos Want?" *Los Angeles Times*, 6 Feb. 1970.

Sánchez, Raúl. "Writing." *Decolonizing Rhetoric and Composition Studies: New Latinx Keywords for Theory and Pedagogy*, edited by Iris D. Ruiz, Palgrave Macmillan, 2016, pp. 77–90.

Spencer, Stephen. *Race and Ethnicity: Culture, Identity, and Representation*. Routledge, 2006.

Sternglass, Marilyn. *Time to Know Them: A Longitudinal Study of Writing and Learning at the College Level*. Routledge, 1997.

Strain, Margaret M. "In Defense of a Nation: The National Defense Education Act, Project English, and the Origins of Empirical Research in Composition. *JAC*, vol. 25, no. 3, 2005, pp. 513–542.

Utt, Jamie. "'We're All Just Different!' How Intersectionality is Being Colonized by White People." *Thinking Race*, 4 Oct. 2018, thinkingraceblog.wordpress.com/2017/04/24/were-all-just-different-how-intersectionality-is-being-colonized-by-white-people/.

Villanueva, Victor. *Bootstraps: From an American Academic of Color*. National Council of Teachers of English, 1993.

———. "Memoria is a Friend of Ours: On the Discourse of Color." *College English*, vol. 67, no. 1, Sep. 2004, pp. 9–19.

———. "The Rhetorics of the New Racism or the Master's Four Tropes." *FYHC: First-Year Honors Composition*, vol. 1, 16 Oct. 2006, pp. 1–21.

Women of Color Faculty. "A Collective Response to Racism in Academia." *Medium*, 8 May 2018, medium.com/@wocfaculty/a-collective-response-to-racism-in-academia-35dc725415c1.

Yancy, George. "Colonial Gazing: The Production of the Body as Other." *Western Journal of Black Studies*, vol. 32, no. 1, Spring 2008, pp. 1–15.

———. "Dear White America." *New York Times*, 24 Dec. 2015, opinionator.blogs.nytimes.com/2015/12/24/dear-white-america/.

———. *Look, A White!: Philosophical Essays on Whiteness*. Temple UP, 2012.

———. "The Ugly Truth of Being a Black Professor in America." *Chronicle of Higher Education*, 29 Apr. 2018, www.chronicle.com/article/the-ugly-truth-of-being-a-black-professor-in-america/.

INTERCHAPTER DIALOGUE FOR CHAPTER 2

About: Interchapter Dialogues (ICDs) are conversations among the co-authors about each individual author's chapter, in which we further explore various ideas, themes, and contexts that inform their work. They serve multiple purposes that we hope will be useful to our readers. First, as we argued in our introduction (Chapter 1), cross-cultural communication and collaboration among scholars is an essential practice of antiracist research. Next, the ICDs provide our readers with additional ways to access our research. Both the audio and textual formats complement and enrich our single-author chapters. These recorded dialogues, as well as their edited transcripts, integrate our perspectives and demonstrate that our work is grounded in real, lived experience. Overall, the ICDs experiment with enacting the intellectual potential of collaborative, multimodal writing processes and building connections among co-authors.

~ ~ ~

Alexandria (Alex): First, I want to delve into your work on disciplinary history and how race and racism appear in the field. You've provided us with this really nuanced chapter to give us a sense of how rhetoric, composition, literacy, and communication studies has simultaneously claimed that it is committed to antiracism and social justice, but when we look at how people are actually studying race or talking about race, there seems to be a different story being presented. I'm interested in knowing a little more about what you're working on right now, Iris, and how you see it being relevant to your activism in equitable online communication and CCCC leadership.

    Iris: Well, let's see, there are a lot of different pieces to the puzzle. The work that I contributed to this book very much builds on the previous work that I've done with critical historiography and how critical historiography is a method of reclamation. As a method of reclamation, it's about recovering history for marginalized populations, which is a manifestation of racial reconciliation, which James discusses throughout his chapter. That's where my work began. I also considered other types of decolonial methodologies which I explore in "La Cultura Nos Cura: Reclaiming Decolonial Epistemologies through Medicinal History and Quilting as Method," a chapter I wrote with Sonia Arellano for *Rhetorics Elsewhere and Otherwise: Contested Modernities, Decolonial Visions.* Thinking about alternative ways to look at some of the most common research methods in the field really informed that particular chapter since we were considering how critical historiography branches into decolonial theory and how traditional methods manifest in the field with little attention to how race plays into that type of method, let alone racial reconciliation.

Alex: Iris, would you please define decolonial, for any readers who might need a little clarity? What's decolonialism, and how is it connected to antiracism?

Iris: This work started back with the Civil Rights movement, which is characterized by nationalist rhetoric that goes beyond a colonial affiliation with the US for people of color. You had the Third World Liberation Front claiming a nationalist identity for colonized peoples. You had Chicanx nationalist rhetoric, you had Black nationalist rhetoric associated with the likes of Malcolm X and the Black Panthers, and, last but not least, you had third-wave feminism, and all of the aforementioned inform and are informed by a broader consciousness linked to the decolonized identity and a reclamation of identities lost through colonialism. These ideas have not ever disappeared, but have been developing with more clear theoretical concepts informed by historical concepts such as "the colonial matrix of power" and "epistemic disobedience," and it's been resurfacing again with these concepts since the mid–90s with the work of Dussell, Mignolo, Quijano, and Walsh. More specifically, the way that we have come to understand it, through the work of Walter Mignolo and Anibal Quijano, is that there is a difference between decolonizing and decolonialism or decoloniality. For example, one of the major issues of narratives about Mexican history is that we think about the decolonialization of that place as when Europeans led the conquest of the Mexican people. We think about the Mexican people being liberated from their colonial presence.

Decoloniality is a little bit different. Decoloniality relates to the study of epistemology and the study of discourse. Decoloniality deals with the question of power and epistemology and the superiority that is attributed to the episteme associated with the body of knowledge that is embedded within Western modernity. When asking the question—what does it mean to be a colonized population?—we must think about the structural aspects of knowledge and its systems, namely, the interdependent production and circulation of knowledge and language.

Chris: Iris, when rereading your chapter, I found myself drawn in by your assessment of how intersectionality theory has been appropriated and diluted. Would you say more about how this connects with your overall analysis of critical historiography in composition?

Iris: Far too many studies misuse the term intersectionality, because their methodology does not fully engage critical race studies. This concern is one of my biggest motivations for doing this type of work. We can't take the term "critical" for granted because assuming its neutrality privileges colonial, racist habits of mind. We need to closely examine methods that claim to be critical and critique them when they fail to be reflective about how they exclude marginalized populations.

Chris: One of the things that I also noticed in your analysis, Iris, is the way you critique euphemisms that are used in place of a real discussion of race and racism—that there's overuse of undefined broad terms that allude to race like *social justice, power, diversity,* and *inclusion* (and increasingly *antiracism*), which masks the field's own history of racist oppression (and beyond). How do we train ourselves to notice this happening, and what kind of work addresses the origin and spread of these euphemisms?

Iris: Fortunately, some studies directly address this issue (Clary-Lemon, Prendergast, etc.). The data is pretty transparent in terms of how many publications are actually engaging with race or racism proper. In my chapter, I call for more research that specifically studies the *CCC* journal and how racism gets talked about. Composition gets racialized through exactly what you said: euphemisms of social justice and inclusion. This is part of what decolonialism is critiquing: the discipline is structured to value and reify a White, hetero-patriarchal discourse since its beginning in 1949. Therefore, when it comes to studying race, we have a hard time with it.

James: I remember a point in graduate school when I started to recognize the field was mostly White men. I picked up what I thought would be transformative text—George Kennedy's *Comparative Rhetoric.* When I read through it, I recognized that it was a great cultural work. However, it also seemed to be reinforcing Greco-Roman tradition. I imagine that George Kennedy was trying to do good by employing comparative rhetoric as a methodology, but its lack of discussion about race and colonialism affects what we think of as Greco-Roman tradition and its so-called exceptionalism. What other work addresses this issue?

Iris: There are definitely people who are trying to devote themselves to social justice pedagogy and social justice methods—for example, studies about actor-network theory. But when I read actor-network theory, I don't see any people of color, I don't see them writing, I don't see them mentioned. I see that kind of work as critical in the sense that it is trying to disrupt disciplinary identity, but when I do not see the mention of marginalized people or any racial issues with technology or information systems, such theories definitely don't exemplify antiracist thought. As James mentioned, this absence reifies existing structures of power, what it means to be credible, and what it means to be legitimate. It has a lot of the characteristics of decolonial theory but is not acknowledging those connections.

Alex: I think another problem involving participation is that there's still a tendency in scholarship to present knowledge from an assumed point of view.

For example, a few years ago, I was at a UNCF-Mellon Teaching Institute in Austin, Texas at Hutson-Tillotson University (an HBCU). Asao Inoue was one of our workshop leaders. Before I continue, I want to acknowledge that he and I are great colleagues and I deeply respect his scholarship. He's done some impactful work on antiracism, putting it into a public sphere of dialogue in the field. But, after reading his work, I asked him, "Who do you imagine that you're talking to?"

When I asked him the question, I was thinking about how he was in an HBCU space and asking *us* whether *we* understand whiteness. "Well, yeah—we do!" So, I decided to flip the script in that workshop and ask him, "If you could write your book in a way that addressed not just the (potentially resistant) White people you imagine reading, but all of us, what would your book look like?" He acknowledged that he had not thought about audience in that way. So I looked at your chapter as helping me grapple with this issue of how we talk about participation and audience in ways that help us start to recraft a more inclusive narrative about who is making contributions to this discipline, and what they look like, and how they can affect knowledge making in the future.

James: I'm glad you brought that story up, Alex. It's great for thinking about how we consider audience. When I'm writing anything, whiteness is always in my mind. In graduate school, I learned that when you're thinking about audience, you're thinking about an academic White audience. I don't mean that as a defense; it just seems like a fact. Whiteness dominates our field in so many different capacities. But you can make the argument that there is an audience out there that we can absolutely speak to. Also, I think it's interesting that you brought up Asao because I've heard great things—and some criticism—about his keynote at CCCC, but audience was very much a part of what he was thinking about at that moment, right?

Alex: Oh yeah. We've had a few conversations since that event. I think that's why he kept in touch with me. He realized that "the issue of audience is a problem, even in my antiracist work." He alluded to our discussion at Hutson-Tillotson in the second footnote in his recent (2019) article, "Classroom Writing Assessment as an Antiracist Practice: Confronting White Supremacy in the Judgments of Language."

James: It does make me think that all the times that I'm talking about race, I think about it in terms of whiteness. And I would love to flip that script and say, "What if I imagine my audience mostly as people of color?" What could come out of that awareness?

Alex: Or how inclusive, or representative, is that "academic" audience—of professionals in our field? As Iris demonstrates throughout her chapter, a racial politics of citation inhibits us from actually seeing the knowledge production of the few BIPOC that have advanced degrees in the field, teach composition, or administrate writing programs. Scholarship is just one form of making knowledge, but it is the highest currency for tenure and promotion despite how racially exclusive the publishing processes are. When the people involved in the review and editing process are predominantly White and trained to see race and racism as ancillary to critique, rather than integral to it, they risk unconsciously reifying their tendency to cite and publish mostly White male authors.

Publishing without support, or access to learning about the process, is very traumatic for graduate students and early career scholars who mistakenly believe that publishing is an equal playing field and that they will solely be judged by the "quality" of their work. Worse, many of our publications are not open access (OA), which affects the likelihood of a person's work being cited. These are some issues that need to be more comprehensively addressed in the field's professional organizations (e.g., CCCC), their resolutions, conference agendas, publication outlets, funding, governance structures, graduate training curricula and resources, etc. One way that our book attempts to intervene is by drawing readers' attention to the importance of multicultural, interracial collaboration. How do we talk to colleagues, like us, while modeling how we might address some kind of racially diverse, integrated audience?

Iris: It's an interesting dilemma because Asao's address tells the audience, "If I'm making you feel uncomfortable right now, this is how people of color feel all the time. If I'm making you feel excluded, this is how we feel all the time." That rhetorical strategy certainly captured the attention of most of the White members there, reminding them that the organization is predominantly White in a mostly White profession. So, when I consider Asao presenting to a whole different audience of mostly people of color at HBCU symposia, it raises the question, "How would the terms of engagement have been altered if he had that audience in mind?" Other than saying whiteness is a thing, whiteness exists, our field is very racist and so therefore, we need to bring in these concepts. Yet if he was thinking, how am I going to connect with *this* audience, a completely different audience of color that was predominantly African American, how would he have better connected with that audience?

Alex: Iris, I'd like to turn our discussion's focus to your critical analyses of the field's origins. One of the things I really appreciated about your chapter is that you clearly demonstrate that disciplinary history needs to be understood within the context of political leadership and association during the 1970s. There's so much different, interdependent, work going on at that exact moment in time. I'm talking about Watergate, the conclusion of Civil Rights, the growth of the Black Panther Party, etc. There was a claim to blackness at that time in the face of racist state-sponsored violence, which was occurring alongside the desegregation of higher education. There were so many things going on at that time that are called for Black cultural preservation and recognition. Few scholars deeply engage with the historical continuity of anti-Blackness. Research about race often fails to increase the value of Black culture and racial literacies. Instead, arguments about race seem to be in a vacuum of predominantly White scholarship. HBCUs, for instance, remain eerily absent from the field's historiographies.

This unfortunate omission inhibits researchers from producing accurate, interesting scholarship. For example, I would argue that we continue to honor our "students' right to their own language" at HBCUs. Here, there can be a lot of respect for home language, Black English, home discourse, or however you want to refer to a student's "own language." But there's also a cultural understanding of eloquence. We always have to switch these codes because you always have to be aware of how your race puts its intelligence on display. It's like the intersectionality question. What happens when something that's highly racialized and highly rooted in cultural preservation and knowledge making ends up being applied to these radically different contexts of social justice work? What do we gain? What do we lose? Iris, I'm very interested in your opinion about that.

Iris: I've written about that quite a bit. I did a lot of research on "Students' Right to Their Own Language" (SRTOL)—who wrote it, the historical moment in which it was produced, etc. I think Scott Wible has done work with SRTOL that is worth engaging. And that's one of the issues I'd like to touch upon briefly, this issue of camaraderie and the issue of multiple generations within the field.

I might not touch exactly upon your particular question, but our book fills in a rhetorical blind spot. One of the things that has been difficult about this work is delving into complex histories without sounding offensive, and/or without being limited by the parameters of scholarly critique. When you're trying to follow the path of an antiracist agenda, you call for these types of engagement, and that's one of the things that I think came across in the chapter. And it's really no different with SRTOL. Here's what we promised we were going to do as a profession. Here's what we decided would be legitimate. I'm sure it was a struggle for the NCTE/CCCC Black Caucus. I'm sure it was a struggle for Geneva Smitherman. I'm sure they had various heated exchanges. All this drama happens around the time the Committee against Racism and Bias in NCTE was formed, several years before that particular statement, and all of this comes out of histories of struggle. It does come directly out of the Civil Rights movement, which is such a complex history with many nuanced but interconnected trajectories to explore. We have to be able to look back on ourselves and be critical of ourselves. What did we promise we were going to do? How did we fail?

Alex: I really like your questions because they further illustrate antiracism as a methodology. They highlight that antiracism as a process that requires constant reflection and continuous reflexive assessment. Your chapter will be very useful to graduate student education, fo' sho. We must consider how people are being trained to understand history, in general, and especially of the actual history of the discipline and the field because it will influence the future of research design. In my personal experience, the whole issue of desegregation of higher education is not part of a wide mainstream conversation about the formation of this field. But, in fact, it is integral to it because most "remedial programs" were located and administered by writing centers and writing programs. The learning mandates of these writing spaces vilified Black students, characterizing them as intellectually deficient and in need of White cultural assimilation. Schools poured millions of dollars into the idea that, "Let's just teach them the right way to talk and that'll rectify the issue of civil unrest." Arguably, the entire modern history of composition studies relied on "basic writing" and the emergence of those kinds of racist programs. I think that's the place upon which we should understand the emergence of SRTOL and those kinds of documents. But I don't know that when people are being trained in the discipline, or learning about disciplinary history, that they're really getting that kind of knowledge.

However, I should mention that my knowledge of this history comes from being situated in one of the most prestigious HBCUs (and women's colleges) in the country, where our field's very own Jacqueline Jones Royster started Spelman's Comprehensive Writing Program (CWP) in notable Black Feminist scholar Beverly Guy-Sheftall's office, where they were also architecting the Spelman's Women's Research and Resource Center. It had never occurred to me that the history of a writing program might actually lie in the development of other curricular initiatives like Black or Women's Studies until Dr. Royster provided her account during a keynote at a writing-intensive (WI) faculty development workshop that I organized at Spelman in summer 2017. More information about such historical collaborations is discussed throughout their article "The Promise and Challenge of Black Women's Studies: A Report from the Spelman Conference, May 25–26, 1990." I plan to continue to work with Dr. Royster to unveil these kinds of hidden narratives of the field to push them towards the center.

Iris: Yes, Alex. As a matter of fact, when we think about civil unrest—even within the histories of Mexican Americans within the United States—rhetorical blindspots regarding the Latinx populations residing within the United States still very much exist. Many Latin Americans living in the United States are largely invisible to the public eye due to their absence in Latin American history lessons. These absences are detrimental to the understanding of these Latin American peoples. The conditions of their absence tell a story of violence, in which colonizers erase a people's history and, in turn, erase a people out of existence. This is dehumanizing education that negates the humanity of real people. These individuals deserve to be a part of the U.S. imaginary. They are contributors to our joint existence on a common land. They should be able to see themselves within the histories of the land they now live upon.

With these thoughts in mind, I'd like to end by saying that Historical Curanderisma can enact a healing methodology; it is a type of medicinal history, which gestures toward healing through critical engagement with competing epistemologies, "polyverses," or "loci of enunciations," which can work toward the recovery of lost knowledges. One of the reasons why we have these misunderstandings of migrants who are coming over from Guatemala and Central America, for example, can be attributed to what we learn and do not learn. We do not learn a critical history of Latin America in high school, for example, and we do not learn the colonial history of the United States in high school. There's a lot of knowledge that we're missing out on, and this knowledge that we're missing out on is very detrimental to how we understand the Latinx population inside and outside of the United States. Children are being separated from their families, being put in detention centers, and how much of these cruel circumstances are based on this idea that they are inferior, or that they are "those people over there"—such misconceptions are not necessarily tied to our history. It's really important to be able to bring up this idea as somebody already operating on the margins of the discipline, as a Latinx scholar, and as somebody already excluded from dominant historiographic representations in common public school history textbooks, with the exception being Ethnic Studies courses. Not reading somebody's experience is the same thing as burning their books. What happens when you basically X out a people's experience is that you also X them out of existence. This is a type of segregation that leads to trauma, but it's also indicative of who we think we are seeing in our classrooms and who is really there. I believe that Carmen Kynard argued that "If there is a physical absence of Conscience Rebels in classrooms, then we got some neo-racial-Jim-Crow admissions standards in our institutions." Let's continue to challenge this *de jure* segregation by using the appropriate research methods to do so.

WORKS CITED

Bell-Scott, Patricia, et al.. "The Promise and Challenge of Black Women's Studies: A Report from the Spelman Conference, May 25–26, 1990." *NWSA Journal*, vol. 3, no. 2, 1991, pp. 281–288.

Clary-Lemon, Jennifer. "The Racialization of Composition Studies: Scholarly Rhetoric of Race since 1990." *College Composition and Communication*, vol. 61 no. 2, 2009, pp. 1–17.

Inoue, Asao B. "Classroom Writing Assessment as an Antiracist Practice: Confronting White Supremacy in the Judgments of Language." *Pedagogy: Critical Approaches to Teaching Literature, Language, Composition, and Culture*, vol. 19, no. 3, 2019, pp. 373–404.

Kennedy, George Alexander. *Comparative Rhetoric: An Historical and Cross-Cultural Introduction*. Oxford UP, 1998.

Kynard, Carmen. "'This the ConscienceRebel': Class Solidarity, Congregational Capital, and Discourse as Activism in the Writing of Black Female College Students." *Teaching Education*, vol. 22, no. 3, 2011, pp. 217–238.

Prendergast, Catherine. *Literacy and Racial Justice: The Politics of Learning after Brown v. Board of Education*. Southern Illinois UP, 2003.

Ruiz, Iris, and Sonia Arellano. "La Cultural Nos Cura: Reclaiming Decolonial Epistemologies through Medicinal History and Quilting as Method." *Rhetorics Elsewhere and Otherwise: Contested Modernities, Decolonial Visions*, edited by Romeo García and Damián Baca, Conference on College Composition and Communication/National Council of Teachers of English, 2019, pp. 141–168.

CHAPTER 3.

TOWARDS RECONCILIATION: COMPOSING RACIAL LITERACY WITH AUTOETHNOGRAPHY

James Chase Sanchez
Middlebury College

Key Terms and Concepts: Racial Literacy, Reconciliation, Essentialism

Around 10:00 a.m. on June 23, 2014, Charles Moore, an elderly White Methodist minister, arrived at the largest parking lot in Grand Saline, TX. Angi McPhearson and Mallie Munn, two white hair stylists at the local salon, watched him pace back and forth in the nearly empty parking lot for several hours, as he moved intermittently from his car to different areas in the open lot. Eventually, around 5:00 p.m., Moore emerged from his car and placed a large blue tarp and couch cushion on the ground in front of him. He poured gasoline all over his body, got on his knees, looked up to the heavens, and lit himself on fire. Moore succumbed to his injuries less than 24 hours later.

A couple of days passed before the public learned about a note he had left on his car windshield titled "O Grand Saline Repent of Your Racism," which detailed his experiences of racism growing up in Grand Saline. In this note, he recalled hearing a resident brag about lynching a Black man off a bridge in town and stories of the KKK, and he even described how, as a young man, he had been kicked out of a church in the 1950s for preaching about racial integration. Moore felt that Grand Saline had never moved past its racism and hoped that his death might shine a light upon systemic racial issues in town. He called for the community to repent, and he chose the flame in hopes that Grand Saline could change and become a more multiracial community.

Researchers often find themselves embroiled in events that matter to them, much in the same way we are drawn to tell stories. We often have to think about the ethics in participating in such events. We are responsible for our stories—beholden to them—and must take to telling them with a lens of personal truth. Yet, this can be difficult when our own stories and histories aren't in the past, when we are still molding them in the present. This issue between history and story happened to me when I heard about Moore's self-immolation because Grand Saline was not some distant place to me. I grew up there. Grand Saline was my home. And as a Latinx man, Moore's death resonated with me in a way I couldn't articulate, and I knew that I needed to explore what his death meant—and how it affected my relationship to my hometown too.

When I think about Moore's self-immolation, I always refer back to *kairos*. I take *kairos* to mean "the right time and due measure," as taken from Kinneavy's definition in "Kairos Revisited." Yet I'm not thinking of *kairos* in terms of how Moore (in)appropriately appealed to Grand Saline to change its culture. I mean *kairos* in terms of my own personal agency in telling stories about Grand Saline. As a kid, I was never interested in issues of race and oftentimes took part in the implicit and explicit racist discourses that were normalized in town. My interest in race and racism did not develop until my B.A. and M.A. English courses at the University of Texas at Tyler, where I read Toni Morrison, Arundhati Roy, Langston Hughes, and other authors of color who I never studied in high school but brought me to see race as an important identity factor in many people's lives—even my own.

However, my understanding of race changed drastically in my rhetoric and composition Ph.D. program at Texas Christian University when I took a course in critical race theory and immersed myself in the scholarship of Patricia Williams, Kimberle Crenshaw, and Derrick Bell, and I began understanding racism as epistemic and everyday. In that class, I remember a specific reading, Derrick Bell's "The Law of Racial Standing," and a quote that stuck with me ever since: "But when blacks suggest racism as a major cause of the problem, our views are lost by the force of a society determined to blame black victims" (120). While many readers might take the truth of Bell's assertion for granted, for me, it represented the budding of my racial awareness, when race and racial issues finally started to make sense. It forced me to come to terms with my memories of people redefining racism in my hometown and blaming victims as the problem—such as saying "rap music is what makes Black people violent" or "people who wear sagging pants are 'asking for it.'"

When I read these theorists, I began to critically reflect on my experiences in Grand Saline and the ways I became racialized, which ultimately impacted the way I connected with Moore's death. This occurred in the summer between my second and third year of the program, again connecting back to *kairos*. If Moore would have self-immolated when I was in high school or in my early years of college, I don't think his death would have impacted me as much. I would have brushed him off as "crazy," as many people in Grand Saline did. In fact, Moore's death did not garner the sweeping change he wanted. People dismissed him as "mentally unstable" and tried to erase any memory of his protest by painting over the burn marks in the parking lot and removing the makeshift memorial to honor his death. The people of Grand Saline refused to have a complex conversation about race. However, his death immediately became a flashpoint for my own research because I saw him empathetically and knew I had to develop a project around his life and death.

Everything occurred in the perfect moment for me, when my research interests and need for a project aligned. In some sense, I believe this illustrates the power of *kairos*, knowing it would be impossible for me to complete my research without Moore's death. Hence, Moore's death became the impetus for my dissertation, *Preaching behind the Fiery Pulpit*, which analyzes the rhetoric of self-immolation globally and the racial public memory of Grand Saline. I also produced a documentary on Moore and Grand Saline, titled *Man on Fire*, which won an International Documentary Association Award in 2017 and became a selection of Independent Lens and aired on PBS on December 17, 2018. The film screened at multiple film festivals and won a few awards. I'll talk more about my documentary and dissertation throughout this chapter because both are central to my racial literacy.

It is important to know that I began to reflect on my own racist upbringing in Grand Saline after Moore's death. I, too, knew most of the stories Moore recited in his letter. Not only that, but his death spoke to me because it unraveled racial memories of my past—moments I hardly remembered but somehow stayed with me, beneath the surface, all of these years. These were stories of me being racialized in Grand Saline because of my Brown skin and stories of me hearing others say racist comments about Black people. (Hell, I actually said these racist things too).

You see, Grand Saline is a town with no Black people. I think a few mixed-raced, Black people live in town now, but historically, when Moore lived there and when I grew up there, no Black people resided in town. When I read Moore's note and saw him describing a lynching that took place in town in the 1940s, I thought of my experience growing up in the 2000s, 60 years after Moore's adolescent years, and hearing similar stories of lynchings and the KKK. I distinctly remember being embarrassed to tell other Texans I was from Grand Saline because of the town's racist reputation. I also remembered my own racialization—how derogatory comments were made about me and my skin and how I brushed them off as jokes. Moore's death reminded me of a past I had forgotten, a painful one I hid from myself, that found its way back to the surface.

~ ~ ~

"You're my taco roll, son!" My coach yelled at me during football practice one day.

"Get in there and be my taco roll!"

I moved to Grand Saline, Texas, in the fall of 2000 (in seventh grade) after living about 12 miles north of town most of my life, in the small community of Alba. I idolized Grand Saline before moving there because the town was known for its football superiority. Football is the epitome of (toxic) masculinity in Texas, and I desired to be a part of this culture. In the fifth grade, I hit a growth spurt and grew to 5' 10". That same year I began playing pee-wee football for my local team. Football came naturally to me as the biggest kid on the field, and though I enjoyed the advantages of my height in all other sports, I cherished none of them as much as I did football. And Alba, simply put, was terrible at football. I often attended Friday night football games in Alba and saw opposing teams beating them by 50 or 60 points. With my size, height, and ambition, Alba did not seem like the place for me.

However, a few miles south, the football players—and community—played and celebrated football differently. Grand Saline earned a reputation as a small-town football powerhouse, which was solidified in its appearance on MTV's *True Life* in 1999. The episode, "I'm a Football Legend," chronicles a forthcoming playoff game between Grand Saline and Celina in the 1999 2A playoffs, a game that Grand Saline lost. Nonetheless, the TV show added to the reputation of the town, a reputation already established with multiple major playoff runs in the 1980s and 1990s, headed by legendary coach Carter Elliott. Thus, by the time I went into the 7th grade and started playing for the middle school, I knew I wanted a change, and my family decided to move to Grand Saline so I could play football for a good team.

"Be my taco roll, son!" My coach yelled.

I didn't know the coach too well before he said this, yet he felt comfortable using this term, for the first time, for the entire team to hear. My teammates busted with laughter. I joined with them, providing a pathetic laugh, one obviously not holding the same racist convictions. I didn't want to piss off my coach and ostracize myself from my peers, so I chose to go along with the "game" my coach was playing and the joke my teammates thought was funny. It was one of the first times I remember feeling like I had no agency in defining myself. Though I don't recall being too upset at the time (this incident hardly affected my everyday relationship with my coach and team), over 15 years later, it still sits with me—a lingering pain that hasn't healed. I see it as one of many racial incidents that constructs my racial literacy.

~~~

This chapter is an autoethnography exploring my racial upbringing in Grand Saline. As a research method, I employ autoethnography on a meta-level. First, after more contextual analysis, I will dive into four racial stories that comprise my autoethnography, concluding with a discussion about the ethics of the method—how it is altered due to positionality, how the autoethnographer can work toward reconciliation, and how essentialism becomes a constraint in the autoethnographic process. I discuss these issues at the end because it is important to situate this chapter with my autoethnography first; however, I do want to preface this work by briefly discussing reconciliation and how I view my work as a racial literacy.

I've written about experiences in my hometown over the past few years and have published them in *Inventing Place: Writing Lone Star Rhetorics* (edited by Casey Boyle and Jenny Rice) and in a forthcoming manuscript tentatively titled *Salt of the Earth: Rhetoric, Preservation, and White Supremacy.* But unlike some of my other published work about Grand Saline, this chapter focuses particularly on the idea of reconciliation—and how I try to achieve it. I define reconciliation as a process in which two parties (one who has done wrong and one who has been wronged) attempt to restore some aspect of their relationship by acknowledging such wrongs. When we think about reconciliation, we often imagine major atrocities and their aftermath, such as the formation of the "Truth and Reconciliation Commission" (TRC) after the end of apartheid South Africa. Erik Doxtader has written extensive critiques of this commission and the idea of reconciliation, stating, "The premise, purpose and value of reconciliation is far more complicated than many critics would lead us to believe. Today, more than ever, it does not suffice to set the idea of reconciliation into the hands of the TRC and then allege that the commission's shortcomings are proof that reconciliation has turned sour" (9). He continues, "Nation-building is a fragile and ambiguous process. In its midst, reconciliation's question is whether we are willing to gather and collectively undertake the work of making history" (9). As Doxtader illustrates, the idea of "true" reconciliation is a complex concept, and even when people use the term "reconciliation," it doesn't mean that actual reconciliation exists. I employ Doxtader's argument to illustrate problems embedded within the "formula" of reconciliation. Doxtader finds that the purpose of the TRC was to begin the reconciliation process through having the oppressors acknowledge their wrongs. However, can reconciliation exist when those who have done wrong never ask for forgiveness or acknowledge their wrongs?

The people of Grand Saline have never asked for forgiveness for their historical, racist misdeeds (which is one of the reasons Charles Moore self-immolated), and no one who participated in racism done unto me has ever asked for forgiveness. Arguably, White privilege might be a key factor in why they don't ask for forgiveness—they don't see anything wrong in their community. Still, I am not asking them to begin this process, especially since I was as much of an agent of racism in Grand Saline as anyone else. However, I view my work in this chapter as being a part of a reconciliatory process that does not fit the normal formula discussed above—one where the wronged is going out of the way to achieve some process of reconciliation without the wrongdoer's permission. By discussing my process of reconciliation, I am asking some very important questions: What is the role of autoethnography in the reconciliation process, especially in terms of a racialized researcher talking about racism? Can autoethnography work toward an ethics of reconciliation? Can we—scholars of color—heal our own racial wounds? As I tease through my autoethnography in this chapter, my goal is both to consider how racial literacy forms and also discuss issues around the ethics of the racialized researcher utilizing an autoethnographic method.

Lastly, before I begin my autoethnography, I want to say that the experiences discussed below revolve around my racial literacy. Racial literacy is a "skill and practice in which individuals are able to probe the existence of racism and examine the effects of race and institutionalized systems on their experiences and representation in the US society" (Sealey-Ruiz 386), and I believe performing autoethnography helps us acquire this skill and practice. Ultimately, a racial literacy allows a researcher to show how race and racism became known to them (typically through a narrative), and I view my racial literacy as better understanding what racism looks like in a colorblind society and the role of the researcher in this autoethnographic process. By referring to my autoethnography explicitly as a racial literacy narrative, I am saying that these moments of racial misdeeds eventually came together to influence my understanding of my own race and of racism in America. None of this happened during high school or during my days in Grand Saline, but rather, they took place years later. Still, I can pinpoint these various memories as being moments that explicitly affected my views on race, racism, myself, and my racial identity. None of these particular stories are necessarily more important than another; they are all small slices of a flowering racial literacy. Yet, their power stems from placing them together and making meaning from their connections.

For example, when I was producing *Man on Fire*, I became acutely aware of my racialized past that I never explicitly connected to my upbringing. I thought of race as a problem for other people when I was younger because I was very well-liked (voted homecoming king, for whatever that is worth) and never thought of racial incidents that happened to me as racism. However, making this documentary and reading more about race forced me to think about my own upbringing and memories of being called racist epithets, hearing disparaging things about Black people, and realizing that my entire upbringing was saturated in racial/

racist discourse. In other words, Moore's protest by fire caused a ripple effect in my life, which led me down a journey of racial self-awareness.

The stories of my racial literacy come together for my reconciliation process as well, becoming building blocks for me to see how I recognize and forgive incidents from my past and how I forgive myself too. But my stories also complicate the reconciliation process because of how they can be critiqued. The problem with racial literacy narratives (as with any narrative) is that they only focus on specific moments of time in which something racialized or racist takes place, which means that we might look back at the culture being described in these stories and might essentialize a people and a place as uniquely bigoted because of the narrative. So what moral obligation do we have in telling these stories? After detailing my racial literacy narrative, I will dive into the complexities of autoethnography, essentialism, and reconciliation to try and untangle the issues embedded within this genre.

MY AUTOETHNOGRAPHY

During my sophomore year of high school, I became a member of the varsity football squad. Not many sophomores made the team, so I was excited to join my older brethren. One day early in the season, I was getting dressed for football practice next to my peers on the offensive line, and somehow, I became the subject of conversation. "Sanchez is basically the Brown version of me," one of the linemen said while putting on his shoulder pads. "Yeah, the wetback version of you!" another lineman laughed. Everyone in the vicinity of this "joke" began to laugh, and I laughed too, wanting to be part of the joke. I didn't think—in this moment in time—that this situation was an explicit form of racism. When my teammates joked about my skin color, I didn't feel attacked racially. I vaguely remember feeling something in the pit of my stomach, knowing that these words were inherently wrong. But I didn't think of it as racism. It was much easier to just try and get along with these older players than stick up for myself, and so I never said anything. I went throughout all of my high school experience being called "wetback" from time to time. But to be quite honest, this nickname was not solely mine to keep. Other Mexican-Americans in school were called by this racial epithet as well.

Soon, being the "wetback version" of one of the graduating seniors of the football team evolved into me being referred to as "Wetback," "Sancho," "Sasquatch," or any other Brown epithet that could be conjured by my teammates. Often times when we were in small groups, in football practice, or in other social situations, people referred to me as some derogatory term for Mexican-Americans (and their intentions for doing this, including malice and ignorance, vary). In other words, people around me were controlling my racial identity in a way that I didn't really notice at the time because I associated more with whiteness and my White mother (I technically only have one quarter Chicanx blood). I was being raised by her and that side of the family's whiteness, yet my Brown skin dominated how people perceived my identity.

My racial untangling does not solely lie within the older White males of my high school designating me as different; much of my high school existence relied upon me feeling different from many of my Brown counterparts as well. This is just as important to understanding my hybrid racial experience, though I do note that any ostracization felt from my Brown peers was not like the White racism I experienced. Othering took place, but it was not oppressive; it did not exist as a way for me to feel subjugated from Brown people. When I really reflect on my experiences, I wonder if my high school interactions with "Browner" people could be referred to as some type of self-othering, a way that I often tried to distance myself from my Spanish-speaking brethren because I felt like a fraud if I were to attempt to join their group. One lunch period, I sat at a table with my friends (most of whom were White because whiteness signified popularity) and stared across the abyss of the cafeteria at a different table, one that was full of people with my skin tone but a bit darker. The table was comprised solely of Mexican-American students, and since there were no Black people in Grand Saline and no sizable Asian-American or Native population, the Mexican-American kids at my school were the largest minority group. (*I can still see me disassociating from them in this last sentence.*)

Many of them created their own communities at our school. If one were to take a bird's eye view of the cafeteria, they would see vast whiteness at most tables with a couple of Brown bodies dispersed amongst them, but there would be one or two tables that were solely Brown. I was one of those Brown spots at a White table, looking at people who resembled me more physically across the cafeteria but feeling exponentially more comfortable with my White peers because I spoke their language—literally and figuratively. Most of the people at the Mexican-American table could speak Spanish and did so often, or at least this was my perception in high school. Yet, when I truly reflect on my experiences, I am unsure if I truly remember them mostly speaking Spanish around me or if this was just a fear I projected onto them, a fear of not being Brown enough to be part of their collective.

Nonetheless, in these instances in the cafeteria, I became aware of my race. I looked at the White people who surrounded me and the Brown people across the cafeteria floor. If we were mostly segregated by race, why was I eating with White people? Instead of panicking and questioning my identity, I rationalized it by saying, "No, this isn't a 'racial thing'" (like I see it today). It's about language. I didn't speak Spanish. I could not sit with the people who could speak Spanish (though all of these people also spoke English on a daily basis). I rationalized my segregation from my Brown peers with this language fallacy, but as I look back at it now, I see that this was not a reasoning that I created only in this moment; rather, it was racist logic that I built into my identity at a young age.

In my early years, I remember people attempting to disassociate me from my Brownness. "You can't even speak Spanish; you're not Mexican," was a common attack levied against me when telling people about my ethnic descent or explaining that my last name actually was Sanchez. To me, it was Sanchez not Sánchez. This was how my family pronounced it for a few generations, and after talking with my dad and grandfather, Pappa (my grandfather emigrated from Mexico), I learned that when Pappa moved to East Texas, his family systematically and purposely purged Spanish nomenclature and accents from their language practices. In his home, my grandfather was taught that being American meant speaking English, and if he chose to speak Spanish, he would alienate himself. Thus, the erasing of Spanish was an act of passage for him, a way to become American, and when his four children were growing up in East Texas, any use of Spanish disappeared. And, the same for their children. Though my parents were divorced when I was young and I lived mostly with my White mother, I still remember questioning my heritage.

Once I asked my father about speaking Spanish and wondered if we didn't speak it since we were Brown: "We just don't need to," he responded. Speaking Spanish seemed like a survival tactic for some, but we had assimilated so well into American culture that we didn't need this language to fit in any longer. I cringe thinking about this now, but my father's words resonated with me at the time.

I learned about race not only through finding and wrestling with my own identity, but also in how White people talked about other people of color. In high school, discussions of Black people always had either explicit or coded racist connotations similar to the ones said of Brown kids. They were more overtly hateful, though, a product of historical racism and the fact that no Black kids went to Grand Saline. Often times, anti-Black racism came from peers and kids who were ignorant (though some were hateful), but sometimes these ideas were spread from people who should have known better: our elders.

During my junior or senior year of high school, our head coach tried to rally the team after a practice early in the season. We were preparing to play our rivals, Van High School, on Friday night, which added an extra layer of intensity to the practice and preparations. After practice, we were at the end of the field listening to our leader tell us exactly how we should mentally prepare for the game, when something odd happened. "One last thing before Friday night," he stated with a serious tone. "Don't try and piss off the Black kids on the other team by jawing at them during the game; they become better athletes when they are pissed off." Students around the huddle nodded in agreement, and then a student replied, "And they have an extra muscle in the legs!" The coach smiled and repeated, "And they have an extra muscle."

That was it. The coach moved on to something else, and all of the students taking a knee in front of the coach didn't react to the situation. I didn't react either. I remember looking at my peers because I knew something was wrong; I knew this encounter wasn't right, but we all sat still. I hope, in reflecting on this moment, that there were others like me who wanted to voice their opinion but couldn't because of the power difference between the coach and us. That's what pisses me off in the present—not that a dumb kid like me said something racist and had no consequences for their actions; rather, an adult, a 50-year-old man who should have known better, not only felt it was okay to have these bigoted viewpoints but to disseminate them as truth amongst other coaches and 50 or so students. This was a minor interaction, one that I'm unsure if others remember, but I believe it is a synecdoche for many racial interactions in Grand Saline. Students and adults alike could spread bigoted misinformation or disinformation about people of color and have no consequences for their actions. This lack of repercussions further created an environment that said racism was tolerated and accepted and was integral to communal knowledge in town.

We travelled to Van High School on Friday to face our rivals. It was going to be a tough game because they heavily outmatched us in virtually all aspects of football. Van was a division above us, and I was a bit nervous before we ran out for pre-game warm-ups. As we did our stretching at one end of the field, I could hear some of my peers talking about our opponents on the other end of the field. "Look at those n****ers out there stretching like they're monkeys!" a leader on our team announced loud enough for most of us to hear. I think he was trying to break the ice and help us ease the tension, but he used the same racist logic that our coach used a few days before, a logic that implied that we should dehumanize Black people, especially when we oppose them in sports. I see now how racism worked in my hometown: passed on from generation to generation, from people who are either ignorant because racism is the only truth they have ever been taught or who willingly choose White supremacy.

However, issues with race and racism extend to scarier concerns, mostly because the Ku Klux Klan has a long history of existing in and near Grand Saline (Loewen; Sanchez, "White Supremacy"). As a kid, I remember hearing stories about the Klan convening in the area. My friends and I often travelled to a spot seven miles north of town called Clark's Ferry. The name comes from an old folklore of a bus flipping and killing a bunch of school children in the area (Sanchez, "Recirculating Our Racism"), and is nothing special: it was just a dried up riverbed in the woods that often attracted kids because it was so far away from town. Yet when we travelled to Clark's Ferry, we did so because it was supposedly a contemporary meeting spot for the KKK.

One weekend, I travelled to Clark's Ferry to drink some beer with my friends while "backroading." Upon arriving at this spot, we got out of the vehicle and began examining the area—as we often did—looking for any clues of the KKK. I ventured to one side of the woods and stumbled across a site that still makes my stomach churn: a disembodied head of a hog was placed upon a cross made out of sticks. I stumbled backwards and yelled at my friends who all ran over to see the disgusting site. "Who would do something like this?" I asked the group. "It was probably just some kids messing around," one friend responded. "Or it was the KKK," someone else said. We were split as a group on this issue. "But you don't have to worry," one of my friends said looking at me, noticing my unease. "The KKK only kills Blacks around here."

My friend was obviously implying that as a Brown person I *should* be afraid of the KKK because of my skin color, but I *shouldn't* be scared in this instance because they "only" kill Black people in this area. I wasn't afraid because, though I did believe the KKK existed in the area, I never felt threatened by them in any capacity. However, I hated the implication: that Black people should be afraid was "normal." My friend wasn't saying that he was upset or ashamed that Black people should be afraid; instead, he just knew from the cultural conversations of the town that they should be fearful. And that was okay to him. I looked at my friend and noticed the inherent whiteness coded into his reaction. The whiteness spread amongst all of my friends at Clark's Ferry. They did not have to be afraid of racial issues because racism didn't affect them—they could tell jokes about it, make others afraid by talking about it, and much more, but they never had to be victims.

I felt upset that my peers believed racism against Brown people was not okay but racism against Black people was fine. I also experienced relief knowing that I was one of the "good ones" to these White folk. How was I supposed to respond to this friend who was telling me racism was normal but not towards me? With my mixed emotions, I should have said a lot of things—maybe telling him off or telling him about the perils of racism and racialized violence. I didn't know any better, though. Instead, I smiled. It was easier to keep harmony when my friends seemed like they would shield me from any real danger.

The racism I discussed in these stories is not always the typical, overt hatred and bigotry that dominates typical discourses of racism. While some of this racism is overt, it is often masked in one way or another. For instance, I was popular in high school. I was mostly a jock and was known for being a class clown. In typical American discourse, we wouldn't use these descriptors to talk about how the systemic racism in a town othered an individual and taught him about racial biases. In this sense, I am not arguing that my memories are more traumatic than someone else's; quite the opposite is true—I use these stories to indicate the everydayness of systemic racism that can affect anyone perceived as racialized. My autoethnography highlights the epistemic nature of racism in Grand Saline.

For example, let's start with the culture of the locker room—a space I was quite familiar with in high school—and how the hyper-masculinity associated with such a space illustrates the ways marginalizing and othering peoples can become naturalized (even though sports pundits might refer to locker rooms as "unifying" spaces). One of the moments when I felt most othered by my peers was in the locker room when I was a sophomore, playing for the varsity football team. I existed in the background of this space because I was one of only maybe a couple of sophomores playing for the varsity squad, and though I had the size of anyone else on the team, I already felt like an outsider because I was younger than all of my teammates. When they made jokes about my skin color, I had to try to fit in no matter what. It was in my best interest to not be outed as a problem. I learned in these moments that race can be a unifying factor—a unifying one that whiteness can circle around and build community around through telling jokes.

The nicknames I had in high school also taught me that it did not matter how I perceived my own body. To many of my White peers, I was always going to be "different," and my silence allowed me to "bond" with my teammates. For instance, when I was first called "the wetback version" of my teammate, I was not conflicted; I was happy my peers were joking about me and allowed me to be a part of the group. However, I was conflicted when it came to the nickname itself. Though I did not speak Spanish and did not fit in directly with other Mexican-American students because I identified with my whiteness, my skin color and my last name signified my racial identity. I knew of the wetback caricature and the various racialized stigmas that correspond with this term and on some level knew the rhetorical distance that was being created between my peers and myself—meaning I could be in the in-group (sort of) but always on the edge, in a liminal space. But ultimately, I never said anything about this nickname because I did not want to be the person causing some sort of division in the locker room. I think I rationalized that this racist encounter actually made me fit more into the collective than not having a nickname would.

A racial literacy doesn't always have to be about the individual researcher though. I learned about race through similar experiences that were not directed at me and my Brownness, but that I took part in as a participant or observer. The last two stories in my autoethnography, about the coach and the KKK, showed me as much.

Racial bigotry can build a community simply through the act of othering, and I often took part in this rhetorical community-building process too. My coach could not have uttered such racism and had no consequences for his actions unless he understood that his audience would not only accept his bigotry but would view it as normalized for the community. In this rhetorical encounter, the coach's goal was to incite his players, which could have been accomplished via a plethora of tactics, yet, he chose this overt racism as a type of rally cry itself. By remarking that we should not "jaw" at the Black athletes on the other team, our coach attempted to provide a tactical advantage in the game—one he had to consider a truth. His racist reality was disseminated to all of the players as not only a tactic, but a racist ideology that we should internalize in some capacity. His cultural knowledge became a truth that we all accepted.

His cultural knowledge also shows how racism is perpetuated. Young, impressionable kids can see a coach make comments about race and understand that such comments are acceptable because no one holds the coach responsible for his actions. Students don't say anything. Other coaches don't say anything. This tells them that, under the right circumstances, racism is acceptable. Maybe they can't call people of color racial epithets to their faces, but when they are amongst their peers, or in "safe spaces" like the locker room, they can be bigoted without consequences. Maybe some of these kids grew up like I did and learned the truth about racism later in life. But it is not too far-fetched to imagine if they never left these "safe spaces" where racism is a commodity for humor and knowledge that nothing would ever change. In some sense, this is how communities like Grand Saline never change. They continually circle the same logic, the same systems of oppression, that have existed in the community for over a century.

My racial literacy emphasizes the epistemic nature of racism—how I was taught to be a racist in a racist environment, how others built knowledge about people of color through myths, and how racist logic made me a "good" Mexican. These memories have never dissipated, 15 years later. They are a part of who I once was, and, in response to that, who I am today. My literacy highlights my own understanding of race in high school to illustrate the fact that my story is not unique. Every kid in Grand Saline learned about race through the same systems—the locker room bigotry, the elders joining in the racism or being silent in the face of it, the ways the community tolerates Brown bodies in relation to Black bodies.

While this racial literacy exists as meta-commentary on autoethnography as a research method, I still hope these stories, if ever read by people related to Grand Saline, compel others to speak their own truths. We need more voices that speak to truth to whiteness, to speak truth to racism.

RACE, AUTOETHNOGRAPHY, AND POSITIONALITY

My own autoethnography illustrates some important issues in relation to racial literacies, essentialism, and reconciliation, but I want to take a moment to focus on the act of writing an autoethnography, especially as it comes to positionality. In their text *Critical Autoethnography*, editors Robin M. Boylorn and Mark P. Orbe (both communication scholars), define autoethnography as "both the method and product of researching and writing about personal lived experiences and their relationship to culture" (16–17). These authors label autoethnography as the relationship between the individual author and culture, in which the author writes and describes his or her experiences. In another context, Carolyn S. Ellis and Arthur Bochner define autoethnography as "autobiographies that self-consciously explore the interplay of the introspective, personally engaged self with cultural descriptions mediated through language, history, and ethnographic explanation" (742). Here, they situate autoethnography as a self-reflexive method that unites the personal with the cultural.

Examining these different interpretations of autoethnography together enables us to gain a better sense of it as a research method, but neither of these definitions focus on positionality. For instance, while Boylorn and Orbe want autoethnographers to connect lived experiences to "their relationship to culture," some questions arise around the definition of culture and the various experiences one might have in relation to a particular dominant (white supremacist) culture. Ellis and Bochner's definition complicates this matter by relating autoethnography to mediated cultural descriptions, but we still need to complicate positionality because of how it alters the subjective nature of sharing stories and how we interpret them.

The definition of autoethnography that best informs the questions I am asking, however, comes from Heewon Chang's *Autoethnography as Method*. Chang, an anthropologist, believes autoethnography "should be ethnographic in its methodological orientation, cultural in its interpretative orientation, and autobiographical in its content orientation" (48). This definition explains autoethnography as a three-prong approach. First, it should situate the individual within the cultural and contextual environments of which they reside (an ethnographic methodological orientation). Second, it should explain and analyze the individual experiences within these contexts (a cultural interpretive orientation). Lastly, it should use the individual author, and their experiences, as the primary subject of inquiry (an autobiographical content orientation). However, I want to complicate Chang's definition. 1) As an orientation, how do researchers of color position themselves for an ethnography in a mostly White, often racist environment? 2) How do racialized researchers position their cultural interpretation when their culture is vastly different than the culture they are analyzing? 3) How does an autobiographical content orientation affect both the method and interpretation?

I'll begin with the ethnographic as methodological orientation paradigm by focusing on two specific texts in rhetoric, composition, and literacy studies, Jennifer Trainor's *Rethinking Racism* and Julie Lindquist's *A Place to Stand*, both of which are ethnographies. Trainor's text focuses on "the causes and origins of white student racism" at "Laurel Canyons High School" (a pseudonym), a school with a 97% White population (3). Most importantly for my research: Trainor is a White researcher who is investigating this racism problem. While Trainor is investigating racial issues in this mostly White high school, I believe her own racial positioning, the whiteness of the skin, helps her in this study. Trainor writes, "Memories of my own racial formation and whiteness ensure that as a researcher at Laurel Canyons, I am not an outsider studying a group of people who appear to me as other. And yet my identity as a researcher and teacher with a commitment to antiracist pedagogies also separates me from the white students" (33). Trainor believes her racial positioning helps her talk with White people about race because it provides her an insider status (though her position as researcher hinders her).

In a similar situation, Lindquist's text looks at the rhetorical practices of a working-class bar in South Chicago, but her positionality is a bit different than Trainor's. Though Lindquist acknowledges the working-class lifestyle she was around as an adolescent, she describes her role in the bar as being an antagonist, saying, "As soon as it became public knowledge that I was a college student and a 'liberal,' I was drawn into performed debates . . . [which] gave me a way, at least, to find a place among others" (18). Lindquist doesn't define herself as a working-class person doing research in this bar, but her research shows the ways she found a "role" to play to open people up to her ethnographic research. In regards to the positionality of the researcher in this methodological framing, it seems that using an ethnographic lens can become muddied due to positionality, especially for a racialized person studying White racism. But finding one's "role" in the research becomes vital. Therefore, we need to be intentional in framing our research because our roles and identities matter.

Culture can be such a tricky word to define. In his famous text, *The Location of Culture*, Homi Bhabha talks about culture as this:

> The theoretical recognition of the split-space of enunciation may open the way to conceptualising an international cul- ture, based not on the exoticism of multiculturalism or the diversity of cultures, but on the inscription and articulation of culture's hybridity. It is the in-between space that carries the

> burden of the meaning of culture, and by exploring this Third
> Space, we may elude the politics of polarity and emerge as the
> others of our selves. (56)

To Bhabha, the hybridity of culture—or its "Third Space"—is what provides meaning. Most importantly for this, Bhabha focuses on culture as not being a fixed set of beliefs and values but rather a spectrum. And this is what leads into issues surrounding interpreting autoethnography with a cultural lens. My racialized identity as a Chicanx man makes my interpretations of a place like Grand Saline much different than how the White person who lives in town might describe the culture. And my own hybrid racial experiences impact these experiences as well. Similar to what Lindquist and Trainor both describe, my specific role as researcher affects my interpretation of culture as well. For the racialized researcher investigating racism, culture must shift to not just be something "other" in relation to their own cultures. Yet, we need to be aware of how our cultural biases might affect the cultures being described in our work, especially when understanding that culture is not a fixed set of values. Thus, we must always indicate how our various values and cultural understandings play into the interpretations of stories, to give readers a better sense of how such work is being interpreted and why it is being interpreted in a certain way.

Lastly, how does the autobiographical content orientation affect both the cultural interpretations and ethnographic methods? In both orientations, positionality is most important, and it often has been upfront in other autoethnographic studies in the field. For instance, in his "A Post(modern)script" from *Bootstraps*, Victor Villanueva describes the various ideological genres that he believes his text fits within, labelling it as postmodern, Foucauldian, and possibly even Derridean. However, when narrowing down the heart of his book, which is largely autoethnographic in nature, Villanueva writes, "The compression of space, time, and motion is the postmodern condition. . . [Yet,] I can only really know and tell about one man of color's conditions" (142). Though Villanueva's book is basically an academic literacy narrative, how a poor Puerto Rican boy from New York found success in academia, it is also "an autobiography with political, theoretical, pedagogical consideration. . . . This is the personal made public and the public personalized, not for self-glory nor to point fingers, but to suggest how, maybe, to make the exception the rule" (xviii). Villanueva's text is similar to my chapter, as both could be described as racial literacy narratives, and the highlight of Villanueva's argument is how vital positionality is in undertaking such work.

Autoethnography is an important method for people to use to study race and antiracism because it gives the individual researcher agency in describing themselves and the culture around them. Researchers who take on this methodology need to focus on their positionality, which is not only vital in the content they are providing audiences but also in the methodological framing and cultural interpreting that are a part of the autoethnographic process. Without a proper positional connection in these framings, the researcher might present a well-rounded, polished framing and interpretation of their experiences. In all three facets of the autoethnographic process, clear-cut descriptions of the researcher's positionality is key.

THE PROBLEM WITH ESSENTIALISM

While positionality is important, we also need to reconsider the limitations within this methodology, especially when it comes to ethics and essentialism. At the heart of the methodology, autoethnography provides the individual agency in telling their story, and when it comes to issues of race, it can define racial issues within communities and cultures that might be overlooked or suppressed. However, how should the autoethnographer tackle the issue of telling their story of racism and their hometown without indicting every single person in their community, especially when racism exists on both implicit and explicit levels? Should that even be an ethical concern for the autoethnographer? In other words, should the researcher be concerned in how the characterization of a community affects all the various individuals in said community? Of course, there is no easy answer to this question, but we need to unpack it.

In theoretical terms, essentialism can be defined as the way "some social groups are represented as if they were collectively defined by some inhering, immutable and group-defining 'essence'" (Hanson-Easey et al. 363). In other words, essentialism is often the way those in power attempt to categorize and define groups through common qualities outside of their inherent social and biological factors. For instance, some White people view Black people as inherently more likely to commit crimes, though, obviously, that is not an immutable trait amongst Black people (Quillian and Pager). Or, for instance, in Grand Saline, we believed all Black people had "extra muscles" that made them better athletes. While often employed to discuss the "essential" qualities of racial groups in critical race theory, others, such as Angela Harris, have demonstrated how essentialism affects other identity groups, such as gender. In her article "Race and Essentialism in Feminist Legal Theory," Harris argues that gender essentialism in feminist legal theory often erases race, and she attempts to subvert it via a multiple consciousness mindset, or stories from the marginalized and silenced (615–16). Over the past few decades, scholars from multiple disciplines have described the problems of essentialism and ways to combat it via anti-essentialist practices, such as multiple consciousness theories, counter-storytelling (Martinez), and other methodologies. Even Lockett's chapter in this book deals with other forms of essentialism surrounding what is or is not "Black Twitter," via linguistic practices and uses of memes.

However, my chapter flips this script, in a way. The problem with writing about racism in Grand Saline isn't that I take a minoritized group and essentialize them based on a certain quality or such. Rather, I take the majority population and characterize their culture and community as inherently racist via my storytelling act. I do this by taking individual racist encounters and talking about the ways they affected me and the ways the silence from my peers and elders also affected me. All of these encounters develop my racial literacy, how I came to know I was Brown in a White town and that race was inherently epistemic. And, by virtue, it presents the people of Grand Saline as racist simply through the act of telling these stories. Thus, an ethical dilemma arises: Where is my responsibility in sharing these stories as a means to discuss my racial literacy but also being weary of how I frame the town?

Of course, it would be easy for me to toss in caveats into all of my stories. I could say, "Not everyone in Grand Saline is racist," "My best friends weren't racist, for sure," "Joe Smith lived in town and said he is not racist, so I want you, reader, to know this." Throughout much of my research on Grand Saline, during my dissertation work and documentary project, I often asked myself questions about essentialism, especially since people often told me I was indicting Grand Saline as racist. These encounters remind me of a recent debate that occurred in Slocum, Texas. For years in Slocum, there were talks of a Black massacre that had occurred at the turn of the century, but there were no historical accounts that illustrated what actually occurred—until historian E.R. Bills wrote a book titled *The 1910 Slocum Massacre* in 2014. Along with the book, Bills applied for a historical marker to be placed in Slocum to remember the dead, whom had been forgotten for over a century. While many in the Black community felt this was justified, some Whites in the area disagreed.

For instance, Jimmy Odom, the White chairman of the Anderson County Historical Commission (where Slocum is located), spoke out against the historical marker saying, "This is a nice, quiet community with a wonderful school system. It would be a shame to mark them as racist from now until the end of time" (qtd. in Madigan). Odom's defense parallels the issues of essentialism in Grand Saline. He argues that by showing these racist misdeeds and attempting to honor the dead, people will only think of Slocum as racist. I believe people in Grand Saline feel the same about my work and would feel the same about my autoethnography: they would say it implies that all people in Grand Saline are racist.

The role of the researcher is to present their truth, even if that truth hurts others. Though I think it is important to note that my truths are solely my own, it would be disingenuous to consistently say, "But not everyone there is racist!" People everywhere are racist. However, I'm not trying to make an essentialist argument about Grand Saline because there are essential, immutable racist tendencies of everyone in town. Rather, I'm trying to say that by recounting my truth through my racial formation, Grand Saline is a microcosm of race in America, and my experiences are not uncommon—these stories are everyone's stories. The goal of my autoethnography is not to essentialize but to illustrate my racial literacy. If I prefaced my racial stories with such "not all" language, I would be practically erasing my stories of their power—giving people in Grand Saline agency in saying that they were one of the good ones. Again, that wasn't my upbringing. There were no antiracists acting in town, just people who were explicitly racist and people who were quiet in the face of racism. This is what made Charles Moore's act so important to me: it was one of the first public acts of antiracism to ever take place in the town and was mostly erased because it was too controversial.

Essentialism is a powerful, rhetorical tool that people often use as a means of oppression. As researchers, we should be more in-tune with the way essentialism appears in our work, especially when it describes marginalized, disenfranchised peoples. In the case of my own research, I bring up essentialism to demonstrate the critiques I often receive about my research, sometimes publicly. A few years ago, a former friend called me a "self-righteous, uninformed, self-serving pseudo-academic," who defamed Grand Saline solely to promote myself on a Facebook newspaper page. He believed my research about Grand Saline labels the entire culture as racist.

I get that sentiment. I think it is important for researchers to be reflexive when it comes to their work. This is a major component of the authoethnographic process, and it should be a more generative discourse that researchers utilize when discussing communities and peoples. Being reflexive won't erase all questions about essentialism we might receive from our work, but it can provide us a stronger methodological positioning to stand.

THE PROBLEM WITH RECONCILIATION

How can an autoethnographic lens create a means of reconciliation? As famed historian Timothy Tyson has stated, "If there is to be reconciliation, first there must be truth" (10), so I share these experiences to first position a cultural interpretation of my upbringing in Grand Saline before investigating the reconciliatory aspects of this autoethnographical lens.

For many of the years during college and grad school—after I began my racial studies—I harbored anger towards Grand Saline because I knew that elders in the community were still spreading a racist ideology, and there had to be other students of color who were at the butt of jokes and harassment. Of course, my pain wasn't a constant presence in my daily life; most of the time I wouldn't even notice it unless I was passing through Grand Saline or had a random moment jog my memory. But all of this eventually changed for me. The moments I described above, these memories that once made me cringe or think hateful things towards some friends and community members for being explicitly racist, are not discharged of emotion, but my anger has quelled. This process of (what I call) personal reconciliation did not develop overnight; rather, I believe it was part of a rhetorical process that stemmed from the autoethnographic methods I utilized in writing my dissertation (and, in extension, this chapter) and producing a documentary about my hometown. But what is my role in the reconciliation process, especially as a researcher of color looking for some resolve in a community not asking for it? Do I have agency in claiming racial healing for myself without communal repentance—or even communal acceptance? Where does my own agency lie in not only being a victim of racism but someone who participated in it?

In his foundational text on the rhetoric of reconciliation, "Reconciliation—A Rhetorical Concept/ion," Erik Doxtader attempts to dissect reconciliation's rhetorical capabilities and limitations. He states, "The reality of reconciliation appears wed to words, the power of logos to turn us from one condition to another and the actions of speech that provoke us to reflect on how we talk and to what ends" (278). In reference to speech, Doxtader argues that the power in reconciliation exists within how words convey meaning and how they have the potential to move an individual from one state (unresolved) to another (resolved). He reiterates his point: "More modest, the claim here is that reconciliation's beginning is an announced call for that speech which tropologically turns justifications for violence toward shared oppositions that contain the potential for communicative understanding. In other words, reconciliation (a) opens a present for speech; (b) performs and advocates the middle voice of an ethos; and (c) constitutes a struggle for recognition" (278). Reconciliation to Doxtader is a window of potential, one that opens access for healing via speech acts, ethos appeals, and recognition. In concluding his article, Doxtader refers to reconciliation as "a working faith in the works of words. . . Reconciliation is a rhetorical memory made, an active re-membering of rhetoric's making, and a remembrance of what rhetoricity might yet make" (284). He envisions the concept of reconciliation living in the hopes that our words can create resolve and a space for healing, and of course, referring to this as a "faith" suggests that all of this resides in a metaphysical rather than a formulaic space. This is where I envision my own chapter intervening in the rhetorical conception of reconciliation.

To achieve reconciliation, Doxtader argues that his three points must be achieved. However, this definition relies upon those who have done wrong attempting to make right their wrongs. In the case of Grand Saline, many in the community have not considered recognizing the pain they have committed against me and others. My discussions of racism and my autoethnography illustrate my own racial literacy and construction of myself in Grand Saline, but they also exist as a personal reconciliation for myself. In one sense, I view the endeavor of writing my dissertation and producing these words on a screen as having faith, faith that my words matter, that they can produce a resolve for me. In this way, I am not solely following Doxtader's formula, because he describes the process of reconciliation existing around a person/community seeking reconciliation and a person/community who has committed "violence." My autoethnography challenges the ways reconciliation forms, suggesting that reconciliation can develop not solely with two or more actors meeting with the potential for resolve and recognition, but can be a discursive process the researcher can unfold, intentionally or unintentionally. Sometimes reconciliation isn't about time or the process but rather about surviving in the muck and doing the work to overcome one's past. Sometimes reconciliation is about having compassion for ourselves and others, understanding that change occurs due to our proximity and understanding of others. Reconciliation is complex.

I view this chapter as another attempt at reconciliation—not just a personal one—where I come face-to-face with my own racial misdeeds in Grand Saline. My hands are not clean. I did not actively try to stop racism in my hometown when it occurred. I also was a participant in it. I said the n-word when I knew it was an acceptable form of communication. When we played against teams with Black players, I participated in fueling hatred towards them. In full disclosure, I don't think I ever led the racist charge. I never was the one who riled up racism. Or at least I hope that I didn't do any of those things. So this chapter not only attempts to reconcile the racism done unto me but also is the recognition that I have done racism unto others as well. I have vilified people of color who didn't assimilate into the "white habitus"[1] as well as I could. I have done all of the bigoted things that I know I am now against. In some ways, maybe this makes me a hypocrite, but I hope it also demonstrates that people can change as well, because I am not that same kid who grew up in East Texas and wanted to be White. And I write these words so others might be moved to change as well.

---

1   Eduardo Bonilla-Silva defines this as a "racialized, uninterrupted socialization process that conditions and creates whites' racial tastes, perceptions, feelings, and emotions and their views on racial matters" (104).

So how do I achieve reconciliation? The answer is as vague as the question. Maybe I have achieved reconciliation. Maybe. For people whom I have wronged—perhaps someone reading this chapter—I want you to know that I recognize that I was an ignorant adolescent who did not have the courage to stand up against racism. I even contributed to it. I am willing to discuss these wrongs with anyone who would like to talk because I believe such discourse is what we need to try and better ourselves and our communities.

But I am unsure if reconciliation exists for me as a victim or me as a perpetrator. On some level, I feel as an agent writing this chapter, talking about my history, and being open with myself, I have on some level achieved some degree of resolve within my community. Maybe this doesn't follow the broad terms of reconciliation that Doxtader promotes because my problem is more nuanced, but I do feel at peace. And I remember the first time this actually took place.

When I was filming the documentary, we had multiple shoots in Grand Saline across the fall and winter of 2016–2017. I often interviewed people in Grand Saline about racial issues for the documentary. This project put a target on the film team's back and made for some awkward encounters with residents about issues of race—where people would call me a liar, ask me to leave certain spaces, and would refuse to talk to me. Since I was the interviewer in most situations, I often had to come face-to-face with big questions about race: "What is it like being labelled as racist?" "Do you believe your community is racist?" "Do you remember anything racist happening in town when you were younger?" Many residents in town refused to talk to us because I had a reputation of being a "race baiter" (whatever that means) and thought our project attempted to defame the town. Others participated in the interviews but skirted around issues of race. And while I was glad to acquire terrific footage for the documentary, I found myself asking particular questions (to myself) when conducting interviews. Was I mad at some of these people for the racism they fostered? Was I only antiracist now because it benefited me academically (as some townspeople told me)? I soon realized that taking on the documentary was as much about myself as it was about the town.

I never had an "aha" reconciliation moment when I felt at peace with Grand Saline during filming the documentary because I don't think this process has an end, but a recent moment helped me realize my thoughts had changed. In March 2018, we held a screening of *Man on Fire* in Tyler, TX, 40 miles south of Grand Saline. It was the first public screening of the film (sponsored by the University of Texas Tyler's Honors Program), and we invited everyone who participated in the project and much of Grand Saline to come to the screening. Two hundred or two hundred and fifty people attended, and a few residents from Grand Saline appeared as well. As we took the stage for the Q&A, I felt nervous.

I had spoken about this film in film festivals and academic settings, which felt natural to me. But to engage with local people who might have grown up in Grand Saline and the surrounding area appeared daunting to me. During the Q&A, I explored some of my own upbringing and received a specific question from a former resident of Grand Saline: "Are you still mad?" she asked me from the back of the theatre. I thought about it for a moment, feeling the eyes of the room looking straight at me. There were people in this room that I knew were racists to some degree or another. Even some of my childhood friends who disagree with my takes on our hometown sat in attendance, and their eyes weighed me down. I looked at the woman and replied: "No."

I don't remember the full explanation I provided this person, but I remember the feeling that made me confident in my response. After a few years of exploring my home community, my racial upbringing, and Moore's death, I felt a sense of relief. But I think this relief is twofold: on one hand, I don't feel angry at these people anymore because I have moved forward with my life, but I also was relieved knowing that I would continually challenge racism and racists in Grand Saline. They could no longer hide beneath the folklore and whispers around town. My documentary and my research would bring them out to the open where maybe they can face processes of reconciliation with others.

I think I never had the "aha" moment because this healing process didn't form through a single moment but through doing the work. The dissertation and documentary made me face my own fears—my upbringing, other agents of racism, and the community at large—and only through the grueling process of the work—interviewing people who made me uncomfortable and challenging my hometown openly and publicly—did I find a sense of healing. By forcing myself to deal with these issues, I was able to find some relief. Of course, I know this isn't possible for everyone dealing with these issues, but it does pinpoint something valuable: if we work on our issues by facing them head-on, we can get the reconciliation process started.

The process might not have a fixed end, but that beginning is better than nothing.

CONCLUSION

Autoethnography is a powerful methodological lens, one that makes the personal cultural, interpretive, and subject to critique. Oftentimes, autoethnographies become academic fodder because of the advantages and constraints built into this method: they afford the individual to claim their own truths (which makes people feel they cannot critique said truths) and rely heavily on subjectivity to make claims. In terms of anti-racism, autoethnography provides a space for the researcher to combat accepted norms and pinpoint realities of racism that might not always be apparent to most audiences. It can be a site of anti-racist power, when used accordingly. Autoethnographies can illustrate the various realities of racism in our personal lives and provide ways to critique normative, institutional structures. My own racial literacy demonstrates this point.

Racial literacies also add to anti-racist research because they inherently demonstrate how the researchers learned that race is a socially constructed phenomenon. My own literacy focuses on the ways I existed within and outside certain categories, becoming Brown in certain situations and relating to whiteness in other ones. And this is where the power of anti-racist methods lies: they can connect the personal with the scholarly and vice versa, drawing clear connections between lived experiences and theoretical or methodical research. We need more scholars doing this work, if only to push the "everydayness" of racism into the forefront of both our research and our lives.

Yet, this power doesn't only exist within making the personal scholarly and the scholarly personal. It can also greatly affect our personal lives through reconciliation. It may not be the formulaic reconciliation that we think of in terms of nations attempting to move past communal atrocities, but personal ones—ones that can help the researcher move past pain and trauma that lingers from their past.

Therefore, the power of autoethnography lies within the ways the research can speak to an audience—sure—but also in how the individual researcher, the one who is speaking their truth, can change due to their own scholarship.

WORKS CITED

Bell, Derrick. "The Law of Racial Standing." *Yale Journal of Law and Liberation,* vol. 2, no. 1, 1991, pp. 117–21.

Bhabha, Homi K. *The Location of Culture.* Routledge, 2004.

Bills, E. R. *The 1910 Slocum Massacre: An Act of Genocide in East Texas.* The History Press, 2014.

Bonilla-Silva, Eduardo. *Racism without Racists: Color-Blind Racism and the Persistence of Racial Inequality in the United States.* Rowman & Littlefield, 2006.

Boylorn, Robin M. and Mark P. Orbe, editors. *Critical Autoethnography: Intersecting Cultural Identities in Everyday Life.* Routledge, 2017.

Chang, Heewon. *Autoethnography as Method.* Routledge, 2008.

Crenshaw, Kimberle. "Demarginalizing the Intersection of Race and Sex: A Black Feminist Critique of Antidiscrimination Doctrine, Feminist Theory and Antiracist Politics." *University of Chicago Legal Forum*, vol. 1989, no. 1, 1989, pp. 139–67.

Doxtader, Erik. "Proper Reconciliation Means a Collective Undertaking to Make History." *Cape Times,* 4 Apr. 2008, p. 9.

———. "Reconciliation—A Rhetorical Concept/ion." *Quarterly Journal of Speech*, vol. 89, no. 4, 2003, pp. 267–92.

Ellis, Carolyn, and Arthur P. Bochner. "Autoethnography, Personal Narrative, Reflexivity: Researcher as Subject." *Handbook of Qualitative Research*. 2nd ed., edited by Norman K. Denzin and Yvonna S. Lincoln, SAGE, 2000, pp. 733–68.

Hanson-Easey, Scott, et al. "'They're all tribals': Essentialism, Context and the Discursive Representation of Sudanese Refugees." *Discourse & Society*, vol. 25, no. 3, 2014, pp. 362–82.

Harris, Angela P. "Race and Essentialism in Feminist Legal Theory." *Stanford Law Review*, vol. 42, no. 3, 1990, pp. 581–616.

"I'm a Football Hero." *True Life,* created by Betsy Forhan, Dave Sirulnick, Jim Fraenkel, and Marshall Eisen, Viacom Media Networks and MTV Studios, 2000.

Lindquist, Julie. *A Place to Stand: Politics and Persuasion in a Working-Class Bar*. Oxford UP, 2002.

Loewen, James. "Showing Grand Saline in TX. . ." *The Homepage of James W. Loewen*, Accessed 21 Sep. 2018.

Madigan, Tim. "Texas Marks Racial Slaughter More than a Century Later." *Washington Post*, 16 Jan. 2016.

Martinez, Aja. *Counterstory: The Rhetoric and Writing of Critical Race Theory*. NCTE, 2020.

Moore, Charles. "O Grand Saline Repent of Your Racism." *Tyler Morning Telegraph*, 2 Jul. 2014.

Quillian, Lincoln, and Devah Pager. "Black Neighbors, Higher Crime? The Role of Racial Stereotypes in Evaluations of Neighborhood Crime." *American Journal of Sociology*, vol. 107, no. 3, 2001, pp. 717–67.

Sanchez, James Chase, producer. *Man on Fire*. Directed by Joel Fendelman, Fendelman Films and New Day Films, 2018.

———. *Preaching behind the Fiery Pulpit: Rhetoric, Public Memory, and Self-Immolation*. 2017. Texas Christian U, Ph.D. dissertation.

———. "Recirculating our Racism: Public Memory, Folklore, and Place in East Texas." *Inventing Place: Writing Lone Star Rhetorics*, edited by Casey Boyle and Jenny Rice, Southern Illinois UP, 2018, pp. 75–87.

———. "Trump, the KKK, and the Versatility of White Supremacy." *Journal of Contemporary Rhetoric*, vol. 8, no. 1/2, 2018, pp. 44–56.

Sealey-Ruiz, Yolanda. "Building Racial Literacy in First-Year Composition." *Teaching English in the Two-Year College*, vol. 40, no. 4, 2013, pp. 384–98.

Thompson, Roger. "*Kairos* Revisited: An Interview with James Kinneavy." *Rhetoric Review*, vol. 19, no. 1, 2000, pp. 73–88.

Trainor, Jennifer Seibel. *Rethinking Racism: Emotion, Persuasion, and Literacy in an All-White High School*. Southern Illinois UP, 2008.

Tyson, Timothy. *Blood Done Sign my Name*. Three Rivers Press, 2005.

Villanueva, Victor. *Bootstraps: From an American Academic of Color*. National Council of Teachers of English, 1993.

Williams, Patricia J. *The Alchemy of Race Rights*. Harvard UP, 1992.

INTERCHAPTER DIALOGUE
FOR CHAPTER 3

Chris: James, I wanted to point out that in your chapter, you explore the challenges of facing racism as a young person and how, as an adult, you've become concerned with the idea of reconciliation. Could you say more about how you define that term? What's the nature of reconciliation? Is it personal or psychological or communal, or all the above?

James: Yeah, so at a certain point of my doctoral studies, I was harboring some serious issues with race. It was hard to negotiate the fact that I had participated in anti-Black racism, but that I was personally a victim of racism as well. When I started doing interviews about race with people in my hometown for both the dissertation and the film project, I was really angry and suspicious. I had no idea how people from Grand Saline would interact with me. I worried because I was like, "These people are very racist!" It was also hard trying to code this data. But somewhere along the way, I realized that I was personally looking for reconciliation. This is somewhat different than the reconciliation that we think about when we think of something like the Truth and Reconciliation Commission (TRC) in South Africa. In that case, you typically have people publicly confessing about how systemic racism caused them to do wrong to members of the community. They formally try to reconcile their misdeeds for amnesty and social progress. It is a bold act of seeking trust. In my experience, people weren't really attempting to reconcile; they didn't really care about my experience or my thoughts on race, racism, and my hometown.

So, this work really is personal. When I was cultivating my own research, I realized that doing historical research rooted in my personal experience was a way for me to reconcile my painful past with racism. I had been called "wetback" during my freshman year in high school. But I was also silent when I observed others using anti-Black racial slurs. At some point, I noticed that I was going through some transformations as a researcher and as an overall adult. Specifically, I was trying to figure out how to make antiracism part of my identity and stance without compromising the integrity of the work. In my case, I started seeing how drawing on my emotions and experience could actually be really vital towards my projects.

Chris: You have definitely devoted a lot of intellectual and emotional energy into making your work accessible to multiple audiences—with your production of *Man on Fire*, the diss, and your current book project. I want to talk a little bit about your methods. What has antiracist filmmaking taught you about antiracist research?

James: That's a really great question! How you interact with your film participants is really important to both of these processes. I focus on Grand Saline because part of my antiracist research agenda is to create a space for White people, especially White people in and around my hometown, to be reflexive about their community.

I didn't want to just claim, "Grand Saline is the most racist town in all of America. But that's just how it is. We can't do anything. Whatever. We don't have to think about it." With *Man on Fire*, we really tried to focus on not showing these very explicit forms of bigotry. If you interview someone for an hour and a half, not everyone is going to say something bigoted, but someone can take a ten-second interview about culturally sensitive topics and twist it in a way that makes you look bad.

Now, I don't deny that these people said things that were very bigoted. But my goal was to highlight my specific experiences with race. I wanted to showcase how implicit racism can be. We wanted to hold up a mirror to Grand Saline to say, "Look, you're not unique in your racism. There's racism like this all across the country. But we're trying to invite this space in for you to be able to reflect on your actions and think about other ways we can move forward with that." And honestly, it hasn't had a huge impact. Occasionally, I've had people from my community reach out to me and say, "Hey, you know, I never really thought about these issues before. But talking with you after watching the film, you know, I have questions and I want to think about it," etc. But I haven't seen a monumental shift.

As a researcher thinking about research practices, I constantly think about how anti-racism might help us become more self-reflexive in our own processes of trying to commit to ending these injustices. I'm always battling with this issue, as I discuss throughout my chapter, as well as the issue of essentialism. I frequently contemplate the risks of antiracist research. Like—how does the focus on race and racism inadvertently oversimplify or essentialize Grand Saline?

I've been asked these kinds of questions. "Are you labeling this town as racist? Are you just following the stereotype of the South being super racist?" And I get that. But ultimately, that's not what we're trying to do. We're trying to be honest about what we see. This ethic should guide the goal of any researcher.

But back to the problem of representation. . . .

Grand Saline is hardly unique for its racism. A whole lot of other communities exist like this, where we need to have these conversations. Don't get me wrong, my research doesn't simply reduce everyone in this community as die-hard KKK racists. However, I'm aware that the work risks this misinterpretation. In writing my own autoethnography, I really tried to work through these major issues throughout this chapter.

Alex: Thanks, James! Can we talk more about the problem of race and representation?

In your chapter, you claim that, "The problem with racial literacy narratives (as with any narrative) is that they only focus on specific moments of time in which something racialized or racist takes place, which means that we might look back at the culture being described in these stories and might essentialize a people and a place as uniquely bigoted because of that narrative, or because of *the* narrative."

I found myself going over that quote and thinking about your ethical struggle with naming racism. Isn't the nature of systemic racism the fact that it is ubiquitous? Like, it is part of our geographies. It is a characteristic of its scene and apparatuses, written into the law and our social codes of conduct. In that sense, why is it a problem to name a place as racist or read race into experience? After all, aren't the practices of racism and the cultures of White supremacy diverse and disproportionate in their scope and scale of damage?

James: You're absolutely right, Alex. That's a really important question!

I think it's all about framing. Ultimately, I'm trying to think about the degree of my impact on public and local perceptions of Grand Saline, as well as the potential for people to be antiracist in that space. Therefore, I am very interested in the audience's reception of my work. In the context of this chapter and our book, overall, I know that the people who will read this are likely to be part of my professional discourse communities. On one hand, I hope this text is something that will be utilized by experienced researchers and graduate students alike. But on the other hand, I would also love for people from my hometown to potentially be an audience for my work and I am constantly thinking about how I need to situate them, given that Grand Saline is an object of critique because it *does* have a problem with racism. However, I don't want to give the impression that Grand Saline is somehow a uniquely racist place where nothing can change and that its residents are all these terrible human beings. Plus, when you say the words race or racism, a lot of people shut down. That's my ethical dilemma: how do I label someone or somewhere as racist?

Because it's true. . . . Grand Saline is a scene where racism is overt enough to directly observe it—and frequently—so it's easy to label the entire town as racist. How do I describe it that way while also finding ways for me to invite in the community to participate in the conversation? How can I be invitational while also telling those people that I'm inviting to a discussion that they have a problem? I don't have a great idea how to do that.

Alex: Well, racism maps on to multiple oppressive systems. If we understand racism as a structural problem, and we say that Grand Saline is a town that exemplifies the systemic nature of racism (e.g., casual use of racist terms in everyday conversation, lack of Black people in the town, etc.), how is the town being essentialized? The value of your work is that you give your audience(s) an opportunity to examine provocative, but typical, racial stories to decide whether, "Yes, we have a problem," or "No, we don't have a problem. That's just who we are." This seems like the invitation you offer. Should you feel that the ethical dilemma is on you or the people from the town who refuse to see or engage the issues of race and racism?

James: Hmmm . . . I'm not sure. Could you elaborate on what you mean?

Alex: For example, did people from Grand Saline respond to Moore's death as a problem? Did some people say, "Man, we need to really talk about what happened here, as a community," or was the reaction simply, "That man's crazy. We are just who we are."?

I'm curious because I'm from (Northeast) Texas, as well. Similar to your relationship to Grand Saline, I understand Texarkana as a "racist" town. My racial literacy about this place is informed by the fact that Northeast Texas is notorious for its history of lynchings (such as that of Henry Smith in Paris, Texas—1893, which was reportedly attended by thousands of people who traveled long distances to see him be murdered). And those lynchings solidified a racially segregated social structure that continues to permeate that location. Given this painful history, I'm wondering about the viability of invitation and forgiveness.

We must concede that we know for a fact that racism causes real violence and trauma, which can literally shape generation after generation of race relations. Unfortunately, we can't transform people's racial attitudes and behavior unless we better understand how racism plays out in towns like Grand Saline, whose size and homogeneity might make it easy to overlook.

James: Yeah, for sure. I understand that point. Basically, I never wanted to create a project that only further alienates me from my hometown, or alienates the town itself. I fear others not seeing my work as helpful. Therefore, I'm interested in using it to create a space to invite these residents in for a conversation. It's really important to me. Not because I am defending my community or giving them an easy way out of being accountable for its racism. I'm far more concerned with *actual* change. Can my small hometown of 3,000 people host real conversations about race, especially when communities with people of color are within 20 miles? What will it take to actually move forward and not hold on to resentment?

I'm wondering about White audiences who might read this book and/or watch my film and choose to focus solely on how I benefited from racism. Maybe they'll say,

"When you were in town you seemed to enjoy yourself."

"You were Homecoming King."

"You're just being a race-baiter."

So I'm always thinking about my skeptical audiences and ways that I can still reach out to them. Perhaps that's the rhetorical problem with essentialism. I don't necessarily think a scholarly (White) audience would think, "Hey, you're essentializing rural America, or Grand Saline, Texas." However, even within this audience—and certainly a more public and local White audience—my work could be challenging to someone who advocates that a "colorblind" perspective is the most appropriate way to solve negative race relations. I want them to read my work and be able to reflect critically enough to reach the point where they conclude, "Hey, maybe James isn't just attacking us and saying we're the worst, most evil people of all time. He's coming at this with a certain nuance. Maybe I need to re-examine my racial experiences here." I think crafting narratives using autoethnography might help researchers bring in that nuance. In my case, it enabled me to simultaneously take responsibility and draw attention to the pervasiveness of racism.

Alex: I definitely understand your concern about y/our audience's racial and economic and cultural backgrounds, James. However, I still don't know how I feel about the way that we ought to talk about White participation in antiracism.

Like you, I wholeheartedly believe that we need as many spaces as possible to talk about our racial literacies. But I still haven't quite figured out your particular vision for antiracist methodology. Why do you care so much about resistant audiences when their racism, literally, may inhibit them from listening to you? Clearly, if they are reading your work, they know that they will be engaging the racial issues. You are from Grand Saline, which gives you some credibility. I mean, are there any nice and neat ways to introduce such an ugly problem as racism? Doesn't silence negatively affect the quality of life of a place where folks don't want to do different cuz, "It's just the way it is." Unfortunately, that's how small towns end up in generational cycles of poverty, regardless of race. I hope we might address this issue towards the end of our dialogue.

Iris: James, your experience in Grand Saline reminds me of my own high school experience in Clovis, California, which is a very traditional institution in a predominantly White city. Therefore, your chapter really hits home with me.

Can you talk a little bit more about autoethnography as an antiracist method? I'd like to know more about how being an embodied narrator affects how we imagine building and creating representations of the epistemology of marginalized populations. Specifically, you introduce the concept of racial literacy. What does this literacy do for you? Why is it necessary for humanities research about race and racism?

James: Sure, that's such a great question. Growing up and playing sports, my nicknames were "wetback" and "beaner." Those were acceptable things to call someone and the White people knew that they could call me that and there would be no action from me. I wouldn't get upset or get angry, whereas I can imagine that some other Latinx people might not go for that. Or maybe they would if they were in the same position I was, I'm not sure. I often reflect about why these memories are so painful and why those emotions make this research so important to me. I don't think my experience was unique. I'm a biracial Latinx person—part White, part Brown—who doesn't speak Spanish. Surely, there have to be hundreds, if not thousands, of Brown people who've had similar experiences: were called similar nicknames and didn't resist racism because they were just trying to fit in, like me.

We knew that in some way, whiteness held cultural capital; it means being "normal" right? I definitely tried to be a "very white" Brown person so I wouldn't be singled out even more. If you could hang out with all the popular White people and sit at their all-White table (literally), and be friends with all these people, you could get better treatment. Maybe you weren't White, but you were better than the Latinx people who sat at the same table together and all fluently spoke Spanish with each other. It is shameful to remember that at one point, I thought that avoiding them and being surrounded by White people meant that I was "better than them." That situation is terrible and what does it mean that millions of non-White people have that experience every single day?

This autoethnography, and the process of acquiring racial literacy, might be viable ways that we can intervene. Even though it's about me, as is the essence of autoethnography, I hope other people read this, Iris, and realize that their experiences aren't so dissimilar. Maybe this recognition will spark conversation and enable us to change communities like Grand Saline. In fact, focused and sustained discussion about race in high school is really vital to social change. In this space, we need to think about how people talk to each other in locker rooms, cafeterias, classrooms, etc.

When I left high school, I had so much racial, racist baggage, especially in terms of anti-Black attitudes. I was taught to be afraid of Black people, that they were dangerous and their culture was deficient compared to nearly all other racial/ethnic groups. For example, rap music was bad, as were their physical features. I was surrounded by negative messaging about the way Black people dressed, did their hair, etc., etc. Their very existence was, in essence, inferior to White people. I had to spend over a decade of my life unlearning that. It's very difficult to consciously work through various processes of unlearning these biases that you're taught throughout your entire existence. I hope my chapter teaches the audience some ways for people to unlearn their racism and/or address their own traumatic experiences with racism.

Iris: Thanks, James! I appreciate how you describe that racial literacy is not necessarily about the individual researcher, but about *collective* experiences.

In my own experience, I learned about race by talking about race through my personal embodied relationship to brownness and blackness. I think your story stands out to me because of how you emphasize race and epistemology. This perspective is interesting because it's a non-traditional view. It challenges the notion of race as a predetermined biological phenomenon. There are specific moments in your chapter that stood out to me, like when you discuss distancing yourself from other Brown people. In academia, we're not necessarily immune from racism, as initiators and recipients—Let's be honest!

Could you talk a little bit more about what that past experience means to you now as a Latinx scholar in higher education where we are very underrepresented?

James: Sure! It's a great question. I actually do have an experience that I don't talk about in the chapter, but I share often.

I was at a concert in Dallas, which is about an hour and a half east or west of Grand Saline, during undergrad. I was leaving the concert, walking down the street by myself. Suddenly, I see two young Black men, around my age or slightly younger, walking down the same side of the street. My automatic reaction was, "I have to cross the street. I'm afraid, I have to cross the street."

I quickly crossed the street and kept going.

I can't shake that memory. On one hand, I was walking down a street in Dallas at night. Why shouldn't I have been afraid of anyone, regardless of color? Years later, I am more willing to admit that race played a role in my decision-making. It pains me that my initial thought was, "Well, you *have* to cross the street. These types of people might cause trouble." Even though I now clearly identify as someone committed to antiracism, I know that unlearning is a continuous process. If that same scenario happened right now, there would probably still be that moment when I might still think, "Hey, maybe I should cross the street. . . ." However, I would draw this conclusion after I ask myself, "Am I being racist? Don't do that." In these tense contexts, I have to be reflexive. I don't know if that process ever ends, but I feel like this is part of the hard work of antiracism. One of the most important things that you can do is fully engage conflicting thoughts and feelings and recognize that you're working through something serious. Antiracism is a goal, but I also define it as a process. This habit of mind, in some ways, reflects the kind of critical thinking any researcher should be doing. What kinds of (previously held) biases might show up in our own work? Do I cite mostly (White) male scholars as a general tendency in my citation practices? When I'm exposed to unfamiliar cultural issues, do I ask, "What is it that I'm missing? Am I integrating everything properly? What would enable me to more comprehensively think about these questions?"

Iris: These are good questions because they really showcase how antiracism as a methodology influences inquiry and epistemological of race. I like the way you describe the challenges of unlearning racism. It took you at least a decade to realize that racist behaviors are not fixed, or even normal (even though they can be normative). As you described, people of color at your high school experience seemed to react to racism in somewhat of an anaesthetized manner. At some point, there had to be at least one instance when you felt like you needed to critically distance yourself from other POC. Likewise, there must have been a moment when you realized that you too were racially coded. Tracing those experiences enabled you to discover something that you needed to know.

Alex: Can we switch back to the issue of how we communicate about race and theorize the concept of reconciliation?

How do discourses of civility reinforce White supremacy? Politeness can be weaponized to inhibit our ability to really address the structural nature of racism. Naming it as a problem may not be considered "nice," which can cause conflict for many people even if they feel morally obligated to antiracism.

A lot of folks are from towns where racist social practices influence how you define your identity. On one hand, it's how you've learned to connect with people there and wield enough power to be treated "like everyone else." On the other hand, that kind of behavior ends up still being very problematic when we consider leaving that place to pursue social mobility.

As you discuss inviting people to join you for conversations about race, I think there's an opportunity to be more critical about how normal it is to disrespect and objectify people in the US. We make fun of people for being fat, gay, disabled, feminine, etc. Bullying is a central feature of American society. From an early age, we learn to compete and connect that way. Perhaps identifying how we participate in such social dynamics, in general, might lower people's barriers a bit when having conversations about race.

James: I wrote a blog post on Grand Saline about four years ago that relates to a topic you brought up earlier. It's entitled "The Historical Truth of Lynching and Racism in Grand Saline." I've had well over 30,000 hits on that blog. It comes up anytime someone searches about "Grand Saline" and racism. When I was making *Man on Fire*, a person actually said flippantly, "Well, you know that everyone in our town is reading your Facebook right now." I was like, "Good! They're seeing my work!" I'm glad people are watching, reading, and listening to me to open up the potential for having these complex conversations. Discussion is progress, but I'm trying to figure out additional ways to organize people (especially from Grand Saline) to take antiracist action.

Alex: That's really cool! Excellent, James. Thank you! So, you have anything else to add before we conclude our dialogue?

James: No, I think we addressed mostly everything. I'm going to continue to probe the idea (and practice) of reconciliation. I invite the audience to build on this work as we shift from merely acknowledging racism exists to trying to change it.

CHAPTER 4.

TASER TROUBLE: RACE, VISUALITY, AND THE MEDIATION OF POLICE BRUTALITY IN PUBLIC DISCOURSE

Christopher Carter

University of Cincinnati

Key Terms and Concepts: Countervisuality, Parrhesia, Surveillance, Body Cameras

As I reflect on James Sanchez's rare, risky work of exposing personal and collective forms of repression, and as I recognize the urgency of Iris Ruiz's attempt to reframe disciplinary histories, I recognize my susceptibility to the critiques they level. Sanchez focuses on the history of Grand Saline, Texas, but the resulting chapter conjures more general scenes in U.S. history. For me, it summons memories of my teenage years in Shepherdsville, Kentucky while also mingling with stories that students told during my time at the University of Oklahoma (OU). Even more specifically, Sanchez's recounting of Clark's Ferry folklore calls to mind Shepherdsville's River Bottom, though such similarities point less to our shared idiosyncrasies than to the consistencies of life in the South. In pleading for truth about these consistencies, he delivers insights that often go missing in studies of ideological reproduction, and he reveals with uncommon precision how racism corrupts our early education, asserting its hold before we know how to fight back.

Like the writers Ruiz depicts as repressing those difficult histories, I have generally kept my positionality in the background, the unfortunate effect of which was to confuse whiteness with disembodied mind. There can be no escape from the body, and no refuge from the violence it witnesses. That violence has followed me across a considerable swath of the country, from my youth in Louisville and Shepherdsville to my early career in Norman, and now to my present position at the University of Cincinnati. I have heard racism express itself in offhand ways and I have felt its more deliberate heat. But to bring Sanchez's and Ruiz's experiences into conversation with my own, I reflect here on racism's visualization, its mediation through hand-held devices and body cameras. The method I describe is antiracist in its effort to disentangle the creative, profoundly rhetorical act of looking from the hegemony of whiteness. This chapter offers more than an antiracist way of interpreting images, however; it makes a plea for critical recording and archiving, urging scholars, activists, and citizens to capture and itemize the ways racism shapes the standard procedures of law enforcement and juridical practice. It describes a cultural and intellectual practice that is fully multimodal, insisting on the enmeshment of visual politics with sound and movement, narrative and physical-theatrical performance. And the method arises from my horror at consistencies that often go unremarked, trends that demand an unflinching gaze at the same time that we acknowledge the dangers of objectification and spectacle.

Shortly after I left Norman for Cincinnati, news broke of OU's Sigma Alpha Epsilon (SAE) fraternity members singing racist chants on a charter bus, a clip of which appeared online with the comment "Racism is alive at the University of Oklahoma." Later reporting revealed that the singers learned the chant, with all its nauseating epithets and references to lynching, on a cruise ship to a fraternity leadership conference. Upon hearing the news, I realized I had passed that organization's house most every day for ten years, likely teaching writing to its members, without ever recognizing its history. Soon afterward, I spoke about the story with Alex Lockett, my former M.A. student and advisee at Oklahoma. During our conversation, I mentioned my frustration with the fact that SAE's bigotry could be so well hidden behind the prominent visibility of their conspicuous real estate on 730 College Avenue. She replied that the bigotry was more apparent to some people than others. Fraternity members were said to terrorize Black students who passed the house, she recalled, and she had personally encountered it—they accosted her with racial slurs several times during her years at OU—enough times for her to take a longer route to school just to avoid "frat row," located on the same block as her apartment. My lack of awareness was no accident but rather an effect of body privilege, one of the ordinary advantages of being White.

Those advantages provide a shield against violence, to be sure, but they also grant specific subjects the benefit of the doubt when violence occurs. Such biases are nothing new, but they announced themselves to me with novel force once I moved to Cincinnati. University of Cincinnati (UC) campus officer Ray Tensing killed motorist Samuel DuBose during a traffic stop in July 2015, claiming that DuBose dragged him with his car, and might have killed him had the officer not fired in self-defense. Body camera evidence contradicted the story, showing the vehicle move little if at all before Tensing delivered the head shot (Ferrell). Still, the video was not enough to convince a jury of the White officer's wrongdoing, as two different trials ended in deadlock. Not only did Tensing escape prison, he received a wrongful termination settlement of approximately $350,000 from the university (Murphy and Curnutte).

Although I attempt, in what follows, to establish the counterhegemonic potential of video, the Tensing trials demonstrate the strength of dominant cultural frames. White desire inhabits those frames in ways that escape notice, or worse yet, ways that viewers actively refuse to accept. Ruiz's "Curandera Methodology" suggests that people who fail to see the operation of whiteness are the same subjects who tend to benefit from it. At times, that benefit has immediate, life-and-death consequences; at others, it limits the contributions of certain cultures to knowledge making and thus threatens the durability of their histories. Ruiz does the double duty of relaying one such history and exposing the processes that aim to suppress her voice; she at once calls out and thwarts the would-be architects of disciplinary barriers. The work of refusing those walls will not be easy. It has not been easy so far.

NOTHING TO SEE HERE

From Geneva Smitherman's meditations on linguistic hegemony to Adam Banks' evocation of politically engaged, multimodal poetics, writing instructors have long debated ways to research and teach the racial politics of public discourse. Wendy Hesford and Robert Hariman and John Louis Lucaites contend that such discourse occurs not just through the spoken and written word but also through visual expression, whether photography, web imagery, television, or feature film. I endeavor to expand current methods of investigating civic dialogue by concentrating on the visual mediation of arrests in South Carolina and Oklahoma, laying emphasis on rhetorics of citizen videography and police camera footage. In an era that finds officers "mistaking" pistols for Tasers and regularly using deadly force against unarmed African American subjects, the question of how to study impromptu documentary appears an urgent methodological concern.

Nicholas Mirzoeff takes up similar concerns in *The Right to Look,* developing a theory of "visuality" that designates not merely the condition of visibility but the historical habits that distinguish publicly seeable events from the unrepresentable and the deliberately hidden. His emphasis on habitual behavior, and on the forms of socialization that distinguish focus from backdrop, center from periphery, locates the operation of hegemony not solely in verbal discourse or civic negotiations but the selective activity of the human senses.

Where visibility designates both the potential for and experience of optical perception, visuality signals the articulation of power relations that focus and limit those perceptions. It suggests that where sight figures into the range of multimodal resources involved in a communicative act, that act unfolds against a backdrop of norms regulating the seer and the seen. Visuality "is an old word for an old project," Mirzoeff explains. "It is not a trendy theory word meaning the totality of all visual images and devices, but is in fact an early nineteenth-century term meaning the visualization of history" (*Right* 2). It "must be imaginary, rather than perceptual, because what is being visualized is too substantial for any one person to see and is created from information, images, and ideas." It requires "permanent renewal in order to win consent as the 'normal,' or everyday, because it is always already contested" (2). Those contested norms come to us permeated with histories of racism and policing, among which Mirzoeff features plantation economies (50–55), political prisons (288, 296), colonialism and fascism (233), and high-tech practices of counter-insurgency (293). We may hear centuries-old modes of subjection, he explains, in officers' admonition to "move on, there's nothing to see here." "Only there is," Mirzoeff remarks, "and we know it and so do they" (1). The return of the gaze, before any recording of specific events, already instantiates a rhetoric of resistance.

But too strict a methodological focus on resistance may inadvertently work to shore up the perspective of the overseer, the position to which others must respond. While such privileging neglects wide varieties of knowledge production, Vorris Nunley articulates its specific disregard for African American epistemologies. In *Keepin' It Hushed: The Barbershop and African American Hush Harbor Rhetoric*, Nunley challenges ideas of public discourse that are "too concerned with and dependent upon Black life and culture as resistance and opposition," and he accentuates instead the "productive, epistemic, and affirmative qualities" of rhetoric while validating the "terministic screens of African American life" (34). Those screens, while inflected by the histories of visuality Mirzoeff details, frame ways of knowing that nourish the collectivity from which they derive. Nunley's rhetoric of affirmation may at first appear unsuited to Mirzoeff's demand for "the right to look," as Mirzoeff chronicles deliberate resistance to the totalizing aspirations of visuality. It may be productive, however, in a time of heightened media attention to the politics of policing, to consider Mirzoeff's and Nunley's positions as complementary rather than opposed. Claiming the right to look may counter the regime of visuality, but it also produces and extends ways of knowing while sustaining the lives and cultures of those doing the looking.

Such looking addresses visual rhetoric not merely as a mode of representation but as a process of epistemic mediation. Within that process, images convey information, condition subjectivity, participate in public discourse, and establish filters through which we make judgment.[1] Images thereby cohere with Nunley's

---

1   In *No Caption Needed* and *The Public Image*, Robert Hariman and John Louis Lucaites explain how pictures help create contending publics through the event of address, rather than merely appealing to an undifferentiated mass of preexisting actors. Those images mediate issues

definition of rhetoric, which calls up the ideas of James Berlin by linking the term to "knowledge generation" and the circulation of ideology while resisting its historical conflation with "eloquence and deceptive speech" (6–7). Rhetoric may manifest as speech, image, or a range of modes that include the sonic, the haptic, and the kinetic, yet it denotes not just the consequences of those modes-in-action but the social, cognitive, and material fabric that enables communication. Positing a dynamic relationship between that fabric and public discourse, Nunley associates rhetoric with broadly distributed forms of pedagogy that proceed through "film, music, commercials, books, churches, newscasts, the Internet, and cable," suggesting that each platform works with and sometimes against technologies of neoliberalism to cultivate "the very ground of human subjectivity" (158). He resists the trend wherein neoliberalism reduces the subject to "*homo economicus*," concentrating his analysis on "forms of intelligibility that alter the terrain of meaning necessary for a messy, but vibrant, democracy" (13, 158). Adam Banks expresses similar interest in democratic interchange in *Digital Griots*, tracking how remix culture in musical, visual, academic, and popular forms works to generate knowledge and remediate longstanding habits of perception. As African-American rhetors perform acts of epistemic mediation, he conceives of them as "archivists" and "real-life documentarians" (79) engaged in the historical and political work of sustaining the collective self.

Insofar as the archive includes not just words but moving pictures and other images, we do well to investigate how images mediate perception and afford distinctive ways of framing experience. Such investigation might attend to the viral circulation of documentary footage that exposes links between violent arrests, racist ideology, and visuality. Citizen video and police body cameras clarify those links in ways that contest unidirectional models of surveillance. To track the politics of what Mirzoeff calls countervisuality, and the insights that flow from videography, I concentrate on two arrests occurring two days apart, each of whose disastrous circumstances involve a Taser gun.

In the first of the arrests, Tulsa deputy Robert Bates purportedly confuses his Taser with a revolver, resulting in the death of Eric Harris. In the second, Charleston officer Michael Slager shoots Walter Scott with a pistol from behind, claiming later that a struggle over his stun gun precipitated the slaying. Although the officers provide oral defenses of their actions, viral video reveals numerous details that either differ from or are not acknowledged by the official narrative. I dwell here on three of those areas: 1) neither Harris nor Scott poses an immediate threat to the officers; 2) police begin to construct a rationale for the gunfire

---

of broad concern, whereupon varied audiences distinguish themselves as publics by interpreting the details, arguing over them, drafting them into ongoing political controversies, and even altering their details in critical or comical ways to advance specific principles and epistemologies.

almost immediately after it occurs; and 3) attending officers continue to mistreat the subjects as they are dying or after they are dead, extending the practice of racist brutality well past the act of shooting.

By concentrating on those three tendencies, this chapter specifies patterns worth watching as public discourse about racism and policing plays out in the coming years. That method of seeing enacts the forms of resistant affect Mirzoeff associates with the right to look, but it also accentuates the knowledge-making practices of African American citizen videographers, itemizing trends that their communities have long understood. The method defines looking as a creative, life-affirming act, even in the most lethal of circumstances. While my argument attunes itself mainly to brutality cases in Oklahoma and South Carolina, it suggests that rhetorical topoi within the associated videos have nationwide significance; and although the argument highlights the visual mode of communication, visuality intersects with numerous other expressive channels while hinting at far-reaching, if at times deeply submerged, currents of U.S. political discourse.

VIOLENT ANTICIPATION

The videos support forms of knowledge construction that defy normative visuality insofar as such visuality codes African American suspects as posing an imminent danger to other civilians or police. The dissonance is especially prominent in the Harris case, for by the time Bates catches up to him, Harris lies mostly immobilized as officers hold him down. A voice calls "Taser!" as Bates arrives on the scene, pepper spray in hand, a stun gun and revolver at his sides. He then grabs the revolver instead of the Taser and shoots Harris in the back near his left shoulder. As the unarmed Harris sprawls facedown beneath the weight of the arresting officers, the bullet travels through his internal organs and stops near his right armpit (Schuppe). A deputy's camera-equipped sunglasses capture the chase, the sound of the gunfire, and Bates blurting out, "I shot him! I'm sorry!" Harris begins to convulse, gasping, "Oh, my God. I'm losing my breath." Another officer accuses Harris of precipitating the shots by running away, dismissing his cries of pain with "Fuck your breath" (Ortiz). The officers pin Harris down throughout the ordeal, one placing a knee atop the dying man's head as he lies face down on the concrete.[2]

---

2   The scene holds uncanny similarities to the killing of Oscar Grant III in 2009. Camera phone footage of the Grant arrest formed the basis of Ryan Coogler's *Fruitvale Station*, which dramatizes the day leading up to the event while incorporating the documentary video into the narrative. As with Harris, multiple officers hold Grant down as Johannes Mehserle draws his weapon. Like Bates, Mehserle grabs his gun instead of his Taser, and later frames the death as an accident.

Two days later, Officer Michael Slager kills Walter Scott in another arrest involving the purported mishandling of a Taser. As in the Harris case, the officer shoots the suspect from behind. But rather than firing one fatal shot with the wrong weapon, Slager knowingly discharges his handgun eight times, hitting Scott with five bullets (Lerner). No more a threat than the prone Harris, Scott shows no sign of being armed, and he attempts to escape the shooter rather than advancing toward him. The Taser trouble arises not during the killing itself but from the act that follows, as Slager drops his stun gun by Scott and accuses him of stealing it. Feidin Santana's cellphone video offers little to corroborate Slager's story but fully captures the shooting—an act of such cruelty that Slager's first lawyer renounces the case once he sees the footage (Graham).

Later lawyers, however, and a defensive sector of the U. S. populace would interpret the incident as yet another example of criminals bringing violence on themselves. That self-inflicted harm comes not just from running, it seems, but from the basic fault of being an African American man. Byron B. Craig and Stephen E. Rahko consider the problem at length in "Visual Profiling as Biopolitics: Or, Notes on Policing in Post-Racial #AmeriKKKa," focusing especially on Darren Wilson's killing of Michael Brown in 2014 Ferguson, Missouri. Craig and Rahko dwell on Wilson's description of the confrontation, in which the officer regards himself as "like a five-year-old holding onto Hulk Hogan. . . . That's just how big he felt and how small I felt from grasping his arm" (291). Brown's size became even more terrifying when Wilson noticed his "most intense aggressive face. The only way I can describe it, it looks like a demon, that's how angry he looked" (291). For Craig and Rahko, that depiction recalls bell hooks' analysis of "neocolonial white supremacist patriarchy," wherein "the black male body continues to be perceived as the embodiment of bestial and violent hypermasculine assertion."[3] In the cases of Harris and Scott, the threat of hypermasculine physicality became so apparent that Bates and Slager did not need to see their faces when firing. The policemen apparently sensed the unarmed suspects' capacity for violence despite them facing away, and, in one case, being held down, as the deadly exchanges transpired.

Those assumptions connote ways of seeing that are socially and historically conditioned, sometimes in overtly bigoted fashion, but often through the more subtle and pervasive operation of institutions like the family, school, news and social media, and popular entertainments. "No one approaches images with an innocent eye," Sue Hum remarks in "'Between the Eyes': The Racialized Gaze as Design" (193). The routine character of the approach to visual objects makes

---

3   Craig and Rahko include hooks' language in "Visual Profiling as Biopolitics" (289). Her original wording appears in *Art On My Mind* (202).

the process feel innocent while its very banality helps reproduce ideology at both optical and affective levels. When Hum delineates a racialized gaze, she addresses not only ocular processing but an array of normalized habits grounded in dominant cultural epistemologies, belief systems, and orthodoxies of desire. Frameworks of knowledge, faith, and longing, she implies, converge in ways that direct and limit what subjects can see. Mirzoeff's idea of visuality invokes the smooth functioning of that social machine. To describe how the machine works, and to isolate the forms of racialization it undertakes, means attempting to see the hegemonic lens itself rather than peer through it. This meta-optics enacts one version of Mirzoeff's countervisuality, his theorization of an antiracist form of looking that confounds sensory habit. *The Right to Look* suggests that even if there exists no neutral gaze, we can look with eyes schooled in the history of race relations, and with senses keyed to the decentralization of power as well as the pursuit of just, intercultural dwelling.

Such a reflexive sensibility involves alertness to the dehumanizing topos that influenced Wilson's view of Brown as well as Bates' and Slager's attitudes toward their victims. Like Hum, Alexander G. Weheliye associates that topos with a racist epistemology that bars "non-white subjects from the category of the human" (3–4). That epistemology codes Brown as a hulk and a demon while enframing Harris and Scott as brutish, unreasoning threats in need of extreme restraint. This topos is so insidious that it even informs attitudes toward African American children, yielding what Alex S. Vitale terms the "superpredator myth" (51) while abetting the murders of Trayvon Martin and Tamir Rice. Those predispositions guide the actions of self-styled community servants like Bates and George Zimmerman—the so-called neighborhood watchman who killed Martin—while coursing powerfully through the law enforcement cultures those men imitate.[4] In *The End of Policing*, Vitale documents how officer training instills aggressively preemptive attitudes in its subjects, repeatedly exposing them to "scenarios in which seemingly innocuous interactions with the public, such as traffic stops, turn deadly" (9).

Even police check-ins at children's pool parties can end in disaster, as when White officer Eric Casebolt tackled Dajerria Becton, a 14-year-old African American girl, "repeatedly slamm[ing] her face on the ground, forcefully straddl[ing] her while thrusting his knees into her back and neck" (Ansari). Becton's lawyer, Kim T. Cole, argues, as I do in relation to Harris and Scott, that

---

4   The topos of blackness as a prodigious threat has attained what Fleetwood describes as "hypervisibility." In Black cultural studies, that term signals "the overrepresentation of certain images of [B]lacks and the visual currency of these images in public culture" (16). The poignant irony is that despite the overexposure of these myths, neither Wilson nor the jurors in the Brown case recognize how such clichéd formulas shape their decision-making, and how they reproduce the myths in legal contexts.

her client "was not a threat to the officer at any point throughout that event" (Ansari). No one at the party accused her of a crime, nor did local authorities charge her with one. Even as the city of McKinney, Texas rejects the charge that it improperly trains its police force, Casebolt's chief, Greg Conley, describes the event as "indefensible" while depicting his trooper as "out of control" (Fantz et al.). Brandon Brooks, the 15-year-old boy who captured the attack on video, underscores its racist dimensions: "I was one of the only White people in the area when [the arrest] was happening. ... You can see in part of the video where [an officer] tells people to sit down and kind of skips over me and tells my African-American friends to go sit down" (Bellware). He also notes that the event verged on something much worse: "As soon as he pulled out his gun, I thought he was gonna shoot that kid. That was very scary" (Bellware). Even a bikini-clad 14-year-old, it seems, stumbles close enough to the superpredator mythos that a cop quickly adopts his battle posture.

The absurdity of that situation indicates how deeply the ideology of anticipatory aggression penetrates the collective consciousness of law enforcement. As we might anticipate, teaching people to expect life-or-death escalation often ends up triggering the very violence it aims to suppress.[5] Worse yet, such pedagogy persistently sparks antagonism in the context of White-on-Black policing, establishing a cycle whereby the racialized interpellation of officers and citizens yields mutual suspicion and the realization of both groups' fears. That pattern besieges African American people from across socioeconomic categories, as even Sterling Brown of the NBA's Milwaukee Bucks found himself tased over a parking dispute in January 2018 (Smith and Hoffman).

The self-fulfilling projection of fierce and even lethal conflict produces a slippage between law enforcement and treating citizens as enemy combatants. Ideals of public service and peacekeeping give way to vigilant surveillance and heavily armed regulation of so-called problem areas. Radley Balko captures the dynamic in *Rise of the Warrior Cop: The Militarization of America's Police Forces*, tracking the soldier ethos among officers to the nation-state's putative wars on drugs and poverty and its emphasis on security in the post–9/11 world. Drawing on Michel Foucault's critique of state security rhetorics, Craig and Rahko draw a direct line between police militancy and high-intensity patrolling:

> The rising body count of unarmed Black and Brown citizens
> killed by police, under the auspices that they were deemed

---

5   The often fatal character of this violence reflects a peculiarly American problem, which comes in part from the mass circulation of firearms and the fantasy of guns as a means of maintaining social order. Vitale notes that "since 1900, the police in Great Britain have killed a total of fifty people. In March 2016 alone, U.S. police killed one hundred people" (25).

threatening and on the verge of aggressive violence, is indicative of the systematic permeation of pre-emptive postures in
policing on the racialized body. (289)

Broken-windows policing, stop-and-frisk tactics, military-grade weaponry,
trucks and aircraft, and the donning of riot gear all signal the overlap of civic
and battlefield mentalities.[6] Worse yet, the violence at times transpires in ways
that fit neither police nor military profiles. In May 2018, for example, a Miami
resident captured an officer handcuffing David Vladim Suazo as he lay prone in
the grass. A second officer, Miguel Figueroa, takes a running start at Suazo and
kicks him in the face. The videographer observes that the officer treated Suazo's
head "like a football" (Jacobo), while reporters Charles Rabin and David Ovalle
note that Figueroa kicked "so hard he almost fell over." Although the trooper
received suspension for a "clear violation of protocol," the frequency of such
violations casts doubt on the efficacy of law enforcement training while raising
concern about the abuses that take place off-camera.[7] Figueroa's action suggests
a subject schooled in the spectacle of the ring or the cinematic bar brawl rather
than in public safety. That visible malice, when combined with the suspicion
of Black and Brown bodies as formidable adversaries, generates a toxic national
affect along with overcrowded prisons and a steady toll of needless deaths.

Citizen videography helps clarify the needlessness, documenting the militaristic tactics that precipitate rather than diminish conflict. What Craig and
Rahko call visual profiling coheres with a larger history of U. S. visuality by at
once performing and reproducing the racist gaze as normative behavior. The
camerawork of quick-thinking witnesses, and occasionally the lively functioning
of officer bodycams, can establish friction within that process of normalization,
raising questions about which mindsets fuel the violence and which institutions promote those modes of seeing. The camera thus serves as a technology for
researching what Nicole R. Fleetwood calls the "rendering" of African American
bodies. She attends to multiple meanings of "render," including "to deliver a
verdict" and to produce an "image through computer software," while stressing
its particular inflection as "to make or become somebody" (7). *Troubling Vision:*

---

6   For reflections on "broken windows" policing, see Rai. She recounts the view that broken
windows, when left unrepaired, suggest that "this is a place where we tolerate crime…where we
have given up, where no one cares, where bad things happen, where we are scared, where you,
too, should be afraid" (154). The theory risks stoking public fears so as to authorize heightened
police presence in certain areas. That presence may trigger the conflict it supposedly guards
against. Herbert and Brown warn that "broken windows" policing may disguise its racist motivations with environmental ones (771).

7   Less than three weeks later, two troopers in Mississippi lost their jobs for repeatedly kicking
a suspect in the face (Associated Press, "Man").

Performance, Visuality, and Blackness gives extensive attention to how technologies of visual production contribute to such making and becoming. The most incisive uses of those technologies to show how law enforcement frames blackness, and to simultaneously render a contrary vision, have typically not come from self-identifying scholars. But antiracist students of public rhetoric might nevertheless attend to what those citizen-cinematographers produce, and how it documents state-sponsored warfare on the populace.

As with most widely disseminated media, the images may be susceptible to appropriation by authoritarian interests; worse yet, their rampant circulation may further naturalize (by rendering too familiar) the warrior cop's actions. Armond R. Towns details that possibility in "That Camera Won't Save You! The Spectacular Consumption of Police Violence," observing how readily the practice of critical videography yields "the commodification of black death" while proving lucrative for White advertisers on Facebook and Twitter. Aided by trends in television and cinema, Internet memes "normalize something that should be abnormal: watching people die."[8] The determined spread of critical interpretations thus becomes a political necessity, as does the meta-optical examination of what, how, and why we see. Whether reflexive analysis can alter the habits of self-satisfied, commercially driven viewers remains uncertain, and given the Trump administration's reactionary attitudes toward Civil Rights gains, the outlook appears dim. But insofar as video evidence led to the convictions of Bates and Slager, it holds a measure of material and juridical value for the antiracist movement against police brutality.[9] Moreover, it helps us enumerate the otherwise inconspicuous forms such brutality takes.

THE ARTFULNESS OF SELF-DEFENSE

In the Scott and Harris footage, the moving image instantiates visual rhetoric working to elude, however temporarily, the hold of visuality. In the Harris case, the sunglasses camera aligns with the perspective of police authority but ironically documents the abuse of that authority. The viewpoint and point of audition aim to conflate themselves with just and necessary action, but what unfolds in

---

8   In an incisive turn, Towns relates such commodification to Amy Louise Wood's scholarship on lynching souvenirs.

9   Critics might rightly question whether a 20-year prison sentence for Slager (Osunsami and Shapiro) and a four-year sentence for Bates (Associated Press, "Ex-Deputy") constitute just decisions given that their victims are both dead. To complicate matters further, Bates served less than half his sentence before being released. There may even exist legitimate questions as to whether the prison system serves in any appreciable way to mitigate structural racism, or mainly works to keep it in place. Still, it is unlikely that either man would have undergone trial at all if not for the video evidence.

the sensory field frustrates that smooth fusion. Soon after Bates apologizes, an attending policeman restores the order of authority by shifting the blame from Bates to Harris, screaming "You ran!" and disparaging Harris's cries of pain. The process of faulting Harris suffuses the video and continues after it ends, as police later construe his running-gait as "consistent with trying to maintain control of a gun" (McGlaughlin and Brumfield). In another explanation that evokes the killing of Oscar Grant at Fruitvale Station in 2009, a policeman observes that Harris kept his left arm under his body throughout the arrest, producing suspicion of a hidden weapon. For those already ill-disposed toward Harris, the subsequent findings of methamphetamine in his system only strengthen their convictions.

When not reviling the dead, police defenders cite the stress of the situation as a reason for Bates' action, claiming that he suffered a form of "inattentional blindness" that caused him to confuse one object with a more familiar one. Sgt. Jim Clark compares the phenomenon to a long-time driver of a manual-transmission vehicle reaching for the stick shift when driving an automatic (McGlaughlin and Brumfield). The clarity of Clark's example undermines his rhetorical purpose, however, by casting Bates as someone whose muscle memory under stress compels him to draw his sidearm, or attempt to incapacitate someone who has already been subdued. His conflation of the gun and Taser, whether instinctive or not, accentuates the ways both weapons work to dominate the unruly body—not just to punish the subject for supposedly hiding his hand, but to exert total mastery over a perceived social and historical threat. As we have seen, that perception is so persuasive that the threat appears urgent even when the subject's back is turned.

Subsequent narratives work to preserve the culture of visuality in response to disruptive acts of looking. While Feidin Santana makes his way to work at a North Charleston barbershop, he passes the confrontation between Slager and Scott and immediately raises his camera phone as an assertion of the right to look (Almasy). At once claiming and enacting that right, he documents the slippage from racist oversight to outright murder, and subsequently records an attempted cover-up. Neither the shooting nor the subterfuge constitutes a break with historical routine, but their circulation on digital video contributes to the ongoing process of epistemic mediation, especially among those communities who are most threatened by the forms of bodily and narrative violence Santana's clip displays. That form of epistemic mediation hinders Slager's effort to sustain the ethos of the overseer, who either wants us to observe him without engaging in the critical act of looking, or who attempts, as in Mirzoeff's accounts of state-sponsored torture, to operate completely out of view (249). When the political practice of looking destabilizes that ethos, it triggers authoritarian efforts to reestablish longstanding power relations through narrative intervention: Slager insists that Scott tried to take his Taser and even posed a threat to the officer's life; Slager's eventual attorney emphasizes the drugs found in Scott's system during autopsy and argues that an off-screen struggle preceded the gunshots (Melvin; Reuters). When confronted with the image of Slager planting the Taser, the lawyer blames the act's sinister appearance on suspicion aroused by other recent allegations of police brutality and reminds us that the officer quickly re-holstered the weapon (Melvin). In combination with Santana's footage, such narratives mediate public knowledge of the violence that both inhabits and follows encounters between White officers and African American citizens.

The attempt to locate exonerating evidence in the video footage indicates the malleability of audiovisual rhetoric. Impromptu documentary does not displace or obviate politics, but rather gives a kairotic boost to interpretive exchange. The video serves at once as a catalyst for political discourse and the evidence on which discourse proceeds. Such an appraisal of videography echoes Hariman and Lucaites' considerations of iconic or otherwise popular photography, which they see as participating in the formation of collective identity. Mass circulation permits the images to contribute to the production of interested publics, with the idea of "interest" connoting both sustained attention and value-laden conviction. Insofar as photography invites us to negotiate our interests, Hariman and Lucaites regard it as a democratic medium (*Public* 4). The meaning of the medium, they contend, is "radically plural" (48). Such are the risks as well as the advantages of public rhetoric, which thrusts us into wrangling with strangers.[10] The same goes for videography. The damning image of an execution-style slaying might appear, from a differently interested perspective, to corroborate Scott's history as a drug-abuser and a fugitive. To recall Nunley's phrasing, such readings demonstrate the unruliness of democracy, with all its unpredictability and tendency toward irresolution.

But even with the prospects of recontextualization, appropriation, and outright misinterpretation, citizen videography generally does not constitute good news for authoritarian police officers. If it posed no threat, those officers would not so often attempt to obscure the view or intimidate people holding camera phones, nor would legislators try so persistently to criminalize the recording process.[11] Susan Buck-Morss may well be right in her contention that "meaning

---

10   Hariman and Lucaites share Michael Warner's view of public discourse as grounded in stranger relationality, suggesting that such discourse invokes agents mostly unknown to each other, and that there can be no public without the attendant uncertainty.

11   See American Civil Liberties Union; Arsenault; Campbell; Kelly; Meyer; Woolf. The efforts to block videorecordings and confiscate cameras suggest that the stakes of the conflict between visuality and the right to look include "the form of the real, the realistic, and realism in all its senses" (Mirzoeff, *The Right* 8). The effort to channel the flow of circulation, and to establish the realm of legitimate interpretation, doubles as an attempt to regulate truth. In the Trump era, that often involves White authorities describing any emergence of unflattering information as fake news.

will not stick to the image" (228–29); viewer perspective and the material situatedness of reception delegitimize assertions of pictures' monolithic or unchanging significance. But Buck-Morss is also right that meaning depends on the "deployment" of images rather than their inherent qualities. And with any given text, some deployments are more plausible than others. It takes no acrobatic imagination, no convoluted logic or artfulness, to see the inhumanity in Santana's video recording. Explaining the officer's behavior away, however, takes work.

Whether Slager's lawyer or one of the millions who identify with the strongman ethos that characterizes the Trump White House, people are clearly eager to perform that work. When the U.S. President can posit equivalence between the rhetorical tactics of white supremacists and those of Black Lives Matter activists, the capacity for contortionist interpretation of public images appears nearly limitless.[12] Those aggressive misinterpretations coexist with what Doreen St. Félix identifies as a troubling trend in national media, in which coverage of police killings of Black citizens "has dwindled in the Trump era compared to just a few years ago, even as the rate of these shootings remains as depressingly regular."[13] Border communities also report intensified violence against Brown people whose citizenship may be in question, though little of it draws nationwide attention (Haag). It thus becomes necessary for antiracist activists to insist on details that cynical interpreters willfully ignore. When it comes to violent arrests, this chapter has so far emphasized the lack of threat posed by the suspects, and officers' strained attempts to explain their own actions even as they occur. Now, I turn to how police abuse and disrespect Black people once they are unconscious or already dead. Underscoring those details deploys the video for urgent political ends, instantiating what Ariella Azoulay depicts as a civic mode of seeing (95–97). Proceeding in materialist fashion, both Buck-Morss and Azoulay imply that images intervene in public debate in ways that human agents cannot anticipate or control. The contingent eventfulness of those images requires a similar liveliness on the part of viewers who

---

12   At a "Unite the Right" Rally in Charlottesville on April 12, 2017, white supremacist and alt-right activists gathered to protest the removal of a statue of Robert E. Lee from a plot in Emancipation Park. When counter-protesters gathered, James Alex Fields, Jr. plowed into them, killing 32-year-old Heather Heyer. When Trump addressed the violence, he deflected questions about the alt-right by excoriating the "alt-left," and then attempted to reassure listeners that "You also had some very fine people on both sides" (Gray). His effort to distribute blame among the protesters and counter-protesters, and his insinuation that "Unite the Right" demonstrators included good, misunderstood people, feeds interpretation of the Trump White House as a bigoted operation. On the very day he announced his presidential campaign, he lashed out against Latinx immigrants as "bringing drugs. They're bringing crime. They're rapists." As if briefly aware of the sweeping, overtly racist tenor of his comments, he followed with "Some, I assume, are good people" (Reilly).

13   St. Félix draws here on the work of Wesley Lowery.

are attentive to the interwoven histories of race and social power. In *The Public Image*, Hariman and Lucaites frame the exigency in this way:

> What is needed are citizens who are willing to take responsibility for what they see. Spectators who are willing to be changed by seeing, to see themselves as part of the same community as the victims and as part of the same community as the perpetrators. (226)

Such seeing means not allowing the perpetrators to define the community, and refusing to stand by while the voices of its members are silenced forever.

That refusal constitutes an antiracist methodological precept. It means keeping a lookout for efforts to make police violence appear warranted and unrelated to race, when that violence is itself a phenomenon that works to reproduce racial categories. It also means questioning the idea of the stressful situation in which officers make deadly decisions based on general, work-related anxiety rather than fears grounded in racial animus. Such explanations extract violent arrests from long-established trends in U.S. history, positioning the officer as a victim of psychic turmoil instead of a subject hailed by the ideology of whiteness.[14] To return to Hariman and Lucaites's phrasing, taking responsibility for what we see means working with images to protect certain obvious narratives from delegitimation. Such an approach does not construe the human agent as the heroic savior of the dumb image, but insists instead on the vital rhetorical work the image already does. It involves active participation in a techno-human assemblage that preserves material evidence of systemic racism against mystification and deceit.

STANDARD SAFETY PROCEDURE

The violence of systemic racism includes not just the self-protective invention of misleading narratives, but the mistreatment of people who have suffered potentially fatal wounds. Given the Scott and Harris cases, we should extend the rhetoric of police brutality to include forms of neglect as well as direct attacks. Santana's video shows a lengthy period of time elapsing before anyone attends to Scott, and it documents Slager taking the victim's pulse more than two minutes after he fired the shots (Laughland et al.). Police Chief Eddie Driggers claims that Clarence Halbersham

---

14   Mirzoeff locates an influential condensation of that ideology in Thomas Carlyle's *The French Revolution*, which exemplifies the epistemology's trans-Atlantic range. "For Carlyle," Mirzoeff explains, "to be Black was always to be on the side of Anarchy and disorder, beyond the possibility of Reality and impossibly remote from heroism" (13). Reading Carlyle as a philosopher of visuality, he argues that the anterior right to look coevolves with the history of "blackness" and slavery.

tried to save Scott's life, but the video suggests instead that the officer only ascertains the location of the bullet holes (Laughland et al.) and dresses the wounds. The footage shows no evidence of the officer trying to revive Scott, nor did Santana witness any such effort after turning off the camera (Almasy; Schmidt and Apuzzo). In the Harris video, we see policemen blaming the wounded where we might expect them to administer life-saving procedures—or at least call for them. And in the Scott arrest, Slager applies handcuffs after the deadly gunshots transpire.

In cuffing the mortally wounded, police call attention to the rhetorical distinction between standard safety procedure and brutality. Standard procedure treats shooting a suspect as a form of arrest, and it dictates that officers cuff arrested persons. So when Slager demands that the lifeless Scott "put [his] hands behind [his] back," it conveys a confirmation of Scott's arrest (Neyfakh). Police defend the practice in two ways: it protects law enforcement from unexpected harms and keeps wounded subjects from further injuring themselves (Baker; Neyfakh). Reporter Al Baker uncovers a patrol guide imperative to place wounded suspects in leg restraints, though officers appear to spare Scott that indignity. A Justice Department research project called Preventing Violence Against Law Enforcement and Ensuring Officer Resilience and Survivability, or VALOR, features interviews with police who describe suspects "who appeared to be dead—for example, from multiple rifle rounds to the head—but who were still alive" (Singal). Law enforcement officials also find, on occasion, that apparently incapacitated subjects harbor weapons (Baker). Such instances purportedly justify the handcuff policy.

There exists no evidence in the report, however, that those who turn out to be alive ever harm officers or themselves (Singal). Unconvinced by the kind of logic VALOR advances, civil rights attorney Lawrence L. Kuby argues that "what you lose in public support and approval is far greater than any marginal, negligible fraction of safety that [police] may gain," and he insists that cuffing a dead or dying person "is one of the ugliest, most barbaric, unnecessarily horrifying things that the police do, and they do it as a matter of course" (Baker). The act appears especially horrifying in the case of Scott, whose wounds rendered retaliatory violence highly implausible if not impossible.[15]

The further abuse of already violated bodies proceeds in tandem with the construction of rationalizing narratives and extends the logic that codes African American suspects as menacing even when subdued or facing away from police. While

---

15   A similarly disgraceful scene occurred in Brooklyn on April 4, 2018, when police cuffed Saheed Vassell after shooting him to death. Based on 911 calls, arresting troopers expected Vassell to have a gun, though the object turned out to be a metal pipe with a knob on it (St. Félix). According to St. Félix, Vassell had been diagnosed with bipolar disorder and the police department was aware of the condition. Interviewees from the neighborhood refused to give their real names for fear of retaliation by the authorities.

accentuating that insidious coding, the videos expose the assumptions that too frequently precipitate lethal arrests. The rhetorical tendencies noted thus far—the attribution of latent violence to African Americans, their subjection to extreme cruelty during and after arrest, and the effort to neutralize potentially damning scenarios through storytelling—exist as a dynamic rhetorical mesh rather than discrete phenomena. Slager neglects and dishonors Scott's body during those same moments that he lays blame on him; attending officers attribute Harris' suffering to his running, his gait, and the belligerent arm pinned beneath his body, expending the energies that might be used to save him to shame him instead.

Despite its shocking appearance, the police's behavior should not be understood as especially strange given the dense history of African American dehumanization in legal contexts. That history proceeds all the more readily under the presumption that we have left it behind. Nour S. Kteily and Emile Bruneau point out the phenomenon in "Darker Demons of Our Nature: The Need to (Re)Focus Attention on Blatant Forms of Dehumanization," noting that many U.S. citizens "tend to consider the overt dehumanization of other groups a relic of a distant past—far beyond the pale of our civilized modern societies"—even as White authority figures regularly participate in processes of Black de-individuation and stereotyping while constructing African Americans as an "undifferentiated mass" (487). The stark parallels of the Bates and Harris cases, along with the overt horrors and casual cruelties visited upon Black people across the lifespan of the republic, signal the range of the problem. With views similar to those of Kteily and Bruneau, Akwasi Owusu-Bempah laments that "despite gains made by the Civil Rights Movement in the 1960s, contemporary evidence suggests that Blacks have not yet escaped the sub-human status bestowed upon them during the earliest period of American formation."[16] The continued imposition of that sub-human status plays out in the cuffing of a mortally wounded body, the lack of immediate medical aid, the cursing of a dying man's breath.

Although Harris and Scott fit the profile of latent criminality and visually express their status as subjects-to-be-regulated, they otherwise fall outside what Owusu-Bempah terms the officers' "universe of obligation" (27). The contradiction catches African American subjects in a space of desperate vulnerability, as the agents of social order feel bound to regulate, restrain, and punish without any reciprocal responsibility to protect them from disciplinary excess. It is in part this paradox of obligation, with all that it implies about the definition and parameters of humanity, that produces predictably disastrous consequences during daily patrols.

---

16   See Owusu-Bempah (28). He traces the rhetoric of sub-humanity to "the earliest periods of American development," when "racial taxonomies emerged to justify the enslavement of Black people in which Whiteness became associated with freedom, civilization, and superiority, while Blackness was associated with bondage, social death, the uncivilized, and inferior" (26).

In methodological terms, studying those consequences involves tracing relationships between racism and dehumanization. As Santana shows, those relationships can be made visible and otherwise available to sensory investigation. And through those investigations, scholars and larger U.S. publics might recognize dehumanization as the current procedural norm, not happily remote but near at hand in both temporal and geographical senses. Documentary evidence of its immediacy is troubling both for what it makes manifest and for what it does not show. Being sensitive to the absences requires asking more than what exists outside the visual frame (though such questions have their own theoretical urgency) but looking stubbornly at what fails to reveal itself—namely, police efforts to save Black lives or give any assurance that they matter. Rather than viewing wounded suspects as needing help, law enforcement constructs them as bodies that still have the capacity to strike. Cuffing them unfolds as part of a preemptive logic that neither marshals precedent for offenders' last-gasp retaliation nor seems to need any. The preemptive approach indicates a contradictory practice that deems the subject at once subhuman and superhuman, unworthy of care or respect and yet capable of death-defying acts of aggression. The officers' universe of obligation, to recall Owusu-Bempah's terminology, requires protecting society against that contradiction, which implies that those who bear the contradiction in their bodies find themselves excluded from the social—and in the Scott and Harris cases, excluded once and for all.

From a broad view, the consequences of this thinking include U.S. police killing a Black person every 28 hours (Ifill). From a closer vantage, Officer Daniel Pantaleo continues to apply pressure to Eric Garner's throat as he pleads for air; "Officers 1 and 2" cuff Kajieme Powell after shooting him to death (Singal); Ray Tensing reaches into Samuel Dubose's vehicle so as to kill him with a head shot and later insists that Dubose attempted to run him over, even though Tensing's own body-camera contradicts the story. To claim the right to look is to claim critical access to such footage and thus permit the discernment of patterns that indicate systemic behaviors rather than anomalies. Locating those patterns constitutes an act of countervisuality, to return to Mirzoeff's terminology, and thereby represents a form of antiracist resistance to the ideology that poses as compulsory technique. But such critical looking involves not just resistance or negation. On the contrary, Mirzoeff contends that "the right to look came first, and we should not forget it" (*Right* 2). Visuality, or the imaginative practice that frames history as a transparent affirmation of "autocratic authority" (3), constantly strives to obscure its own secondary character, its belated attempt to appear disinterested and inevitable. Against such inevitability, the right to look affirms creativity and community, dignity and ethical sensitivity, constituting a necessary dimension of what Nunley lauds as vital, unruly democracy. It builds knowledge for that democracy, which exists not as some perfected state but a virtual condition that both motivates and eludes public discourse.

ARCHIVING FOR ANTIRACIST RESEARCH

As researchers describe connections between countervisuality and the antiracist striving toward democracy, I encourage them to consider the following approaches to citizen videography:

1. Stay alert to impromptu video of officers and what it reveals about the ties between race and law enforcement. Catalog and preserve the digital images so as to track behavioral trends.
2. Examine the relationship between optical and aural rhetorics in documentary footage. Ask how people in the field of view attempt to frame that field with speech and narrative.
3. Record all physical actions that officers undertake at the crime scene. Such details could serve to disrupt (or support) their framing of events, which might involve "staging" the scene by placing affectively charged items in view. Also note any police efforts to shut down videography altogether (so as to prevent inhospitable frames from forming). Consider sharing recordings live or with a friend to document any seizure of your camera.
4. Uncover the rationale for officers approaching people or pulling them over. Consider whether the stated reason for the stop matches the details of the interrogation. If there appears to be a disconnect, ask how race or racism might explain it.
5. Isolate tensions between appeals to routine procedures, such as handcuffing wounded suspects, and the purported threat those suspects pose to officers, onlookers, or themselves. Locate overlaps between standard operating procedure in police and military contexts, and situate that convergence against the backdrop of institutionalized training procedures.
6. Watch and listen for the reproduction of myths about race and physical power, and how those myths mediate officer-community relations as well as the outcome of specific arrests.
7. Attend to how political intrigue in the White House steals media attention from deadly acts of racism and how that supports White dominance of the visual field.
8. Compare "official" media accounts of police violence with citizen footage uploaded to websites that advocate the "right to record." For example, the living archives FatalEncounters.org, Free Thought Project (see https://thefreethoughtproject.com/; the Project has a Facebook page entitled "Police the Police 3.0" at https://www.facebook.com/PoliceThePolice3.0/),

Copwatch.com, and PINAC (Photography is Not a Crime, see http://photographyisnotacrime.com) are among many active efforts to engage the problem of free speech and citizen journalism.

9. Research historical archives of citizens' surveillance of police to learn more about how citizen videography initiatives have been organized and supported. Information about relevant faculty, organizations, and funding sources regarding this issue could be discovered that could enable scholars to network with their communities to provide legal and social resources for antiracist action. Some examples of websites that offer a comprehensive archive, but are no longer active, include Harvard University's Berkman Center's Digital Media Law Project (2007–2014, see https://www.dmlp.org) and the Guardian's The Counted project which contains archives from 2015 and 2016 only (see https://www.theguardian.com/us-news/ng-interactive/2015/jun/01/the-counted-police-killings-us-database).

Adopting those research techniques means examining how diverse rhetors contribute to dialogue, or attempt to suppress dialogue, through a range of modes and media. Drawing on the ideas of Cornel West, Nunley advocates for forms of dialogic action associated with "deep democracy," which features "the kind of African American *rhetorical membership* in the nation-state of the American imaginary that would broaden the range of the sayable and the intelligible" (164). The social activists who populate Black Lives Matter and the Black Youth Project embody that kind of rhetorical membership, intervening in politics-as-usual through argumentation that depends as much on visual as oral communication. Black Lives Matters led the North Charleston protests in the days after Scott's death, insisting that the broad U.S. populace continue to grapple with the historical implications of the Santana video (Holpuch and Laughland). The Black Youth Project highlights the legal value of such footage (Ifill), which helped ensure Slager's indictment and brought to light corruption in the Tulsa County Sheriff's Office.[17] Such activism raises suspicion that the shooters' narratives would have prevailed if not for the circulation of the arrest videos, implying that crediting police stories has obscured a long history of abuses. As oppositional as such rhetorics may be, they also constitute ways of generating communal knowledge and infusing that knowledge into the courses of deep democracy.[18]

---

17   Vitale praises the Black Youth Project for its emphasis on economic development and reparations for structural racism, and he remarks how their program rejects the logic of policing and incarceration as solutions to racialized inequality. He gives particular notice to their efforts to raise the minimum wage while supporting unions and labor coalitions (225).

18   There exist certain risks, however, in accepting the idea of video and other images as contributors to democratic discourse on race and racism. Fleetwood shows concern that "visual representations of blacks" might come to "substitute for the real experiences of black subjects,"

Democratic knowledge construction presumes an unsettled visual field in which looking constitutes a political act. Banks' invocation of African American "archivists and real life documentarians" underscores the political exigency of digital artistry, especially that which mixes eras of musical production, though we might also view Santana's work as an expression of archival agency. Impromptu videography manifests such agency insofar as it denaturalizes the operation of visuality, producing powerful anomalies in knowledge production. Philip Stinson suggests that in most historical cases where police shoot a suspect without cause, an officer eventually exposes the crime (Ifill). Impromptu videography has come to displace that scenario, generating marches and rallies, firings and indictments, and forms of public debate that are remarkable for their recent prevalence. Stinson notes that forensic evidence may have led to Slager's indictment, but the video sped the decision while bringing international attention to Scott's death. Santana's footage thus enacts an antiracist rhetoric of parrhesia, which Nunley describes as "speaking bluntly, speaking truth to power," and which he sees as key to deep democracy (1).

The same holds for the footage from the sunglass camera, suggesting that there need not always be an external videographer to expose brutality; a lens aligned with an officer's perspective does the work quite sufficiently. Both kinds of video contribute to a historical and political archive—a database that is now broadly distributed but that still needs powerful forms of organization and concentration—geared toward disclosing relations between race and rhetoric. That archive, both in its current and potential forms, exemplifies the strain of participatory culture that subtends what Mirzoeff describes as visuality in "crisis" (*Right* 34). Amid such crisis, he explains, it is "no longer possible to contain these images within the circle marked out by the police" (290). One methodological challenge with regard to viral circulation is to track the explosion of similar imagery onto the public scene, establishing articulations among the varied visual rhetorics so as to engineer antiracist critique that holds enduring political and juridical value. Douglas Kelly's *Accountability by Camera* and Charles R. Epp, Steven Maynard-Mooney, and Donald Haider-Markel's *Pulled Over* advance such critique in the mode of print. Much work remains if we are to formulate similarly powerful arguments in dynamic, multimodal format, though evidence for those arguments already abounds on digital browsers and social media.

The archive of images may provide analysts with critical purchase on the social and cultural work of stun guns, which figure prominently in the cases

---

and that mediation through a "technological apparatus" might appear equivalent to an "ontological account of black subjects" (13). Whereas the regime of visuality reifies, diminishes, and terrorizes those subjects, practices of countervisuality enact their own forms of oversimplification that require steady reconsideration and revision.

described thus far. In some instances, Tasers function as a less deadly alternative to handguns, but in others they serve to escalate tensions. Beyond the case of Oscar Grant, whom Johannes Mehserle shot to death in California after allegedly reaching for his stun gun (Van Derbeken), we have seen officers tase Philip Coleman into a motionless, catatonic state in his jail cell and drag him out by his handcuffs (Lighty and Mills). We have seen South Boston police shock Linwood Lambert so persistently that he would not recover (Pegues). In Prairie View, Texas, we have heard an officer threaten to "light up" Sandra Bland before manhandling her alongside the highway. She later died by hanging in a local jail, though the circumstances of the event remain obscure.[19] In the same town of Prairie View, Michael Kelley later mercilessly shocked city councilman Jonathan Miller without provocation as Miller knelt on the ground—his crime an attempt to hinder racial profiling by intervening in the questioning of his houseguests, whom the officer suspected of drug possession (Goodwyn). As bystanders, body cameras, and surveillance systems record those events, they suggest that the Taser exacerbates the brutality its proponents aim to mitigate.

However suggestive the commonalities of those cases, analysts of police-community relations rightly probe the limitations of impromptu videography as a corrective technology. Anya Van Wagtendonk underscores those limitations by reminding readers that despite direct video of the chokehold administered to Eric Garner, the courts refused to issue an indictment. Vitale also cautions against overconfidence in police body cameras, which can "reinforce a false sense of police legitimacy and expand the reach of the police into private lives" (222). While the idea of police cameras as a panacea is unsound on its face, it also harbors the assumption that the technology is in working order. That assumption merits critique given that officers sometimes sabotage the equipment or turn off their audio during tense situations (Balko; Lillis and Chavez). Claiming the right to look, then, does not always subvert the operations of visuality, which proceed from centuries of routinized behavior. Kristie Fleckenstein shows in *Vision, Rhetoric, and Social Action in the Composition Classroom* how the act of seeing is an act of social and material conditioning, an experience wherein the learned attribution of significance to phenomena in the optical field dictates what we register, where we focus, how we distinguish figure and ground, and what we ignore. To

19 See Dart. Although the Sandra Bland case has already prompted a book-length study (Lewis), it deserves even greater attention as an indicator of racist arrest procedures. Fleetwood promotes such attention by arguing that "the black visual has been framed as masculine, which has positioned the black female visual as its excess" (9). The present chapter underscores the haunting similarities between two Black men's deaths, which happened in rapid succession and involved the misuse of Taser guns. Bland's death, though it did not take place at the time of arrest, also evokes a certain "Taser trouble" insofar as state trooper Brian Encinia threatened to punish her with a stun gun for purported noncompliance.

return once more to Nunley's favored term, seeing is epistemic: it creates knowledge, and in many cases, it does so by closely adhering to what already counts as knowledge. Little wonder, then, that a jury who inherits deeply ensconced patterns of perception views Garner's death throes as evidence of noncompliance.

A clip of police brutality, or even an archive of clips, will not automatically alter those habits of seeing. State and federal authorities will continue to frame what Jacques Rancière depicts as the "police-principle" as indistinct from history itself; that stealthy conflation inheres in the "now notorious slogan of the New York Police Department: 'If you see something, say something'" (Mirzoeff, *How* 162). The point is so fully to internalize the police-principle that citizens personify it. Transforming that epistemology, where possible, requires persistent circulation of information that fractures commonplace frameworks, and it requires demonstrating, tirelessly and with unfailing rigor, the systemic significance of that information. Vigilant expressions of public memory displace what Nunley names "social death," or the "normalizing surveillance" that impels African Americans to "domesticate, trivialize, or ignore knowledges, performances, and other practices and beliefs. . .grounded in specific ontological orientations to increase the likelihood of individual social and economic access and acceptance" (24).

Keepin' It Hushed laments the limitations on that access and acceptance, detailing how "African American ontology, rhetoric, and knowledge practices have always been and continue to be haunted by the terror of precariousness" (18). Santana's video helps secure Slager's indictment, but those who brutalize Sandra Bland go free.[20] Ray Tensing spends a brief time in jail after murdering Samuel Dubose; Dubose's family experiences irreparable loss, a grief radicalized by the unreachability of justice, no matter the legal outcome.[21] The images capture public attention until the next instance of gun violence takes media precedence. And yet the surge of police brutality videos produces a sense of heightened alert among citizens, a readiness to raise their cameras despite the dangers and despite warnings from officers. These antiracist videographers endeavor to

---

20   Although the Bland case drew a good deal of national scrutiny, similar cases of officers beating and mistreating Black and Brown Women go under-reported. The lack of coverage holds lessons for activists and scholars insofar as those women prove just as vulnerable to the dehumanizing tropes of visuality as do African American men (Capehart).

21   The idea that camera phones and bodycams will support the just resolution of brutality cases is by no means a given. Despite its potential to support antiracist social movements, jurors and complacent publics find ways to interpret the visual evidence in favor of police. As an especially stark example, both Towns and Janet Vertesi point to the acquittal of the four officers whose merciless beating of Rodney King was captured on video. Towns describes how such videos make meaning within a discursive economy that prefigures the Black subject as criminal, thus specifying another instance of how Mirzoeff's visuality mediates perception in preliminary, unconscious fashion.

build knowledge despite the "terror" of its "precariousness," showing faith that initially local forms of epistemic mediation might, in concert with a broadening range of documentary practices, have structural consequences. In the following chapter, Alexandria Lockett further explores the citizens' critical gaze and how it becomes adopted (and appropriated) into journalistic and national intelligence discourses. She situates Black Twitter amid the varied forms of archival techne that hack the hegemony of whiteness. She analyzes #SayHerName and #BlackLivesMatter as innovations in movement praxis and media history alike; she interprets #CNNBeLike and #IfTheyGunnedMeDown as outcries against the racist standardization of information, the body politics of neoliberal news. As a White writer who wants to avoid essentializing communications platforms as well as the bodies they connect, I feel the critique in ways that extend past assent to a quiet tremor, a jolt of recognition.

WORKS CITED

Almasy, Steve. "Feidin Santana on S. C. Shooting: I Told Them What They Did Was an Abuse." *CNN,* 13 Apr. 2015, www.cnn.com/2015/04/09/us/south-carolina -witness-video/.

American Civil Liberties Union. "ACLU Sues D. C. Police Officer for Stealing Citizen's Smartphone Memory Card." *ACLU,* 5 Sep. 2012, m.aclu-nca.org/docket/aclu -sues-dc-police-officer-for-stealing-citizen's-smartphone-memory-card.

Ansari, Azadeh. "Texas Teen Tackled by Police Officer at Pool Party Files Federal Lawsuit." *CNN,* 5 Jan 2017, www.cnn.com/2017/01/05/us/texas-mckinney-pool-party -officer-lawsuit/index.html.

Arsenault, Chris. "U. S. Police Smash Camera for Recording Killing." *Al Jazeera,* 21 June 2011, www.aljazeera.com/indepth/features/2011/06/201162114131825860.html.

Associated Press. "Ex-Deputy Robert Bates Convicted in Death of Eric Harris Released from Prison." *NBC News,* 19 Oct. 2017, www.nbcnews.com/news/us-news/ex -oklahoma-reserve-deputy-roberts-bates-released-prison-n812446.

Associated Press. "Man Makes Police Brutality Claims; 2 Officers Get Fired." *Miami Herald,* 21 May 2018, www.miamiherald.com/news/nation-world/article211643 209.html.

Azoulay, Ariella. *The Civil Contract of Photography.* Zone Books, 2008.

Baker, Al. "Handcuffing the Wounded: A Police Tactic Hits a Nerve." *New York Times,* 18 Nov. 2007, www.nytimes.com/2007/11/18/nyregion/18cuffs.html.

Balko, Radley. "80 Percent of Chicago Dash-Cam Videos are Missing Audio Due to 'Officer Error' or 'Intentional Destruction.'" *Washington Post,* 29 Jan. 2016, www .washingtonpost.com/news/the-watch/wp/2016/01/29/80-percent-of-chicago-pd -dash-cam-videos-are-missing-audio-due-to-officer-error-or-intentional-destruction /?utm_term=.f66a74cdc49d.

————. *Rise of the Warrior Cop: The Militarization of America's Police Forces*. Public Affairs, 2013.

Banks Adam. *Digital Griots: African American Rhetoric in a Multimedia Age*. Southern Illinois UP, 2011.

Bellware, Kim. "Teen Who Filmed Texas Pool Party Cop: 'When He Pulled His Gun, My Heart Dropped.'" *Huffington Post*, 8 June 2015, www.huffingtonpost. com/2015/06/08/brandon-brooks-pool-party_n_7538140.html.

Berlin, James A. *Rhetoric and Reality: Writing Instruction in American Colleges, 1900–1985*. Southern Illinois UP, 1987.

Buck-Morss, Susan. "Visual Studies in Global Imagination." *The Politics of Imagination*, edited by Chiara Bottici and Benoit Challand, Birkbeck Law Press, 2011, pp. 214–33.

Campbell, Andy. "Texas Bill Would Make Recording Police Illegal." *Huffington Post*, 13 Mar. 2015, www.huffingtonpost.com/2015/03/13/bill-recording-police-illegal _n_6861444.html.

Capehart, Jonathan. "Police Violence Affects Women of Color Just as Much as Men. Why Don't We Hear about It?" *Washington Post*, 27 Mar. 2018, www.washington post.com/blogs/post-partisan/wp/2018/03/27/police-violence-affccts-women-of -color-just-as-much-as-men-why-dont-we-hear-about-it/?utm_term=.c0d629cd15e1.

Carlyle, Thomas. *The French Revolution: A History*. Modern Library, 2002.

Coogler, Ryan, director. *Fruitvale Station*. Weinstein Co., 2013.

Copwatch.com. 2020. copwatch.com.

The Counted. *The Guardian*. 2015–2016. www.theguardian.com/us-news/series/coun ted-us-police-killings.

Craig, Byron B., and Rahko, Steven E. "Visual Profiling as Biopolitics: Or, Notes on Policing in Post-Racial #AmeriKKKa." *Cultural Studies<——>Critical Methodologies*, vol. 16, no. 3, 2016, pp. 287–95.

Dart, Tom. "Sandra Bland Dashcam Video Shows Officer Threatened: 'I will light you up.'" *Guardian*, 22 July 2015, www.theguardian.com/us-news/2015/jul/21/sandra -bland-dashcam-video-arrest-released.

Digital Media Law Project. 9 Oct. 2020. www.dmlp.org.

Epp, Charles R., et al. *Pulled Over: How Police Stops Define Race and Citizenship*. U of Chicago P, 2014.

Fantz, Ashley, et al. "Texas Pool Party Chaos: 'Out of Control' Police Officer Resigns." *CNN*, 9 June 2015, www.cnn.com/2015/06/09/us/mckinney-texas-pool-party-video/.

Fatal Encounters. 2020. fatalencounters.org.

Ferrell, Nikki. "Everything You Need to Know about the Ray Tensing Murder Trial." WLWT5, 23 June 2017, www.wlwt.com/article/everything-you-should-know -about-the-ray-tensing-murder-trial/7146075#.

Fleckenstein, Kristie S. *Vision, Rhetoric, and Social Action in the Composition Classroom*. Southern Illinois UP, 2009.

Fleetwood, Nicole R. *Performance, Visuality, and Blackness*. U of Chicago P, 2011.

Foucault, Michel. *Security, Territory, Population: Lectures at the College de France, 1977–1978*. Edited by Michel Senellart, translated by Graham Burchell. Palgrave Macmillan, 2007.

Free Thought Project. 2020. thefreethoughtproject.com.

Goodwyn, Wade. "Prairie View, Texas, Reflects on History of Racism after Police Incidents." *NPR*, 23 Oct. 2015, www.npr.org/2015/10/21/450611772/prairie-view -texas-reflects-on-history-of-racism-after-police-incidents.

Graham, David A. "The Shockingly Familiar Killing of Walter Scott." *The Atlantic*, 8 Apr 2015, www.theatlantic.com/national/archive/2015/04/the-shockingly-familiar -killing-of-walter-scott/390006/.

Gray, Rosie. "Trump Defends White-Nationalist Protesters: 'Some Very Fine People on Both Sides.'" *The Atlantic*, 15 Aug. 2017, www.theatlantic.com/politics/archive /2017/08/trump-defends-white-nationalist-protesters-some-very-fine-people -on-both-sides/537012/.

Haag, Matthew. "Border Patrol Agent Kills Woman Who Crossed into Texas Illegally, Authorities Say." *New York Times*, 24 May 2018, www.nytimes.com/2018/05/24 /us/border-patrol-shooting-woman.html.

Hariman, Robert, and John Louis Lucaites. *No Caption Needed: Iconic Photographs, Public Culture, and Liberal Democracy*. U of Chicago P, 2007.

———. *The Public Image: Photography and Civic Spectatorship*. U of Chicago P, 2016.

Herbert, Steve, and Elizabeth Brown. "Conceptions of Space and Crime in the Punitive Neoliberal City." *Antipode*, vol. 38, no. 4, 2006, pp. 755–77.

Hesford, Wendy S. *Spectacular Rhetorics*. Duke UP, 2011.

Holpuch, Amanda, and Oliver Laughland. "Michael Slager Fired from South Carolina Police Force after Killing of Walter Scott." *Guardian*, 8 Apr. 2015, www.theguard ian.com/us-news/2015/apr/08/michael-slager-south-carolina-officer-walter-scott -fired.

hooks, bell. *Art on My Mind: Visual Politics*. New Press, 1995.

Hum, Sue. "'Between the Eyes': The Racialized Gaze as Design." *College English*, vol. 77, no. 3, 2015, pp. 191–215.

Ifill, Gwen. "How a Bystander's Video Revealed the Truth about a Police Shooting in South Carolina." *PBS*, 8 Apr. 2015, www.pbs.org/newshour/bb/bystanders-video -revealed-truth-police-shooting-south-carolina/.

Jacobo, Julia. "Cellphone Video Shows Miami Police Officer Apparently Kicking Suspect in the Head during Arrest." *ABC News*, 3 May 2018, abcnews.go.com/US /cellphone-video-shows-miami-police-officer-apparently-kicking/story?id=54915684.

Kelly, Douglas A. *Accountability by Camera: Online Video's Effects on Police-Civilian Interactions*. LFB Scholarly Publishing, 2014.

Kteily, Nour S., and Emile Bruneau. "Darker Demons of Our Nature: The Need to (Re)focus Attention on Blatant Forms of Dehumanization." *Current Directions in Psychological Science*, vol. 26, no. 6, 2017, pp. 487–94.

Laughland, Oliver, et al. "Michael Slager Radioed in Taser Claim Six Seconds after Firing at Walter Scott." *Guardian*, 9 Apr. 2015, www.theguardian.com/us-news/2015 /apr/08/south-carolina-walter-scott-shooting-audio-video.

Lerner, Kira. "A Family Fights for the Inconceivable: Convicting a Police Officer for Murder." *ThinkProgress*, 29 Sep. 2015, thinkprogress.org/justice/ 2015/09/29 /3706285/walter-scott-brother/.

Lewis, Marion T. D. *A Girl Named Sandy: Legal Implications of the Arrest and Death of Sandra Bland*. Waterfall Press, 2016.

Lighty, Todd, and Steve Mills. "Judge: Using Taser, Dragging Coleman from Lockup Amounts to 'Brute Force.'" *Chicago Tribune*, 14 Dec. 2015, www.chicagotribune.com/news/local/breaking/ct-philip-coleman-judge-ruling-met-20151214-story.html.

Lillis, Ryan, and Nashelly Chavez. "Cops Muted Their Body Cams after Stephon Clark Shooting: Now They Need to Keep Mikes On." *Sacramento Bee*, 10 Apr. 2018, www.sacbee.com/news/local/news-columns-blogs/city-beat/article208382939.html.

Lowery, Wesley. "Police Are Still Killing Black People. Why Isn't It News Anymore?" *Washington Post*, 16 March 2018, www.washingtonpost.com/outlook/police-are-still-killing-black-people-why-isnt-it-news-anymore/2018/03/12/df004124-22ef-11e8-badd-7c9f29a55815_story.html.

McLaughlin, Elliott C., and Ben Brumfield. "Video Released of Deadly Shooting in Tulsa after Police Chase." *CNN*, 12 Apr. 2015, www.cnn.com/2015/04/12/us/tulsa-police-shooting-video/.

Melvin, Craig. "Michael Slager, Cop Who Killed Walter Scott, Says He Felt Threatened." *NBC News*, 8 Sep. 2015, www.nbcnews.com/storyline/walter-scott-shooting/lawyer-michael-slager-cop-who-killed-walter-scott-says-he-n423672.

Meyer, Robinson. "What to Say When the Police Tell You to Stop Filming Them." *The Atlantic*, 28 Apr. 2018, www.theatlantic.com/technology/archive/2015/04/what-to-say-when-the-police-tell-you-to-stop-filming-them/391610/.

Mirzoeff, Nicholas. *How to See the World: An Introduction to Images, from Self-Portraits to Selfies, Maps to Movies, and More*. Basic, 2016.

———. The Right to Look: A Counterhistory of Visuality. Duke UP, 2011.

Murphy, Kate, and Mark Curnutte. "University of Cincinnati Pays $250k to Ex-Cop Who Killed Sam DuBose." Cincinnati.com, 22 Mar. 2018, www.cincinnati.com/story/news/2018/03/22/university-cincinnati-pays-cop-who-killed-sam-dubose/450587002/.

Neyfakh, Leon. "Why Did the North Charleston Cop Handcuff Walter Scott?" *Slate*, 8 Apr. 2015, www.slate.com/articles/news_and_politics/crime/2015/04/walter_scott_shooting_why_did_michael_thomas_slager_cuff_the_victim.html.

Nunley, Vorris L. *Keepin' It Hushed: The Barbershop and African American Hush Harbor Rhetorics*. Wayne State UP, 2011.

Ortiz, Erik. "Oklahoma Man Eric Harris Fatally Shot by Deputy Who Meant to Fire Taser." *NBC News*, 12 Apr. 2015, www.nbcnews.com/news/us-news/oklahoma-man-eric-harris-fatally-shot-police-accident-instead-tased-n340116.

Osunsami, Steve, and Emily Shapiro. "Ex-Cop Michael Slager Sentenced to 20 Years for Shooting Death of Walter Scott." *ABC News*, 7 Dec. 2017, abcnews.go.com/US/cop-michael-slager-faces-19-24-years-prison/story?id=51595376.

Owusu-Bempah, Akwasi. "Race and Policing in Historical Context: Dehumanization and the Policing of Black People in the 21st Century." *Theoretical Criminology*, vol. 21, no. 1, 2017, pp. 23–34.

Pegues, Jeff. "Death after Taser Arrest Leads to Va. Police Brutality Allegations." *CBS News*, 15 Nov. 2015, www.cbsnews.com/videos/death-after-taser-arrest-leads-to-va-police-brutality-allegations/.

PINAC News. Photography Is Not a Crime. 2020. newsmaven.io/pinacnews/.

Rabin, Charles, and David Ovalle. "Miami Cop Caught on Video Kicking Handcuffed Man on Ground in Head, Relieved of Duty." *Miami Herald*, 3 May 2018, www. miamiherald.com/news/local/crime/article210384404.html.

Rai, Candice. *Democracy's Lot: Rhetoric, Publics, and the Places of Invention*. U of Alabama P, 2016.

Rancière, Jacques. "Ten Theses on Politics." *Theory and Event*, vol. 5, no. 3, 2001. muse.jhu.edu/article/32639.

Reilly, Katie. "Here Are All the Times Trump Insulted Mexico." *Time*, 31 Aug. 2016, time.com/4473972/donald-trump-mexico-meeting-insult/.

Reuters. "Michael Slager's Lawyers Want Him Out of Jail because Walter Scott Had Drugs in His System." *Huffington Post*, 9 Sep. 2015, www.huffingtonpost.com/entry /walter-scott-shooting_55f0650de4b002d5c0778fb7.

Schmidt, Michael S., and Matt Apuzzo. "South Carolina Officer is Charged with Murder of Walter Scott." *New York Times*, 7 Apr. 2015, www.nytimes.com/2015/04/08 /us/south-carolina-officer-is-charged-with-murder-in-black-mans-death.html?_r=2.

Schuppe, Jon. "Eric Harris was on Meth when Tulsa Deputy Robert Bates Shot Him: Autopsy." *NBC News*, 12 May 2015, www.nbcnews.com/news/us-news/ eric-harris-was-high-meth-when-tulsa-deputy-shot-him-n357926.

Serna, Joseph. "With Smartphones Everywhere, Police on Notice They May be Caught on Camera." *Los Angeles Times*, 21 Apr. 2015, www.latimes.com/local/lanow/la-me -ln-feds-probe-video-phone-in-south-gate-20150421-story.html.

Singal, Jesse. "Why Cops Handcuff Dead People." *New York Magazine*, 8 Apr. 2015, www.thecut.com/2015/04/why-cops-handcuff-dead-people.html.

Smith, Mitch, and Benjamin Hoffman. "Video of Sterling Brown's Arrest Shows Milwaukee Police Using Stun Gun on N. B. A. Player." *New York Times*, 23 May, 2018, www.nytimes.com/2018/05/23/us/sterling-brown-milwaukee-police-taser.html.

Smitherman, Geneva. *Talkin and Testifyin: The Language of Black America*. Wayne State UP, 1977.

St. Félix, Doreen. "On the Street in Brooklyn the Morning after the Police Shooting of Saheed Vassell." *New Yorker*, 5 Apr. 2018, www.newyorker.com/news/dispatch /on-the-street-in-brooklyn-the-morning-after-the-police-shooting-of-saheed-vassell.

Towns, Armond R. "That Camera Won't Save You! The Spectacular Consumption of Police Violence." *Present Tense*, vol. 5, no. 2, 2015, www.presenttensejournal.org /volume-5/that-camera-wont-save-you-the-spectacular-consumption-of-police -violence/#note2.

Van Derbeken, Jaxon. "Johannes Mehserle Says He Feared Oscar Grant was Going for Gun." *SF Gate*, 14 June 2014, www.sfgate.com/crime/article/Mehserle-says-he-fired -after-Grant-made-digging-5551691.php.

Van Wagtendonk, Anya. "How and Why You Should Record the Police." *PBS*, 10 Apr. 2015, www.pbs.org/newshour/updates/6-rules-follow-citizen-journalist/.

Vertesi, Janet. "The Problem with Police Body Cameras." *Time*, 4 May 2015, time. com/3843157/the-problem-with-police-body-cameras/.

Vitale, Alex S. *The End of Policing*. Verso, 2017.

Warner, Michael. *Publics and Counterpublics.* Zone Books, 2002.

Weheliye, Alexander G. *Habeas Viscus: Racializing Assemblages, Biopolitics, and Black Feminist Theories of the Human.* Duke UP, 2014.

West, Cornel. *Democracy Matters: Winning the Fight against Imperialism.* Penguin, 2004.

Wood, Amy Louise. *Lynching and Spectacle: Witnessing Racial Violence in America, 1890–1940.* U of North Carolina P, 2009.

Woolf, Nicky. "Arizona State Senator Proposes Bill to Restrict Recording Videos of Police." *The Guardian*, 11 Jan. 2016, www.theguardian.com/us-news/2016/jan/11 /arizona-state-senator-john-kavanagh-recording-police-video.

INTERCHAPTER DIALOGUE
FOR CHAPTER 4

James: Chris, I really love your chapter on this issue of race and surveillance. How does your examination of surveillance affect our understanding of whiteness?

Chris: That's a great question. One of the things that I want to stress is the extent to which whiteness informs the reception of images of violence, images of controversy, and images where there may be a degree of urgency or exigency potentially surrounding the issue of race. Nicholas Mirzoeff's work informs my interpretation of the increasing reliance on digitally-mediated visuals for making "credible" arguments in legal and popular cultural forums. What counts as evidence, as Mirzoeff claims, represents and advances the dominance of White (supremacist) epistemologies. So the idea that the visual itself may be overlapping with the ideology of whiteness was something that was counterintuitive to me when I started reading him. But the more I engaged with his work in *The Right to Look*, the more I thought about the reception of images. What seemed very obvious to me was that blatant acts of police brutality, in which White officers were engaging in both acts of excessive violence and outright dehumanization of unarmed (Black) suspects, are clearly mediated by race and racism. When examining those instances, I can see how they were reframed, and that questions were posed that undermined the straightforwardness of those documents. And so it seems that even when the visual isn't immediately consonant with the interests of whiteness, that White juries and the hegemony of whiteness powerfully reinforce and recreate racial hierarchies.

A rather damning example that comes immediately to mind is the slaying of Samuel DuBose, right here in Cincinnati. He was pulled over for allegedly not having a front license plate. DuBose was questioned, but as soon as Officer Ray Tensing wasn't getting the answers he wanted, he reached to open DuBose's car door to conduct a search. DuBose began to resist. And before he knew it, Tensing had pulled out a gun and executed him on the spot. The entire incident was recorded on his body camera. The district attorney came on TV very shortly after the event, declaring DuBose's untimely death as "a horrific instance" of police work. This admission may have quelled some degree of citizen outrage since there wasn't an outright rebellion during the protests in downtown Cincinnati. This may have been because the district attorney made it clear that this was an instance that was obviously going to be taken to trial and that the police officer was going to serve time. But when the trial actually started, the evidence began to serve a narrative advocated by

Tensing and his lawyer, in which whiteness mediated the images and, thus, what counts as evidence.

James: I'm really connected to this issue of evidence because I teach about the contemporary meaning of surveillance in my Race, Rhetoric, and Protest class. For at least the past five years or so, many people have argued that body cams could be an effective solution to police brutality. They believe that if we had more cameras that could document police activity, we'd "really" know what happened and could "objectively" determine who's at fault when people are shot by an officer.

But as your chapter touches on, that isn't the case, right? The story about how the shootings are filmed affects how the footage is circulated and interpreted. I've seen so many different shootings, which in and of itself reflects the massive scope of America's race problem, and I'll watch the video and think, "Wow, this is damning evidence. How can the officer get away with this?" But then, the police officer uses that footage as justification for their actions during their defense in the courtroom proceedings. And usually they claim, "We're using this visual to justify what you didn't see. This testimony isn't in this footage."

Chris, could you further discuss how visual evidence is used to justify these narratives of "absence," or some story about we don't necessarily see.

Chris: Sure. What you referenced is readily apparent in the case of Michael Slager killing Walter Scott in South Carolina.

If you just look at the images that were produced by Feidin Santana, the barber who was on his way to work and happened to be passing by when he decided to record the slaying as it occurred, it clearly looks like an execution-style killing. However, the lawyers immediately started to suggest, "Well, there was a struggle beforehand. We don't know about that. We need to understand the extent to which Scott was resisting before the video camera was ever aimed at him." They also argued that Slager dropped his Taser gun at the site because Scott was trying to take it and use it against him. In that case, we don't see this narrative in Santana's footage. Nevertheless, the legal defense used by police officers like Slager certainly relies on the idea of "contextualization" to delegitimize what we see.

When teaching and theorizing rhetoric, we often think of context considerations as a very positive thing. We tend to assume that when you contextualize, you get a lot closer to the truth, which may presumably bring you closer to justice. But in fact, the simple question regarding whether the shooting of an unarmed (disproportionately Black, Brown, or Indigenous) person is ever justified challenges the legitimacy of any context that could lead to such an action. Here, racism and authoritarianism is absurd. This idea of backstory or contextualization only amplifies the lack of logic employed by the officer(s) very plainly killing someone who wasn't posing a threat to them in the footage. Fortunately, it didn't work for Slater, but his story is the anomaly. Due to the politics of trials and laws like qualified immunity, most police officers aren't even fired for killing the unarmed, let alone being charged and indicted, much less going to prison for it.

Iris: One of the things that we've discussed throughout the process of doing this work is this idea of positionality. Of course, we talked about it with James' chapter since it's obviously the focus of an autoethnography. In your chapter, Chris, you briefly address your relationship to your research, but not necessarily as comprehensively as James does.

Chris: Right.

Iris: Being accountable to our personal relationship to race and racism is one of the major characteristics of how we are theorizing antiracism as a research methodology. Would you please elaborate on what it means for you to research and write about Black people, and specifically some of the instances that have contributed to the Black Lives Matter movement?

Chris: Absolutely. This was a key challenge during my chapter revision. Explicitly incorporating my personal experiences with race in my research writing is not something I have typically done. However, some of my work has featured my experiences with graduate and contingent labor in the university, such as my first book, *Rhetoric and Resistance in the Corporate Academy*, and editor of *Workplace: A Journal for Academic Labor*. In terms of this project, it was an interesting critical exercise to reflect on a variety of contexts of citizen videography of injustice. I thought about multiple instances of police violence toward African Americans in Louisville, my hometown. After doing my graduate work there, I moved to Norman, Oklahoma. The University of Oklahoma was pretty quiet about problems of racism on campus. But I knew people like Alex—my former advisee—who was an M.A. student at the same time as I came in as an assistant professor. She was vocal about experiencing it very directly.

As I considered that time of my career, I discovered that racism was probably much more prominent than I recalled seeing in my daily experience. That realization was unsettling, to say the least. To write about it, and to engage in conversation about it, and to publicly take a position about systemic racism are part of my attempt to take accountability for doing the labor of transforming how the discipline makes space for more research and professional engagement with antiracism. Working on sharing power and using collaborative multicultural writing to signal my solidarity with victims of racial violence opens up more opportunities for me to really think about and more fully grasp the severity of the consequences of racism.

Philosophical inquiry that centralizes the issues of race and racism syncs well with investigations about all kinds of oppression. I found myself asking, "What good is the work we do as teachers and researchers when people all over the world are experiencing extreme and unnecessary suffering?"

Within a year of moving to Cincinnati from Norman, OK, I saw a horrific example of a campus police officer, not even a city police officer but someone from UC, traveling a mile off campus for the purposes of tracking someone down based on some vague hunches. His racially targeted search was simply "protocol" that he used to justify a murder. Clearly, the fact that he feels like he can do that to another human being as a matter of his job duties indicates the historical continuity of racism. Controlling Black people has been part of U.S. law enforcement's ideologies since the slave patrols of the 18th and 19th centuries. The idea that racism has diminished is a lie that we need to face head-on with an insistence on history.

Telling my story as part of the research starts a crucial conversation in our small, but influential disciplinary networks. Trump's racist vitriol seems to be normalizing a disturbing trend of overt racism, including an uptick in hate crimes. Certainly, the issue of race was getting more attention at the end of the Obama administration. But the Trump administration is perpetually involved in a scandal that sucks up so much of the air time in the broadcast media, distracting people. Unfortunately, racism gets much less attention than it deserves.

Iris: Thank you. I think it's really interesting to know about your own personal history and how this project has been part of your evolution as a researcher answering a call to social justice. I'm sure that you know that some of your colleagues will wonder about the direction of your research. But I do see you having a history of engagement with antiracist literature in the field. You mentioned Geneva Smitherman and Adam Banks at the beginning of your chapter, for example. Could you briefly describe your entryway into this tradition of racial literacy, considerations of race, especially as it relates to digital technology?

Chris: The issue of access was very much on my radar when I started my doctoral work at the University of Louisville. Many scholars were observing racial and economic disparities among internet users. Access to computers and the internet affects who is able to participate in computing and internet cultures.

But even as the internet became more globally widespread, the question of access became a more nuanced one. A person may have access to digital technology, but do they really have access to its literacies? To educational experiences that give them an opportunity to learn how to compose powerful narratives? To cultural authority and cultural capital? These questions have been part of the evolution of my thoughts about the relationship between race and technology. Banks' *Race, Rhetoric, and Technology*, which was one of the works that inspired the title of this book, was certainly part of this process. But I look to the ways in which African American ways of making meaning and communicating have been marginalized. In our own disciplinary history, vernacular is placed at the periphery and understood as a form of error. Geneva Smitherman powerfully critiques the notion that Black American English (BAE) is underdeveloped. In *Talkin' and Testifyin'*, she looks at its sophistication. By identifying linguistic characteristics of BAE and how it flows throughout the American experience, Smitherman disrupts the idea that standard White edited English (SWEE) ought to be the "default," or the standard for "professional" communication and in general. I think those conversations still matter when we think about how the internet is documenting and influencing our current language practices.

Iris: Awesome! Thank you.

Alex: I am particularly interested in your chapter's articulation of some of the challenges embedded in truth-telling today, as well as what it means to bear witness to injustice with these contemporary technologies. Bearing witness obviously comes with all kinds of responsibilities such as documenting, sharing, and defending one's testimony. Tell us a little bit more about the researcher's ethical duty to disclose how they are bearing witness to oppression throughout their processes of knowledge making.

What does it mean to bear witness to racial logics that inhibit the public's ability to value truth—as a guide, as a principle? And what role does trust play in antiracism and especially antiracism as a methodology?

Chris: To answer that question, we may need to insist on believing what our senses are telling us in the wake of the influence of postmodern theory. During the 1990s and early 2000s, the humanities and social sciences increasingly emphasized anti-foundationalism and the constructedness of truth. It's terrifying to see the extent to which that logic has now been adopted and appropriated by white nationalist and/or far right-wing groups who successfully troll. Fox News, for example, has mastered the art of "spin" by re-contextualizing its chosen facts to serve their political agenda.

When I researched the Trump administration's attitudes toward police body cameras, I figured that they would advocate doing away with the body cameras. Certainly, Trump doesn't want to imply that the police might be doing something criminal since they are part of his base. But the more I researched, the more that I saw him saying that the police departments can decide for themselves whether to use body cams. Trump would say that they were an asset to the police because when suspects end up getting killed or harmed, you can actually use the footage to exonerate the police officer. "We look at that footage, and then we discover, hey, the police officer wasn't doing anything wrong. He was provoked." This response suggests that Trump is so confident in the ethos that he has helped create that the police will be able to reorient those images to reinforce their authority to kill people. And that's really terrifying to me. As James and I were discussing earlier, even if a piece of evidence seems to clearly indicate overkill and/or murderous intent, it can be manipulated to suit the interests of a certain voting constituency.

Alex: Right. I want to further discuss how you talk about racial logics in your article. The recent trial of Amber Guyger has been on my mind a lot these past several days. I'm wondering about that case because it connects so seamlessly with you and James' chapters. Here is this off-duty police officer, a young thin blonde White woman, who killed a Black man in his apartment. Botham Jean's family gave her so much compassion after she received that light (10-year) sentence. The news focused extensively on a photograph of Jean's younger brother, Brandt, hugging Guyger. She also received a long embrace from Judge Tammy Kemp. These images generated all kinds of public conversation about forgiveness, empathy, and reconciliation. And I just kept thinking about how Guyger appeared to receive more sympathy than the man she killed. White supremacy, in that case and so many others, demonstrates particular racial logics embedded in criminality, policing, victimhood, and truth.

How do researchers negotiate the problem of discovery and invention when the prevailing racial logics make it so clear that what's true isn't necessarily going to be persuasive?

We live in a culture where it's increasingly not persuasive to, say, call someone out for being racist (as you mentioned with Trump). Police occupy a militaristic role, ordering the public to submit to their absolute power. There's little to no accountability when law enforcement misuses force, fails to intervene on behalf of the public when they observe wrongdoing, improperly documents citizen complaints, etc. The culture of secrecy, of "(White) brotherhood," protects the "few bad apples," as do multimillion-dollar budgets for large city precincts that don't seem to require any oversight. Police killing unarmed persons is hardly a matter of "good" vs. "bad" cops; it is simply part of the design of policing: slaying Black people might just "happen," and if it does, the judicial system will be kind. But it probably won't even get that far.

Given that we must live and work in this culture of violence that is powered by the logics of White supremacy and authoritarianism, how is a researcher supposed to make knowledge? What do scholarly audiences expect from us, besides the most basic act of naming and verifying a problem or pointing out the obvious.

Chris: I have two responses, and they may be conflicting, but they illustrate my immediate thoughts.

First, I'm intrigued by the fact that people don't seem to know what to make of a person who wants to embrace a person who has killed their loved one. There is something like a sort of superhuman level of forgiveness on display there. And the mainstream news media doesn't know exactly what to make of it. But I'm not sure I do either. To your point Alex, we don't really have a language for this social and emotional conflict.

This problem connects with James' analysis of reconciliation. Amber Guyger embracing Brandt Jean conveys an image of people engaging in some kind of gesture of reconciliation that is hard for me to identify with. The same culture of violence that made Botham Jean's murder possible is the same culture that has socialized me to desire harsh punishment for the criminal. Likewise, that same culture would have me "more naturally" envision criminals as Black (more than Whites) and tacitly consent to a double standard of accountability for citizens and police officers.

How should I talk about that as a researcher and as a citizen?

How should these issues be incorporated in graduate instruction, and K–16 education, more broadly? In philosophies of research design and methodologies for studying culture, language, rhetoric, etc.? In community building and organizing initiatives, and so on?

The other part of me worries that we move too quickly to justify and forgive people in power. How does this response fully acknowledge the dignity of a person who gets slain just for being an African American person sitting in his living room because a white woman was "confused and made a mistake"? The horror, of course, is that these incidents are not exceptions. They are numerous enough to be considered somewhat typical. I am worried about the extent to which we try to find ways to tell stories that make us feel better and distract us from pursuing hardcore reform, perhaps even abolition.

Alex: It really is a horror story to live with these realities, especially while Black or if bearing witness to abuses of power. One of the witnesses for the Guyger case was shot right outside the apartment complex. That, of course, has people wondering, "Why do all these horrible things happen to befall witnesses or critics of police brutality?" Several Black Lives Matter activists have been mysteriously killed or found dead. Ramsay Orta, who recorded Eric Garner's death by chokehold, seems to be facing a lot of legal issues. Feidin Santana was interrogated about his race and ethnicity during Slager's trial, as if his racial identity might make him automatically "anti-cop." I think that we have a major problem when it comes to claiming an antiracist positionality. Of course, people want to do what is "right." But I think that we still have to deal with these troubling politics of civility and the very real risks and dangers of bearing witness to injustice.

Chris: Absolutely.

Alex: The dominance of policing, and the notion that most cops are "good," is so embedded in American culture and discourse that the idea that they could *systematically* do wrong fundamentally threatens the fabric of a "good" society. And I think that even for antiracist researchers, there are probably many people who still long for the good old days when the cops were good guys, even as they empathize with Black Lives Matter and countless instances of police misconduct. I can't help but wonder how film, entertainment, and social media contributes to that perception. Crime drama dominates TV. We literally consume it for entertainment. Researchers should further explore how they are socialized to perceive the police. Shows from *Law and Order SVU* to documentary style programs like *Snapped, See No Evil, Fatal Vows, For My Man*, etc. position police solely as champions, heroes, and servants of the public. Rarely do crime dramas, fictional or nonfiction, depict any cases involving police officers engaged in crimes or corruption. The sad reality is that the pervasiveness of the "real evil" of legal and criminal justice systems, which is racism, means that we want to escape into a world where law enforcement actually protests and serves us without racial prejudice. I think these are some reasons that we're entertained by cops in protagonist roles.

Chris: It does appear that, even if Guyger tells the story, "I thought I was in my own apartment and this was an intruder," it sounds too wrong to be believable. Clearly, the jury believed that she needed to serve some jail time . . . maybe it wasn't enough. Yet, there are still so few instances in which police end up on trial for murdering unarmed civilians.

Alex: In the Guyger case, I think what we're seeing is a fundamental conflict between the cultural value of police officers as public servants who might need you to comply with their policies (e.g., oblige a warrant) so they can "do their jobs," vs. the individual freedom we are supposed to be granted to protect our homes and other property like our vehicles. If we are conflicted about our relationship with the police, or if we notice that we have a hard time critiquing their actions without feeling as if we are taking a risk, we need to recognize how such a dilemma illustrates the challenges of doing research as Americans.

Chris: Thank you very much. I agree.

Alex: James, Iris—do you have any concluding remarks?

James: The last thing I want to say is that what bothered me about the Amber Guyger case was also the expectation of forgiving a White (woman) murderer. It was both the immediate response and assumed to be the Christian thing to do. Race clearly impacts the optics of forgiveness as much as it does the likelihood of being randomly, but disproportionately, killed by law enforcement. I know that, inherently, if the racial identities and professional roles were reversed that we would never, ever see anything like that.

Chris: That's right.

James: There is no way they would be sharing that video as well!

Alex: Black people are conflicted about it. You can find tons of conversations on Twitter where folks are vigorously debating how we, as a people, should be responding to these public displays of compassion for people who would clearly rather have us dead than reason with the fact of our humanity. But this is a long conversation that goes back to the history of fugitive slaves and the slave revolts all over the world. In modern U.S. history, we could go back to the issue of non-violent protesting and revisit how Malcolm X and MLK Jr. debated about self-defense.

Iris, what are your thoughts?

Iris: I am thinking about the exoneration of police who kill Black and Brown people and media depictions of African Americans as criminals. I'm also thinking about the history of Civil Rights. In one interview of Angela Davis during her incarceration, she says, "You're asking me about violence?" And she reflects on her experience witnessing the devastation from racially motivated church bombings. Davis declared that, "Those were my neighbors, and there's limbs all over the place, and people were blown apart. You know, those were my friends. Those were my neighbors. So for you to talk about violence, it just doesn't make any sense to me that you would ask me that question."

And I have to ask the question: how does a society normalize racism to the point where there is a perception that only one group exhibits violence whereas the other group is completely immune from ever being violent? When mass murders happen, they are characterized as the efforts of a mentally ill "lone wolf," not a white nationalist domestic terrorist who is well connected to other groups of White people.

It's so illogical. And because it's illogical, its going to continue to produce "facts" and evidence that support absurdity. I think that's exactly where Chris is trying to intervene. He's pointing out that racism enables irrational explanations to prevail over clear right vs. wrong situations.

Alex: Given your last comment, Iris, it seems that racial violence is ultimately going to produce self-destruction. And self-destruction is going to assure mutual endings. And in so much as we notice the same racist state-sponsored violence over and over and over and over and over and over again, I think what will happen—and what has happened, let's be clear, is total collapse. Police brutality is so out of control that as more people utilize mobile technologies to document what they see, the less radical police reform and abolition efforts will seem to the general public. We must remain steadfast in our faith in sharing what we believe and know is true when so many lives are at stake.

WORKS CITED

Mirzoeff, Nicholas. "The Right to Look." *Critical Inquiry*, vol. 37, no. 3, 2011, pp. 473–96.

Mirzoeff, Nicholas. *The Right to Look: A Counterhistory of Visuality*. Duke UP, 2011.

CHAPTER 5.

WHAT IS BLACK TWITTER? A RHETORICAL CRITICISM OF RACE, DIS/INFORMATION, AND SOCIAL MEDIA

Alexandria Lockett

Spelman College

Key Words and Concepts: Black Rhetoric, Blackness, Surveillance, Disinformation, Information Warfare, Hashtags

"I TWITTER, THEREFORE I AM BLACK, OR AM I BLACK AND THEREFORE I TWITTER?"

Black Twitter tells a powerful story about emerging digital racial literacies and their relationship to a long history of anti-Black information warfare. Through a constellation of hashtags, Black Twitter maps onto archived demonstrations of Black cultural discourse. Its users critically exchange stories about bearing witness to the absurdity of race and racism. These include having humorous discussions about shared racial experiences (#Growingupblack and #ThanksgivingwithBlackFamilies), critiquing Black mis/representation in media and entertainment (#OscarsSoWhite and #CNNBeLike], putting racist White folks on blast (#AskRachel and #PaulasBestDishes], and making structural anti-Black racism more publicly visible (#Icantbreathe, #NotJustUVA, #reclaimOSU, and #BlackLivesMatter]. Such hashtags have generated countless conversation threads that appeal to a vast global network of (presumably and predominantly) Black social media users.[1]

Throughout this chapter, I argue that Black Twitter should be read as a text comprised of narratives about digitally mediated Black cultural preservation and expression. I will show how Black Twitter serves as a living archive of collective

---

1   #BlackLivesMatter has been the most extensively studied hashtag that is associated with Black Twitter. According to one report, "[#BlackLivesMatter] has been used nearly 30 million times on Twitter—an average of 17,002 times per day—as of May 1, 2018." (Anderson et al. Activism in the Social Media Age).

memories of Blackness. It enacts and represents experiences of misidentification, disinformation, alienation, belonging, forgetting, and remembering. These stories represent various forms of testimony that articulate different accounts of how one experiences being Black—our sharing of joy, suffering, and survival through a world that exploits, overlooks, and erases us.

PURPOSE OF RESEARCHING BLACK TWITTER

Although Black Twitter has been researched from various disciplinary perspectives, few studies in rhetoric, composition, and writing studies (RCWS) have examined the significance of this rhetorically complex space. Some notable exceptions include Jacqueline Schiappa's article "#IfTheyGunnedMeDown: The Necessity of 'Black Twitter' and Hashtags in the Age of Ferguson;" Catherine L. Langford and Monténe Speight's "#BlackLivesMatter: Epistemic Positioning, Challenges, and Possibilities;" and Elaine Richardson and Alice Ragland's "#StayWoke: The Language and Literacies of the #BlackLivesMatter Movement." As the titles indicate, this body of research connects Black Twitter to social movements and political protest. In addition, scholarship like Pritha Prasad's "Beyond Rights as Recognition: Black Twitter and Posthuman Coalitional Possibilities" focuses on the multidimensionality of Black Twitter by exploring it as a tributary. She argues that "Black Twitter functions not just as a tool or accompaniment to 'real' protests elsewhere, but rather as an alternatively embodied, relational rhetorical imaginary that affords multiple simultaneous spatialities and temporalities" (7). As Prasad claims, Black Twitter operates variously, its multiple purposes leaking out like several tributaries moving from and towards larger streams.

Furthermore, Keith Gilyard and Adam Banks' rhetorical examination of #BlackTwitter demonstrates the importance of Black English and digital publics in their 2018 book *On African-American Rhetoric.* Their focus on language, power, and persuasion as they relate to the process of recognizing Black identity performance online renders Black Twitter a more culturally rich subject of research. Overall, many rhetorical studies about Black Twitter seem exclusively focused on making claims about the political relationship between blackness and protest. Given the popularity of #BlackLivesMatter, and how this movement has been co-opted by Russian operatives like the Internet Research Agency (IRA), such an emphasis is understandable and necessary. However, I integrate critical technological discourse analysis and rhetorical analysis to more comprehensively study how Twitter and its (human and nonhuman) users reflexively mediate the rich intellectual, aesthetic, and ultimately *persuasive* value of Black Twitter (Brock 1017).

OVERVIEW OF THE CHAPTER

This chapter considers how studies about Black Twitter benefit from "insider knowledge" about Black English (BE), or African American Vernacular English (AAVE). The meaning-making breadth of BE could be easily underestimated by researchers who don't know the cultural contexts and references communicated between users (Abreu). Moreover, researchers studying blackness online, regardless of their race, must check their linguistic biases. BE, or AAVE, continues to face ridicule in the public sphere. Journalists, for example, are quick to show screenshots of "funny" or "woke" tweets without crediting authors.

More problematic still, the fact of Black Twitter affects public opinion about "publics," which influences the credibility of Twitter itself—as a media. Some may casually dismiss the space when comical Black tags like #AskRachel or #Paulas BestDishes are used, but take it extremely seriously when they see #BlackLives Matter or #HandsUpDontShoot. In addition, Black Twitter and its related networks are subject to political sabotage. In 2016, Russian hackers focused primarily on infiltrating and disrupting Black online communities via Twitter, YouTube, Instagram, and Facebook, among several other personal websites, for the purposes of dissuading Black voters from voting for Hilary Clinton, or going to the polls altogether (Carroll and Cohen). Studying Black Twitter, then, offers value to a growing body of scholarship about how social media affects racial identity, political affiliation, and civic engagement. This chapter considers the significance of these contexts through its presentation of a rhetorical criticism of Black Twitter. This method focuses on how Black Twitter functions as a Black rhetorical object, as well as identifies and analyzes key challenges involved in such an investigation.

THEORETICAL FRAMEWORK AND METHODS

But __what__ exactly is Black Twitter? We know it is significant, but the internet scales its categorical multiplicity, affecting the range of its meaning and meaning-making potential. In Zygmunt Bauman's *Liquid Life,* he argues that we live in an age of "Liquid modernity," in which "the conditions under which its members act change faster than it takes the ways of acting to consolidate into habits and routines. [Such a] society, '[. . .] cannot keep its shape or stay on course for long.'" (1). Black Twitter thrives on uncertainty, or the happening, which is why journalists rely on its texts. It enacts the ebb of spontaneous collective response through turbulent forces as movement, place, discourse—sometimes all at once. It is adaptive, dynamic, diasporic, and its traces lead to a stream (Royster). Therefore, I utilize the language of liquidity throughout this chapter to make claims about the "leaky style" of Black Twitter.

To illustrate, Black Twitter leaks on racial injustice and White fragility by starkly representing these realities in virtual and offline worlds. As an alternative media, counter-public, and cultural production happening in real-time, Black Twitter disrupts White hegemony by communicating in Black cultural codes to the masses. It transfers analog cultural practices into memes and messages of up to 280 characters, simultaneously enacting and documenting blackness all up in Twitter. Drawing on Alessandra Raengo's concept of *liquid blackness,* I argue that Black Twitter "emphasiz[es] fluid interchanges between past and current experimentations in the context of transnational artistic and intellectual flows" ("About Liquid Blackness").

On one hand, Black Twitter resists objectification through its liquidity. Its visibility cannot be predicted, nor can the longevity of its content. #BlackLivesMatter, for instance, is a rhetorical statement about how race affects the meaning of political concepts like equality, freedom, democracy, citizenship, and liberation. It articulates that simply inhabiting a Black body constantly puts one at risk of fatal contact with the state. As long as unarmed people continue to lose their lives to police and white nationalist violence, the #BLM hashtag is part of a rich digital media ecology, where the circulation of visual archives produced by citizens and law enforcement influence its significance. As Christopher Carter shows in Chapter 4, discrepancies between citizen and police testimonies are increasingly exposed by the affordances of mobile devices. Feidin Santana made the ethical decision to document Michael Slager shooting Walter Scott in the back (Edwards and Angone; "Michael Slager"; Powell; Helsel).[2] He also testified against Slager in court during a rare instance of a police officer going on trial for killing "on the job." Santana's media intervention strengthened #BLM's persuasive power to verify the truth of injustice. His footage adds meaning to #BLM, which records and contextualizes preventable deaths.

On the other hand, some of Black Twitter's content could be systematically surveillanced and appropriated by organized political agents like the Internet Research Agency (IRA). Blackness, in this virtual public social scene, is just information to weaponize factions among users. The Russian hackers used an assemblage of certain usernames, memes, and hashtags that they imagined represented and signified Black cultural identity (Romano; Starr; U.S. Senate Select Committee on Intelligence). Consequently, Blackness via the internet can be replicated even when it is essentially disconnected from a person who is living while Black. Some have dubbed this practice, and its variations, "digital

---

2   See Feiden Santana, "Man Who Taped Walter Scott Murder Comes Forward," WERE-AM 1490 (http://bit.ly/2LKWg7p); AP News Articles about Michael Slager (https://apnews.com/MichaelSlager); "Ex-South Carolina Cop Michael Slager Gets 20 Years for Walter Scott Killing" (http://cnn.it/3ae5D91).

blackface," which I will discuss later in this chapter (Harmon; "Is It OK to Use Black Emojis and Gifs"; Jackson; Sommer). Nevertheless, Black Twitter and its facilitation of Black folks in conversation can give some users life, which Raengo sees as critical for our survival. She claims that "What is at stake for blackness is not simply a condition of vitality but life. Not liveliness but living. Not simply vibrancy but physical as well as social, cultural, and existential mobility—a life, existence, and mobility that might never register as such" ("Black Matters" 259).

My observations about how Black Twitter exemplifies the dynamics of emergent, leaky contexts of cultural production informed my selection of two methods that are informed by antiracism as a methodology: critical technocultural discourse analysis (CTDA) and Black rhetorical criticism. CTDA, a critical approach developed by communications scholar Andre Brock, can be adapted to address intersections between "technology, cultural ideology, and technology practice" (1014). Brock defines CTDA as a flexible method that depends on critical frameworks like critical race theory and Black feminist theory—as well as "queer theory, critical feminism, Latin@ studies, intersectionality, pan-Africanist, postcolonial, or gender and women's studies"—to disrupt research about technology that fails to decenter whiteness and recognize that the design of technology and information architectures aren't neutral or deterministic (1014; 1017). Brock's discussion of CTDA features an analysis of Twitter, in which he takes into account how Twitter's character limits and SMS capabilities enabled Black people to "retrofit Twitter's brevity, ephemerality, and performativity to signifying' discourse" (1025).

Like Brock, I also analyze Black Twitter's numerous implications for scholarly research about race, racism, and technology. His study about CTDA, however, focuses on theorizing CTDA as a robust method that can adapt to a range of critical frameworks and methodologies that facilitate our understanding of how human beings integrate their cultural discourses with an information communication technology's (ICTs) technical affordances. In this piece, Brock's examination of Black Twitter illustrates how cultural expression operationalizes Twitter as a platform, service, archive, artifact, and text—transforming the website's technical design and usability (1023). These functions also serve both Twitter and its users' multiple discourses, which are used for varying (but often dominant) ideological purposes (1024; 1026). My work seeks to demonstrate that RCWS researchers need to develop more language to communicate about the reflexive relationship between racial ideology, language, culture, and technology. Therefore, this chapter builds on Brock's concise, but comprehensive, look at the analytical depth offered by a CTDA of Black Twitter (1017–8).[3]

---

3   Brock offers a more detailed textual examination of Black Twitter in his article "From the Blackhand Side: Twitter as a Cultural Conversation."

In particular, I extend Brock's CTDA of Black Twitter by using Black rhetorical criticism to further illustrate the importance of resisting characterizations of Black internet users and their discourse as deficient—a point that he discusses in his review of historical literature about the digital divide. As Brock notes,

> These studies reduce the cultural aspects of ICT use to a technologically limited "social" aspect (e.g. "user") while privileging ICT usage of elites as a "norm," leaving unspoken the environmental, social, or cultural ideologies shaping ICT design, expectations, or use. (1014)

In the next few paragraphs, I will discuss how Black rhetorical theory can be incorporated into CTDA for the purposes of studying how Black discourses are performed, preserved, and circulated via Twitter. This analysis "(. . .) focus[es] on the ways that technology users perceive, articulate, and ultimately define the technocultural space in which they operate and exist" (Brock 1016).

First, the "Black" in Black Twitter is a fundamental characteristic of this phenomenon that warrants further analysis. Black is defined by "Black Twitter" in particular ways that emphasize how the condition of being Black is tantamount to possessing a critical consciousness. This kind of mindfulness is expressed by wit, which must bear weight under the restriction of minimal characters. This digital performance of blackness, as such, suggests that Black Twitter needs to be studied as a rhetorical object, and more specifically, as a *black rhetorical object*. Its racial character affects how it makes meaning and the kinds of audiences capable of understanding those meanings enough to engage in those meaning-making processes, or its discourses. Likewise, technologies mediate this blackness in ways that draw our attention to the meaning of being human, belonging to a community, and innovating language.

Next, it matters that I am a relatively young (mid–30s) queer Black Woman researcher from the South. My cultural identity affects how I understand the power of language and communication. In fact, I grew up very close to Grand Saline, which is at the center of James Chase Sanchez's racial literacy narrative (see Chapter 3). Living in Northeast Texas as an adolescent fundamentally shaped my complicated relationship to Black cultural expression. As a result, elements of autoethnography leak throughout this chapter because I will be illustrating my claims to both my "blackness" and "professional identity" through deliberate stylistic shifts. My positionality, then, provides me with some insider knowledge about Black Twitter. I will take rhetorical risks to animate my personal experience and philosophical understanding of its dynamic life. Towards this end, readers should expect my style to occasionally flow between academic standard edited (White) English and Black English.

As previously mentioned, my use of CTDA occurs alongside Black rhetorical analysis. I build upon Adam Banks and Keith Gilyard's rhetorical analysis of Black Twitter as an illustration of contemporary Black rhetoric. Extending their effort, I will demonstrate how Black Twitter defines blackness as fluid, vital, torrential, ubiquitous, and uncontrollable through an examination of specific cases in which its categorical leakiness resulted in authorial conflicts and/or viral user participation. These instances will highlight how Black Twitter articulates blackness through an aesthetic of flowing analog and digital Black expression. Furthermore, these multimodal streams affect the design of cultural critique, which affects "what" is recognized as Black culture and the human beings who produce and circulate it.

The next section of this chapter will discuss key challenges that face RCWS scholars who study race, technology, and rhetoric. The chapter will conclude with a brief summary of recommendations for future research about these topics.

KEY CHALLENGES RESEARCHING "BLACK TWITTER"

Defining Black Twitter

A time comes in nearly every Black internet user's life when they must confront their relationship to this nebulous, powerful entity the grapevine calls "Black Twitter." When I heard the term "Black Twitter" several years ago, I was uncomfortable because I knew that even if I wasn't part of whatever it was, the "Black" in "Black Twitter" could have implications for all us Black folks, whether we wanted it to or not. After all, a major aspect of what it means to be Black is to be denied the ability to be judged as an individual outside of an entire cultural group, and thus unable to speak from a universal "default" perspective. Consequently, I needed to see what Black Twitter was about.

I wondered, "What, categorically, is Black Twitter? Is it a person, place, or thing?" It can be referred to in all three capacities:

1. Black Twitter has the agency of a person.

    Example: "Black Twitter said. . ."

2. Black Twitter, or #BlackTwitter, is a location. It is a "place" in which the hashtag marks a textual digital location that users reference to create archives that can be retrieved to discover how folks be talkin about/making/remembering culture.

    Example: "If you go on Black Twitter. . ."

3. Black Twitter is a happening of certain kinds of talk that occurs often enough that it leads to the creation of a hashtag. The hashtag enables that talk to become recognizable as a thang, or a speech event. It is an unfolding of activity that represents Black interpretations of popular culture (#OscarsSoWhite), current events (#BlackLivesMatter), cultural norms (#GrowingUpBlack), and controversial public figures (#PaulasBestDishes and #AskRachel).

Example: "Black Twitter is blowing up right now. . ."

Investigating Black Twitter was much more difficult than I imagined. Its unpredictable, fluid, and collective nature makes it a bit of a grammatical mess. In addition to its various capacities as a noun, some characterize it as a political movement, a journalistic outlet, and a counter-public (Chatman et. al; Durrani; Freelon et. al; Graham and Smith; Sack). Others denied its existence altogether, as evident in scholarly dialogues and news outlets responding to the question "Does Black Twitter exist?"[4] Categorical debates about whether Black Twitter is real, its agency, and impact reinforced my initial reaction (Neuwitz; Manjoo; McDonald; Mitchell and Hitlin; Opam; Thomas, "Is 'Black Twitter' Dead?"). The fact that Black Twitter is such a virulently contestable rhetorical object reflects that digital performances of blackness intensify similar issues as embodying analog blackness.

For example, one of the primary characteristics of Black Twitter is that it increases the visibility of race, which defies the idea of a post-racial world. The very name "Black Twitter" racializes the entire media of Twitter, as some of its users engage all kinds of public social conversations about race, racism, rhetoric, and culture. On one hand, it functions as a discourse community. "Insiders" seek to make themselves recognizable as Black through symbolic production and exchange with enough layered meanings to differentiate themselves from those who fail to convincingly "pass" as Black because they lack knowledge of this experience. On the other hand, the very fact of its existence invites criticism. Some Twitter users argue that the "Black" in Black Twitter segregates and divides people. This colorblind perspective suggests that talking about race is "racist," or that racial identity has no business in this century.

Other Twitter users, who may also happen to be Black, are concerned that Black Twitter will be misinterpreted as representative of all Black people. These issues align with the offline Black experience as well, since our cultural expression of what it means to be Black via how we talk, dress, wear our hair, walk, create art, consume entertainment, and make a living seems to always be up for

---

4   This question has surfaced in a number of locations including a University of Michigan virtual chat (Szymanski; http://bit.ly/2Ordcki) and a PBS Digital Studios video entitled "The Reason #BlackTwitter Exists (And is Totally Awesome)" (http://bit.ly/3pi1oO3).

a debate. Whether we are too loud, ugly, uppity, unkept, athletic, combative, angry, and/or criminal, these signifiers are ultimately racial. Cultural rituals signifying Black identity tend to measure authenticity on a spectrum of extremes: are you too White or too *Black*? These racial markers of difference apply to actual skin tone (too dark or too light), hair texture (too "nappy" or "good hair"), how you walk (too saggy or too stiff), your name (too ghetto or too proper), and, again, especially whether you talk "ghetto," or if you "sound White."

As racism threatens Black lives, some of Twitter's Black users recognize that Twitter can amplify their voices and provide a space to organize and develop their own distinctive discourses (Florini). They have engaged in so much activity that Black Twitter has become a proper noun. However, as the previous examples illustrate, it can also mean any sense of a noun. Certainly, the rhetorical power of Black Twitter results from its leakiness, or its conceptual ability to move through multiple kinds of message forms, channels, etc.

Confusion over Black Twitter's public image provides the existence for these meditations about its definition. Does it exist? How can we know? Stereo Williams, a writer for the *Daily Beast*, reflects, "So is Black Twitter real? Very much so. But it's interesting to see how the mainstream and 'traditional' media spaces have responded to this relatively new, quite active and dynamic voice." Implicit in this definition is an interest in how various media outlets describe and respond to Black Twitter. If it is a voice, whose is it? How should Black Twitter's users be acknowledged, engaged, and credited by traditional journalistic outlets? By researchers like myself? Others?

Global networked platforms reflect and mediate racial differences, as well as influence the meaning of culture. Such transformations warrant rhetorical study. Social media and its online communities are affecting language practices, and even grammar. In particular, these technologies and their collective users are increasingly granted the same linguistic agency as individual human beings (e.g., "Black Twitter says X"). Therefore, we must pay close attention to how we attribute actions to, as well as how we make claims about the persuasive power of the internet and those who "speak" there. Before I present my rhetorical analysis of specific cases about/involving Black Twitter, the next section will provide some background information about the site Twitter to further contextualize major challenges with researching Black Twitter and contemporary media in general.

ABOUT TWITTER'S TECHNICAL FEATURES

According to its own website's definition, Twitter is "an information network made up of short messages (including photos, videos, and links) from all over the world" (Twitter Glossary). It is comprised of over 300 million users representing over 40 countries (Molina; Perez). Founded in 2006 by Jack Dorsey, Noah Glass, Biz Stone, and Evan Williams, Twitter has managed to survive well into its adolescence. As of 2018, approximately 24 percent of American internet users are on Twitter (Greenwood et al.; Smith and Anderson).[5] Of this percentage, a disproportionate number of users are young, Black, and/or educated (Wojcik and Hughes). Some reports indicate that a significant number of Black people use Twitter—28 percent of total internet users who use Twitter (Duggan et al).[6] However, reports on userd' cultural diversity are limited and vary widely. For example, Pew's latest reports on social media use do not include demographic information about race or ethnicity.

Arguably, Twitter's demographics have led journalists and researchers to associate the medium with deliberative rhetoric. Some argue that it is unreliable for gauging public opinion because almost half of its users identify as politically "liberal" and/or between the ages of 18–29 (Byers). Nevertheless, news outlets recognize its users as engaged in conversations about political campaigns, elections, social protest (#BlackLivesMatter), and controversial social issues (#MeToo). Twitter transforms journalism because as a platform, it is a publisher that affects the mass circulation of texts. In fact, the Apple App Store has been categorizing Twitter as a "news" app since 2016, whereas it had previously labeled it a "social networking" app (Rashidian et al. 91).

The association of Twitter with news and politics likely influences how "Black Twitter" is interpreted. In particular, Twitter is one of the most marginalized social networks. One study found that Twitter is considered an outlier to the U.S. general public for three reasons: its demographics do not represent the population, less than 15 percent of adults use Twitter, and less than five percent reported that they use it regularly (Mitchell and Hitlin). Furthermore, a small percentage of users can control a major topic. A recent 2019 study estimates that "97% of tweets from U.S. adults that mentioned national politics over the study period came from just 10% of users" ("National Politics on Twitter").

Additionally, Twitter's demographics may contribute to Twitter being associated with radical, progressive discourse. The visibility of Black Twitter as a racialized community that often produces counter-discourses might also account for Twitter's marginalization among similar sites. Although it is a popular social media network, it is the least popular among slightly older networks

---

5   See Figure 5.1. It is important to note that these estimates do not include frequency of use. According to one report, "Just 13% of adults said they ever use Twitter or read Twitter messages; only 3% said they regularly or sometimes tweet or retweet news or news headlines on Twitter. [Thus] Twitter users are not representative of the public" (Mitchell and Hitlin).

6   This is the most recent report with demographic information available.

like Facebook (2004), YouTube (2005), and LinkedIn (2003), as well as newer platforms such as Instagram (2010), Pinterest (2010), and Snapchat (2011).

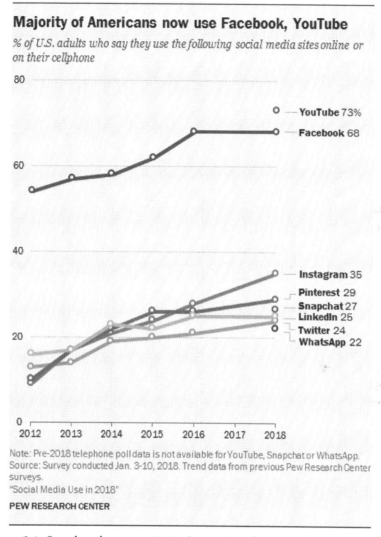

Majority of Americans now use Facebook, YouTube

% of U.S. adults who say they use the following social media sites online or on their cellphone

YouTube 73%
Facebook 68

Instagram 35
Pinterest 29
Snapchat 27
LinkedIn 25
Twitter 24
WhatsApp 22

Note: Pre-2018 telephone poll data is not available for YouTube, Snapchat or WhatsApp.
Source: Survey conducted Jan. 3-10, 2018. Trend data from previous Pew Research Center surveys.
"Social Media Use in 2018"

PEW RESEARCH CENTER

Figure 5.1. Social media use in 2018. Source: Smith and Anderson. Screenshot.

Socio-Technical Features of Black Twitter

Black Twitter interacts with Twitter's socio-technical features in various ways. First, Black Twitter's rapid flow of exchange drives its content to the top of Twitter's trending list, despite occurring among small networks (Brock; Guo; Sharma). Therefore, the feed design of Twitter affects the visibility of Black expression. As

Twitter notes, "Top Tweets are selected through an algorithm, we do not manually curate search results" (Twitter Search Result FAQ).[7] The company's response raises questions about how Twitter's proprietary algorithms work.

Sanjay Sharma further investigates this problem in his article "Black Twitter? Racial Hashtags, Networks and Contagion." He explains that, "[Nonetheless], the *exact* operations of Twitter's *value-laden* algorithm remain hidden by the company, and studies attempting to discover or model its inner-weighting and statistical calculations reveal highly complex computational processes involved in determining which terms trend" (57). Sharma's point is significant because researchers can never be completely sure how users are exposed to different kinds of information. Black Twitter is comprised of a small network of users that are highly networked and very actively engaged for certain durations of time. This means that if the majority of the "Black users" start rapidly talking about a subject at the same time (e.g. #ThanksgivingwithBlackFamilies), the conversation will appear more prominently in their followers' feeds. The more users respond to the content, it will probably start trending—regardless of what other people are talking about on Twitter, and regardless of how many people are talking about those subjects. This affordance of Twitter could play a role in Black Twitter's visibility and presumed popularity.

DISCUSSION OF ADDITIONAL RESEARCH CHALLENGES

Studying race in a place like Twitter presents several additional challenges. First, how do you look for racial identity online? Black Twitter's geography extends beyond the United States since Twitter is a global social network. South Africans could be communicating with Black Twitter alongside African Americans or Puerto Ricans. This potential for international participation inspires diasporic research with a focus on language. For example, some scholars like Taylor Jones and Ian Stewart have used Black Twitter to chart linguistic diversity and location throughout the diaspora (Taylor Jones; Stewart).

Next, RCWS scholars have long needed to innovate the way that our field talks about race, technology, and communication. Claims of a democratic society via a more racially distributed internet were all the rage during Web 1.0 and at the turn of 2.0. Well into the Millennium, internet use was discussed in terms of racial disparities involving access, or the "digital divide" (Banks; Monroe; Wajcman; Warschauer). However, Pew documents that only a marginal gap exists between White, Black, and Hispanic users in the US (Internet/Broadband Fact Sheet 2019).[8]

---

7   Twitter Search Results FAQs. (URL: https://bit.ly/3rJGpFw]

8   See http://pewrsr.ch/3vGxQOt.

Demographics and Internet Use

The fact that some of the access gaps between races have nearly closed affects how we ought to be talking about race and technology at present (See Table 5.1). A study of Black Twitter could help fill gaps that were opened by some of this research. Since nearly every racial group in the US is networked, we must broaden what we mean by "access" on the level of how social media transforms its users' relationship to "the news."[9] For example, "One-in-five U.S. adults say they often get news via social media, slightly higher than the share who often do so from print newspapers (16%)" (Shearer). Increased reliance on social media redefines what counts as news and how internet users will interpret its racialized content.

Table 5.1. Demographics of Broadband Access in the US (2000–2019)[10]

Year	White Users (%)	Black Users (%)	Hispanic Users (%)
2000	53	38	(no data available)
2006	72	59	(no data available)
2012	84	77	79
2018	89	87	88
2019	92	85	86

Another issue with place involves the challenge of discovering information within the platform itself. Re-finding what happens on Black Twitter is far more difficult than it may seem. One might imagine that the scale of Twitter's data capacity would serve researchers well when they are investigating its social functions. However, users should be wary of Twitter's capacity to serve as a reliable archival device.

In their study of 606 Twitter users, Meier and Elsweiler discovered that retrieval rates are very poor. They observed, "58.3% (of respondents) reported having been frustrated by challenging or unsuccessful re-finding task in the past" (137). They also noted that "About 70% of our respondents hold the opinion that Twitter's features for returning to previously viewed content should be improved" (138). Indeed, we must keep the limitations of Twitter's own archival capacity in mind when researching its users' social behaviors (boyd).

Meier and Elsweiler's findings suggest that Twitter generates so much data that some of it ends up lost in an ocean of information. The hashtag, which is employed as an index marker for countless taxonomies of convo streams, isn't

---

9   See http://pewrsr.ch/3s50qqz.

10   Adapted from data in Pew Research's report, "Internet/Broadband Fact Sheet," published on June 12, 2019. See http://pewrsr.ch/3vGxQOt.

always going to yield accurate sortable quantities of results. Black Twitter, then, depends on some degree of synchronicity for its life. Black Twitter's users produce discourses that flow within and outside of the Twitterverse, leaking into mainstream news articles, cross-platform posts, and even the Library of Congress. The scaled collective, distributed nature of Black Twitter's knowledge production makes it difficult to attribute authorship to any single user.

The problem of "who" an author is on Twitter is connected to another socio-technical issue that affects researching race and rhetoric online: the matter of human and non-human users. For example, bots introduce the issue of race and reality (Friedberg and Donovan). The report "Bots in the Twittersphere," published on April 9, 2018, by Pew, defines bots as ". . . accounts that can post content or interact with other users in an automated way and without direct human input" (Wojcik et al.). Bots, apparently, are fully integrated with most internet users' experiences via online social environments. An estimated "two-thirds of tweeted links to popular websites are posted by automated accounts—not human beings" (Wojcik et al.).[11]

How much information is produced by online users that are really even people? Can bots go viral? Can they reproduce texts? When are they questioned? As Wojcik et al. argue, bots participate on social media in numerous ways, including "answering questions about a variety of topics in real time or providing automated updates about news stories or events. . . . they can also be used to attempt to alter perceptions of political discourse on social media, spread misinformation, or manipulate online rating and review systems" (Bots in the Twittersphere). Apparently, "500 most-active suspected bot accounts are responsible for 22% of the tweeted links to popular news and current events sites" (Wojcik et al.). Bots can be programmed with racial biases, as well as to post controversial content about race and racism (Benjamin; Daniel, Cappiello, and Benatallah; Garcia; Noble).

When we browse through political coverage that shows up as trending topics and on prominent features of popular news websites' articles and comment sections, we may not immediately know whether a real human person even authored the information (Stocking and Sumida). The fact that bots, which are created by humans to autonomously generate information, compete against the live active human users remediates racial representation in ways that make truth and reality nearly impossible to know. Who is the folk? How much talk emerges from real life users engaged in a moment of spontaneous deliberation about their experiences and interpretations of reality? How much of that talk is facilitated

---

11   To conduct their study, Wojcik et al. ". . . used a list of 2,315 of the most popular websites and examined the roughly 1.2 million tweets (sent by English language users) that included links to those sites during a roughly six-week period in summer 2017."

by machines persuasively performing human talk? What kinds of human actions does the bot-human interaction generate?

The problem of bots relates to three additional issues with racial performance online—identity tourism, straight-up fraud, and cyber-security. If bots are indistinguishable from human life to some users interacting with them, profile images and cover photos offer additional ways to manipulate users. A Twitter profile that displays an image of a young Black Woman may not necessarily represent its offline user's identity. Identity politics has been unsettled by convincing performances of marginalized identities being expressed by White male users, such as the notorious case of the blog A Gay Girl In Damascus (Hesse).[12] In that bizarre drama, Tom MacMaster—a straight White man in Georgia—ran a popular blog as Amina Araff, a gay Syrian female (Young).[13] After his offline identity was discovered, he was criticized by Paula Brooks, who was supposedly a deaf lesbian editor of Lez Get Real—another popular website (2008–2014).[14] However, similar to MacMaster, Brooks turned out to be Bill Graber—a straight man living in Ohio (Flock and Bell). The hoax baffled internet users because the persuasiveness of their performance sustained communities with thousands of users for years.

A similar fraud occurred on Facebook with a Black Lives Matter group, but with a more familiar motive—money. The group was being administered by a White man living in Australia.[15] Ian Mackay embezzled over $100,000 from the group's approximately 700,000 members (Lockhart). It was the largest #BLM page on Facebook, even after Patrisse Cullors officially reported that it was fake. In addition, Mackay ran numerous #BLM groups, some of which were also popular (well over 40,000 people). He also bought and sold various domains with "pro-Black" language (e.g. blackpowerfist.com). Mackey attempted to justify his fraud, claiming that online racial performance was simply his "personal hobby" (O'Sullivan).[16]

This case of #BLM organizational impersonation powerfully illustrates that studying Twitter cannot occur in a vacuum. The cross-platformed nature of social media means that users navigate these various platforms simultaneously. Moreover, the hashtag serves as both an archival tool, as well as a powerful sign of intertexting among media networks. For example, the CNN report about this massive fraud mostly implicated Facebook for its structural inability to remove the fake group sooner. Facebook claimed that the page didn't violate their "community standards." This inaction occurred alongside Facebook's compliance with

12   See http://wapo.st/3c1Y4Dl.
13   See https://bit.ly/3pogm52.
14   See http://wapo.st/3s7qdia.
15   See http://bit.ly/3s9sgCo.
16   See http://cnn.it/3tzMiWM.

Russian hackers' meddling in U.S. elections, as #BlackLivesMatter was one of the hashtags that the hackers frequently employed to troll and generate divisive deliberation. In addition, scandals like the Cambridge Analytica leaks, which revealed that 50 million users' psychographic profiles were sold to this company despite Facebook's claim to protect user information in its terms and conditions, offer a partial glimpse of a much wider scope of the vulnerabilities inherent in social media design (Cadwalladr and Graham-Harrison). I will analyze these cybersecurity issues in more detail in the next section on specific case studies.

Interestingly, the "woke rhetoric" and movements associated with Black Twitter ended up internationally co-opted in ways that eclipsed the actual size of authentic organizational activity. Who knew the difference between the real/ fake, bot/human performances of racial identity and solidarity? How many scholars and teachers were duped into joining Mackay's groups? Dr. Ethan Zuckerman, Director of MIT's Center of Civic Media, further elaborates on this issue: "Tribalism, manipulation, and misinformation are well-established forces in American politics, all predating the web. But something fundamental has changed. Never before have we had the technological infrastructure to support the weaponization of emotion on a global scale" ("Bigger than Facebook.").[17] To illustrate, the Mueller investigation resulted in several indictments of Russian hackers working for the Internet Research Agency (IRA) to interfere in the 2016 U.S. Election through widespread disinformation campaigns via Twitter, Facebook, YouTube, and Instagram. As I will further discuss later in this chapter, the IRA focused most of its energies on systematically targeting online Black communities by using human users to impersonate Black cultural identities. Their hacking methods are part of a much larger ecosystem of political and financial fraud that depends on users' reliance on social media. This scene and its rhetorical power needs to be addressed more comprehensively by RCWS researchers. These platforms are hardly neutral, as their design affects how users participate and their epistemologies about identity, performance, and technology. We need to know more about the extent to which users trust these networks' (to vet its) published content, as well as how much fraud and corruption affects their behavior, attitudes towards truth, etc. The rest of this section further examines how these ethical issues contribute to the leakiness of race online.

In her article "Cyberrace," Lisa Nakamura challenges readers to consider how digital performances of race during Web 1.0 authorized White users to downplay the reality of racial identity. She explains that "The ability to manipulate the 'look and feel' of race by online role-playing, digital gaming, and other forms of digital-media use encouraged and fed the desire for control over self-construction

---

and self-representation" (1675). The architecture of the internet favored much more anonymity than Web 2.0, which made it easier for users to imagine themselves operating in a democratized space that could work towards destabilizing race and ethnicity.

In Web 2.0, a proliferation of memes and GIFs that present Black people looking "funny" compete for users' attention. Users routinely circulate images of Black celebrities, women, and children showing "attitude"—eye rolling, sucking teeth, and making disapproving glances. This social practice conjures dark memories of the minstrelsy that pervaded the late 19th century throughout the Jim Crow era. Thus, some writers have dubbed it *digital blackface* (Dickey; "Is It OK to Use Black Emojis and Gifs?"; Jackson, "We Need to Talk about Digital Blackface," "Memes and Misogynoir").[18] Memes play a major role in digital identity performances, as their ease of replication and ability to convey memorable "insider" cultural messages make them a very persuasive form of communication. In their report *The Tactics & Tropes of the Internet Research Agency*, DiResta et al. claim that not only are memes "the propaganda of the digital age" but that "the Department of Defense and DARPA has studied them for years because they are a powerful tool of cultural influence, capable of reinforcing or even changing values and behavior" (50). Proving the "authenticity" of one's racial identity when online, then, becomes a major burden on historically marginalized populations, as we will observe in the case of the subreddit BlackPeopleTwitter. It would also be problematic for researchers to uncritically assume that users will utilize their "real names" and that profile photos and meme usage will reveal their actual cultural backgrounds.

ANALYZING THE *LEAKY STYLE* OF BLACK TWITTER

Case Study: The Black Twitter Beat

In 2015, the *LA Times* hired Ph.D. student Dexter Thomas to cover Black Twitter. Before I discuss this story, it is worth noting that during this time, "real journalists" questioned the existence and/or relevance of Black Twitter. The fact that the *LA Times* was willing to devote space to Black Twitter sparked headlines like NPR's 2015 story "'Los Angeles Times' Recognizes Black Twitter's Relevance" and had numerous people hopeful (and doubtful) about what the beat could mean (Bates; Black Enterprise Editors; Opam).

But the gig was legit, according to S. Mitra Kalita, Managing Editor for Editorial Strategy at the *Times*. Kalita argues that "Black Twitter is not a standard journalistic beat. But over the last year, it has emerged as a force in shaping the national

---

18   See https://techcrunch.com/2017/10/01/thoughts-on-white-people-using-dark-skinned-emoji/

discourse about race. It's truly been an emblem of democracy." She continues her praise for Black Twitter, noting that "If folks on Twitter had not shared the body of Michael Brown lying in the street for hours [in Ferguson, Mo.], would we have seen the mainstream media coverage that we later saw?" (Gourarie).

Of the hundreds of verifiable users that actively engage Black Twitter, who are probably more than qualified to write about Black Twitter for a newspaper, the *LA Times* hired Dexter Thomas for the scoop. Thomas seemed skeptical of the job. When Chava Gourarie, from the *Columbia Journalism Review*, interviewed Dexter Thomas about his new gig with the *Times*, Thomas remarked, "As soon as somebody named Black Twitter, it became a thing that could be exploited." His words culminated in a self-fulfilling prophecy.

Thomas' gig with the *LA Times* was very short-lived. His first (and last) article for the *LA Times*, "When Black Twitter Sounds Like White Twitter," critiqued the liberatory potential of Black Twitter because numerous memes and tweets mocked the rapper Tyga for having a sexual relationship with a transgender porn actress. Folks clapped back hard at Thomas for oversimplifying Black Twitter as transphobic with evidence that consisted of some bad tweets (Eromosele; Kenneally; Magee).

For these critics, Thomas wasted an opportunity to represent the complexity, depth, and cultural impact of Black Twitter (Bossip Staff; Clark, "The 'Black Twitter' Beat"; Lemieux; Vasilogambros and the National Journal). Even if Thomas would have only highlighted that the fact of his position vividly showed that whatever Black Twitter was, it was a fierce journalistic force, and probably for the better (than the mainstream!). Needless to say, the Black Twitter beat was an example of what academics and journalists ought not do.

One major reason that the *LA Times* failed to effectively report on Black Twitter is because Black Twitter itself is referred to as a journalistic source. As previously discussed, the popular hashtag #BlackLivesMatter (aka #BLM) continues to drive media coverage about race, culture, and violence. Through #BLM, Black Twitter came to be associated with the torrents of global antiracist protests, which generated considerable news coverage. In their lengthy report *Beyond the Hashtags*, Freelon, McIlwain, and Clark argue that "Black Twitter" is a widely-discussed cultural phenomenon that overlaps with BLM but remains distinct from it" (8). Thus, examining the power of this hashtag enables us to observe how Black Twitter influences racial discourses across platforms and media. For instance, one computational analysis claims that

> #BlackLivesMatter has become an archetypal example of modern protests and political engagement on social media: A new Pew Research Center analysis of public tweets finds the

hashtag has been used nearly 30 million times on Twitter—
an average of 17,002 times per day—as of May 1, 2018."
(Anderson et al.)

Throughout their report, Freelon et al. trace the evolution of #BLM. Trayvon
Martin's death in 2014, alongside the deaths of other unarmed Black persons,
including Renisha McBride and Marlene Pinnock, inspired Alicia Garza, Opal
Tometi, and Patrisse Cullors to dub the hashtag #BlackLivesMatter. Freelon
et al.'s study examined 40.8 million tweets happening over the course of a year—
from June 2014-June 2015 (10). They break up their analysis of these tweets
into nine phases that mark major spikes in tweet activity, which is indicated by
the hashtag #BLM and affiliated hashtags like #Ferguson, #ripericgarner, #mike-
brown, #handsupdontshoot, #shutitdown, #tamirrice, #icantbreathe, #walter-
scott, #michaelslager, #ericharris, #freddiegray, #policebrutality, etc. users.

#BlackLivesMatter appeared in almost 30,000 tweets in the month of June
2014 that year before blowing up to over 200,000 tweets by early August 2014
(Freelon et al. 36–37). Eric Garner's death on July 17, 2014, was intensified by Michael Brown's death, which culminated in a torrent of tweets about
#BlackLivesMatter. Brown's death on August 9, 2014, inspired over 20,000,000
tweets (42). After the Ferguson protests, BLM tweets don't spike again until a
few months later when Tamir Rice is gunned down in the park by police officers, an event which corresponded to the non-indictment of Officer Darren
Wilson, who killed Michael Brown. Almost 10,000,000 tweets emerge during
this time, and of particular note is that the date of Wilson's release "[November
24, 2014] saw the highest total tweet volume of any single day in the entire
dataset: 3,420,934 tweets" (55). BLM activity didn't increase because of police
killings again until Walter Scott was shot in the back in April 2015.

Freelon et al. claim that "BLM is an apt test case for the idea that social
media uniquely benefits oppressed populations" (8). They also argue that "YBT
[Young Black Twitter] serves as young Black people's CNN, to paraphrase Public
Enemy frontman Chuck D" (40). Indeed, several researchers have focused on
the liberatory uses of Black Twitter (Bonilla and Rosa; Chaudhry; Hill; Langford and Speight; Richardson and Ragland; Schiappa). I hesitate to call Black
Twitter radical, however, because nothing is more radical in offense or detriment
to human survival than white patriarchal cultural supremacy and its norms of
violence, which most intensely coerce compliance—also known as respectability—from Black, Brown, Red, and other persons of color. Resisting radical acts
such as racial segregation and colorblindness should not be considered inherently radical, but a logical response to surviving in a racially, gendered, and
economically segregated society.

Race and racism are more publicly visible in the past several years than a few decades ago (Horowitz et al.). However, Black people are more likely to connect these issues to their cultural identity (Barroso). As one study notes, "Blacks are especially likely to think social media magnify issues that are not usually discussed in other venues. Fully 80 percent of Black people say the statement 'social media highlight important issues that might not get a lot of attention otherwise' describes these sites well" (Anderson et al. 11). This view of Black Twitter as necessary sharply contrasts with a polling of White users who ". . . are more likely than either blacks or Hispanics to assert that social media distracts people from issues that are truly important or that these sites make people believe they are making a difference when they really are not" (11). Although Black Twitter might inspire political movements like #BlackLivesMatter and #SayHerName, this communication remains part of the archives of a racially mixed Twitter. As a corporation with an obvious interest in brokering data, Twitter in and of itself liberates no one. Its users participate for all kinds of purposes, enlivening it, which will animate, reflect, and perpetuate all kinds of stratification and resistance to it.

Moreover, the inextricable relationship between journalists and what the general public understands as Black Twitter is critical for the preservation of #BlackTwitter activity itself. Screenshots provide the most reliable method of documenting tweets that recirculated the most during the dialogue life of a given hashtag. The specific hashtags that I have analyzed throughout this chapter were ones that I was personally familiar with. As a Black Twitter user who rarely participates in #BlackTwitter's languaging, I certainly lurk on my feed when a hashtag about Black life starts to trend. My networks may start posting about a trending hashtag, which was definitely the case with #BlackonCampus. As an academic representing historically oppressed populations, I'm especially interested in how we talk about race, oppression, and education. As Carter describes in chapter four, I routinely observed and experienced racism in our shared location of the predominantly white public southwest institution—University of Oklahoma. Our discussion about me being #BlackonCampus occurred before Twitter became widespread. My testimony remained local, and even suspicious, before its plausibility exploded through the imagery of SAE's white male fraternity members joyfully singing in praise of lynching Black people. Researching digital blackness then, or topics involving race and technology, relies on mixed methods of interpretation (Brock, "Critical Technocultural Discourse Analysis"; Prendergast). On one hand, I need to understand the limitations of Twitter's retrieval mechanisms. Additionally, I need to know a thing or two about Black cultural communication and lived experience.

Case Study: Russians Hack COINTELPRO 2.0

This section briefly explores two major events that will illustrate how being Black online and being Black in real life will subject a person to scaled oppression. First, Russian hackers disproportionately targeted Black online communities during the 2016 U.S. presidential election. Second, the moderators for r/BlackPeopleTwitter, a subreddit community of four million members, asked its members to verify their race. During the Robert Mueller investigation, he issued an indictment against the Internet Research Agency (IRA) and twelve of its operatives.[19] The IRA was indicted for multiple counts of fraud and theft (Internet Research Agency Indictment). These include:

1. Conspiracy to defraud the US (count 1)
2. Conspiracy to commit wire fraud and bank fraud (count 2)
3. Aggravated identity theft (counts 3–8)

According to the indictment, the IRA successfully infiltrated numerous online communities via social media, including Twitter, and other internet-based media. They began executing their strategy to create discord in the U.S. political system in 2014. This operation included meddling in the 2016 election, specifically for the purposes of supporting then-candidate (now former president) Donald J. Trump. To accomplish this objective, they developed and executed a vigorous anti-Clinton campaign (Mueller 17). Equipped with millions of dollars from organizations controlled by Yevgeny Vitasovic Prigozhin (Пригожин Евгений Викторович) and hundreds of operatives, the IRA's activities were vast.

In particular, some of the defendants lied about their identities to obtain visas to enter the US for the purposes of gathering intelligence (12). These defendants gathered intelligence from Nevada, California, New Mexico, Colorado, Illinois, Georgia, Michigan, Louisiana, Texas, and New York (Mueller 13). All of the defendants directed, developed, and/or administered methods for concealing and inventing identities. They used virtual private networks (VPNs) to conceal their identities, stole social security numbers, dates of birth, and email addresses

19   The IRA concealed its political and electoral interference operations through several Russian entities "including Internet Research LLC, MediaSintez LLC, GlavSet LLC, MixInfo LLC, Azimut LLC, and NovInfo LLC" (Mueller 5). Funds were supplied by an organization called Concord Management and Consulting, LLC, as well as multiple affiliates (e.g., Concord Catering) that are "related Russian entities with various Russian government contracts" (6). Concord concealed funds through 14 bank accounts in the names of these affiliates: Glavnaya Liniya LLC, Merkuriy LLC, Obshchepit LLC, Potentsial LLC, RSP LLC, ASP LLC, MTTs LLC, Kompleksservis LLC, SPb Kulinariya LLC, Almira LLC, Pishchevik LLC, Galant LLC, Rayteks LLC, and Standart LLC (7).

from real people, as well as created and used fake driver's licenses and email addresses (4–5). This information was used to open social media and PayPal accounts, which were used to purchase ads and maintain accounts (4–5, 15–16). They also coordinated political rallies with real political organizers in New York, D.C., Florida, North Carolina, and Pennsylvania (20, 22–23, 30).

The IRA began targeting Black online communities in 2016. The effort was part of the "translator project," which focused specifically on the U.S. populations on social media. More than 80 employees were assigned to this project.[20] The purpose of this strategy was to "encourage U.S. minority groups not to vote in the 2016 U.S. presidential election or to vote for a third-party U.S. presidential candidate" (Mueller 18). The defendants appealed to expressions of "political intensity"— "supporting radical groups, [and engaging] users dissatisfied with [the] social and economic situation and oppositional social movements" (Mueller 14). For example, some of the ads they purchased featured text such as "You know, a great number of black people support us saying that #HillaryClintonIsNotMyPresident" and "Hillary Clinton Doesn't Deserve the Black Vote" (20). They also created at least a dozen websites "with names like blackmattersus.com, blacktivist.info, blacktolive.org and blacksoul.us" (Shane and Frenkel). In 2017, the IRA shifted its focus on online Black users from Facebook and Twitter to Instagram. "Approximately 40% of its [Instagram] accounts achieved over 10,000 followers (a level colloquially referred to as 'micro-influencers' by marketers); twelve accounts had over 100,000 followers ('influencer' level)" (DiResta et al. 26).

The IRA learned how to cultivate online personas through detailed surveillance. They focused on certain group pages and individualized posts (Mueller 15). The defendants "tracked certain metrics like the group's size, the frequency of content placed by the group, and the level of audience engagement with that content, such as the average number of comments or responses to a post" (12). They also "tracked the size of the online U.S. audiences reached through posts, different types of engagement with the posts (such as likes, comments, and reposts), changes in audience size, and other metrics" (15). Moreover, they relied on human feedback, regarding how to make posts seem more "authentic." They frequently consulted about "[the correct] ratios of text, graphics, and video to use in posts; the number of accounts to operate; and the role of each account (for example, differentiating a main account from which to post information

---

20   The indictment describes the various defendants' participation in the IRA's targeting of U.S. minority populations. This specific strategy was directed by Dzheykhun Nasimi Ogly Aslanov (Асланов Джейхун Насими Оглы) a.k.a. Jayhoon Aslanov a.k.a. Jay Aslano. and coordinated by Gleb Igorevich Vasilchenko (Васильченко Глеб Игоревич), Irina Viktorovna Kaverzina (Каверзина Ирина Викторовна), and Vladimir Venkov (Венков Владимир).

and auxiliary accounts to promote a main account through links and reposts)" (15). These methods enabled some of their social media accounts to grow to hundreds of thousands of followers. For instance, @TEN_GOP received over 100,000 followers (15).

Unfortunately, big tech companies did not provide enough information on detailed interactions to draw accurate conclusions about which of the IRA's communication tactics worked best. As DiResta et al. point out, "None of the data sets provided by [the] Facebook, Twitter, or Google included comments, and it is impossible to gauge how many followers the pages attracted— or how many disagreements they provoked—through the strategic use of either inter-linking, or divisive hashtags" (49). Nevertheless, Table 5.2 summarizes some of the impressions the Russian hackers obtained from their racialized disinformation campaign.

Table 5.2. IRA's Targeting of Online Black Communities—Social Media Impressions

Date of Operations	Platform	Accounts/Pages/Personas	# of Followers/ People	# of Engagements
2015–2017	Twitter	3,841 accounts	1.4 million	73 million
2015–2017	Instagram	@blackstagram	300,000	187 million
January 2015– August 2017	Facebook	30 pages Blacktivist	1.2 million	76.5 million
September 2015–July 2017	YouTube	1,063 videos • Don't Shoot • BlacktoLive • Black Matters • Starling Brown • Stop Police Brutality • A Word of Truth (Williams and Kalvin)		

Notes: (1) Adapted from Shane & Frenkel and DiResta et al. (2) Follower totals are approximate.

The IRA's successful cyber-operations resemble a long tradition of the U.S. government's own tactics for disrupting and dissolving "radical" political movements. Their objective of launching "information warfare against the United States of America" was made possible by our own government's historically continuous use of race and racism to create disinformation that destroys trust in communities (Internet Research Agency Indictment; Moore). As of March 1968, at least 41 field offices were directed by J. Edgar Hoover to expand the operations of COINTELPRO (counter-intelligence-program) (Church Committee 87; Federal Bureau of Investigation).

This program sought to destroy "militant," or "extremist," Black organizations, as well as a number of other "subversive" domestic groups such as the American Indian Movement (AIM) and the Ku Klux Klan. In the letter, Hoover explains that the program's purpose is to "expose, disrupt, misdirect, discredit, or otherwise neutralize the activities of Black nationalist hate-type organizations and groupings, their leadership, spokesman, membership, and supporters, and to counter their propensity for violence and civil disorder" (Churchill and Vander Wall 58; Federal Bureau of Investigation[21]). According to its final report on domestic spying during the entire 20th century, the Senate Select Committee to Study Governmental Operations with Respect to Intelligence Activities concluded that "Between 1960 and 1974, the FBI conducted over 500,000 separate investigations of persons and groups under the 'subversive' category, predicated on the possibility that they might be likely to overthrow the government of the United States" (Church Committee 22).

COINTELPRO was atomically destructive to the Black community. It annihilated our ability to organize against the status quo without an extreme state-sponsored retaliation (Brown; Shakur). The FBI approved nearly 40 proposals for their targeting of "black nationalists" (Church Committee 98). The Church Committee argued that "These operations utilized dangerous and unsavory techniques which gave rise to the risk of death and often disregarded the personal rights and dignity of the victims" (98). Alongside the physical "neutralization" of Black Power movement leaders like Alprentice "Bunchy" Carter, John Jerome Huggins,[22] and Fred Hampton,[23] Hoover's methods included the most powerful uses of information—discrediting an individual (Shetty). Distorting others' perception of a person's character would enable Hoover to direct the program towards "Preventing groups and leaders (nationalists) from gaining 'respectability' by discrediting them to the 'responsible' Negro community, to the white community and to Negro radicals" (qtd. in Churchill and Vander Wall). Creating intra-racial divides was also a central part of the FBI's COINTELPRO practices—countless examples of requests to write "anonymous" articles to disrupt Socialist Worker Party (SWP) activity

---

21   See http://bit.ly/313NdT2.

22   See http://bit.ly/38Zx31F.

23   See http://bit.ly/2Pdp4qI.

are further discussed in Blackstock's *COINTELPRO* and Ward Churchill and Jim Vander Wall's *Agents of Repression*.

COINTELPRO's tactics have also been utilized by misogynist groups organized across online platforms like 4Chan, Reddit, Tumblr, and Twitter. For example, in 2014, #EndFathersDay was a popular hashtag that originated on 4Chan to create discord within and among Black and White feminists. At the same time as the IRA was in the process of executing its translator project, and several months before Gamergate, Shafiqah Hudson noticed that the #EndFathersDay hashtag was circulating with messages composed in badly written Black English. According to Rachelle Hampton, the post didn't sound like anyone she knew and the account wasn't following anyone in her Black feminist networks or Black Twitter. One read, "#EndFathersDay" . . . "until men start seeing they children as more than just 'fuck trophies'"(Hampton). Fake Twitter accounts included handles like "@NayNayCantStop, @LatrineWatts, and @CisHate, and bios like "Queer + black + angry'" (Hampton; Caldwell).

Hudson organized her efforts to expose these fake accounts with the hashtag #YourSlipisShowing, which is a double entendre that most Black people might recognize as a caution issued to you by your grandmother. Don't get caught slipping cuz you being leaky. In other words, the phrase "refers to something that's meant to be concealed but is, embarrassingly, on full display" (Hampton). Quoting Hudson, Rachelle Hampton reports, "One of my favorite aspects of #YourSlipIsShowing is that it's funny," [she explained.] "It's something that your meemaw would say, it's church. I love that something that your big ma would say to you is essentially weaponized. That's the kind of world I want to live in, where you can combat true maliciousness and racism and ick with good manners and good humor." Indeed, the hashtag also captured the attention of To l'Nasah Crockett, who noticed the #EndFathersDay posts on Tumblr and started searching for the source.

Crockett found and posted screenshots, with the hashtag #YourSlipisShowing, of 4Chan threads describing their info war against Black Women on no uncertain terms (Broderick). Hampton references various examples in the following quote. "Users said things like 'I've had hundreds of nigs chimp out at me over this [fake tweet]. This turned out way better than expected :)'" and "'the more you do it the less effective it is going to be when we launch a proper attack. making them question each other is great but i want to make them hate each other.'" Fortunately, #YourSlipisShowing gained major traction among Black feminists with a popular social media presence (e.g., Feminista Jones and Jamilah Lemieux). It also enabled Crockett and Hudson to connect outside of the Twitterverse. Through Hudson's invention and determination, "[Black feminists] had documented a small army of fake accounts numbering in the hundreds—accounts that users could not only cross-reference with their followers but also mass-report to Twitter" (Hampton).

The #EndFathersDay hoax provides a useful case for further study about how racism and sexism are exploited as a rhetorical and political strategy. However, these same systems are a liability. The trolls revealed their disdain for Black Women through their poor imitation of them. It was their reliance on stereotypes that alerted and appalled Hudson, Crockett, and others who knew full well that they were being attacked. Meanwhile, Hudson credits her academic training for enabling her to exhaustively research #EndFathersDay and establish links between the fake accounts. Unfortunately, Hudson has mixed feelings about the exigencies for creating the hashtag and being erased for her digital labor—work that misogyny and racism compelled her to do for free as a matter of survival. Although #YourSlipisShowing received some national attention through celebrities like Samantha Bee, who only acknowledged the hashtag—not its founder, Hudson felt "sadness . . . and vindication . . . as well as 'extra broke' and at a loss as to how to turn this work into income" (Hampton).

Black feminists like Hudson and Crockett should be credited with the massive amount of work they do to correct misinformation. Despite their coverage in Hampton's article, "The Black Feminists Who Saw the Alt-Right Threat Coming," Black feminists lack positive and significant mainstream attention. As the scope of data warfare includes more and more globally distributed and expansive campaigns, however, Black Women's experiences are fundamentally shaped by being routinely subject to surveillance and harassment in any digital or analog environment (Barlow; Sherri Williams). Black feminists have always had to use emerging media to labor over counter-strategies to combat both physical and informatic violence, especially negative representations of Black Women (Davis; Lockett; E. Richardson; Royster). Our critical perspective derives from being forced to consciously protect ourselves at all times, which prepares us to defend ourselves against anti-Black Woman data.

The vitriolic speech of radical conservative online groups has been downplayed for years. Arguably, the IRA's strategy was made possible by the silence surrounding the large and disproportionate amount of harassment experienced by women and racial/ethnic minorities via social media. In addition, examining the IRA's disruptive tactics within the context of COINTELPRO's history reminds us to recognize how racial division has long been institutionalized by the U.S. government's defense policy (Blain; Harriot; Mock; Starr). If living under the heavy weight of racial tension were not Americans' sociopolitical reality, the IRA would not have been able to secure large audiences that distrust the government enough for their hackers to leverage users' suspicion of "others." The IRA's intense focus on destroying Hillary Clinton's reputation, combined with its impersonation of Black internet users, builds on a surveillance paradigm from the auction blocks of the 18th century to COINTELPRO of last century. The problem of misinformation has long made Black people suspicious of the political system and each other. In the 21st century, Black internet users must face the general challenges of discovering truth while drowning in oceans of data. However, they are also subject to systematic manipulation that amplifies the global scale of anti-Black violence. In the next example, I'll examine another instance of how Black users have resisted information warfare.

CASE STUDY: DIGITAL SKINFOLKS, RACE, AND ONLINE SPACES

Similar to Hudson and Crockett, many Black Twitter users have been critical of how White Twitter users appropriate Black Twitter's language practices—of "talking back and talkin' Black." It frustrates them to spend time and energy doing emotional and intellectual work such as entertaining trolls, bots, and fake user accounts. Moreover, it is exhausting to engage and avoid people who casually use BE and express themselves with Black people in memes even though their experiences with Blackness may solely be digital. On Reddit, a large Black community had absolutely had it. r/Black People Twitter is Reddit's 59th most popular subreddit—consisting of approximately four million users—that "relies on a simple idea: screenshotting tweets, usually jokes, from black Twitter users" (Sommer).[24]

As an April Fool's joke, in 2019, the moderators of the group asked users to verify their race by sending in evidence of their skin tone by taking a photo of their forearm with their Reddit username and a timestamp. Users were told that they may also include certain food, educational, household, and personal items in their photos to prove that they are Black in offline reality (/r/BlackPeopleTwitter is Open).[25] The joke did its critical work, receiving outcry from White Reddit users who quickly commented that the moderators' actions were racist, even as it sparked the creation of the (now deleted) group /r/SubforWhitePeopleOnly.[26] However, the moderators defended their actions, claiming, "We cannot turn off the screens of our blackness or unsubscribe from racism" (/r/BlackPeopleTwitter is Open).[27] In response to the call to prove their analog Black identities, thousands of Black Reddit users sent in pictures of their forearms for verification. The moderators put a checkmark beside the users' names to confirm their identity and make it easier for users to filter their online experience. Users with a checkmark are permitted to participate in restricted forums via the r/BPP's Country Club—named

24 View the subreddit at https://www.reddit.com/r/BlackPeopleTwitter/
25 See http://bit.ly/3skEUi1.
26 See http://bit.ly/3r7X3hw.
27 See http://bit.ly/3skEUi1.

after a space that has historically excluded Black people and continues to do so.

The moderators' controversial surveillance practices attracted some national journalistic coverage in *The New York Times* and *The Daily Beast*, as well as the conservative blog *Pluralist*. The headlines illustrate the writers' discomfort with the idea. Amy Harmon wrote two articles about it: "Discussing Blackness on Reddit? Photograph Your Forearm First" and "Prove You're Not White: For an Article About Race-Verification on Reddit, I Had an Unusual Request." Will Sommer composed "Reddit's BlackPeopleTwitter Forum Wants to Know If Its Users Are Actually White," and the *Pluralist* published "Anti-Racist Reddit Forum Asks Users to Send in Photos to Prove They're Not White." Harmon's and Sommer's articles discuss the racism that drove the moderators' willingness to take dramatic measures to express its users' refusal to continue being digitally "gaslighted" (language used by former moderator Wesley Moreno) by scores of White users who would belittle the Black experience (Harmon).

For instance, "The forum's millions of subscribers have been able to stay friendly in the comments on a post about cooking or dating, but if someone mentions a political issue like racial profiling, white people have flooded the comments to say they didn't see what the big deal was" (Sommer). Harmon offers more specific examples:

> A comment on a post about a first-generation black college student's entry to Harvard Medical School—"you'll be attending thanks to affirmative action"—received hundreds of "upvotes" before it was removed by a moderator. In conversations about police violence, allusions to "black on black crime," carrying the false implication that black people break the law more often, would float to the top. ("Discussing Blackness on Reddit"[28])

The *Pluralist* acknowledged, but minimized, the moderators' concerns, focusing on how "everybody" finds the policy to be too exclusive. They reported that "The decision has sparked heavy backlash from Reddit users—Black and white—who feel that the policy exemplifies the same type of discrimination the moderators are protesting."

The nature of the r/BlackPeopleTwitter policy, and the moderators' desire to provide a "safe" space for the group's users in the absence of a site-wide policy against hate speech, exposes numerous issues that summarize the key challenges discussed in the prior section of this chapter. Black internet users must put in a considerable amount of unpaid cultural, intellectual, and emotional work into how they communicate in predominantly White platforms like Reddit and

---

28 See https://bit.ly/3rbOv97.

Twitter. Moderators spend hours and hours removing inflammatory posts. Fortunately, r/BlackPeopleTwitter illustrates that social media ecologies integrate platforms in ways that help us retrieve data. The group consists of Twitter screenshots, offering a record of what Black Twitter be doing. Without the group, amid Twitter's imperfect retrieval capacity, we'd have to rely on even more limited representation of "Black Twitter" via anonymous handpicked lists and blogs (66 Most Hilarious Posts; Arceneaux; Lewis; OMG Black People).

The desire to connect with other Black folks and allies situates many Black users in a conflict between online and offline racial embodiment. The fact that hundreds of users were willing to sacrifice their anonymity and privacy in exchange for "real" communication online illustrates that we have hit a critical impasse for reckoning with the realities of living in Marshall McLuhan's "global village," or what Martin Luther King Jr. dubbed the "world house." King recognized that racism and technological "progress" could not co-exist and lead to integration and liberation. He argued, "Our hope for creative living in this world house that we have inherited lies in our ability to re-establish the moral ends of our lives in personal character and social justice. Without this spiritual and moral reawakening, we shall destroy ourselves in the misuse of our own instruments" (*Where Do We Go from Here*). King further claimed that "As early as 1906 W.E.B. DuBois prophesied that 'the problem of the twentieth century will be the problem of the color line.' Now as we stand two-thirds into this exciting period of history we know full well that racism is still that hound of hell which dogs the tracks of our civilization." At present, we are over twenty years into a new century, and information warfare based on racial divisiveness has scaled to match the nuclear power from which contemporary information communications technologies emerged.

Overall, each of these case studies exposes the precariousness of our economic position and anxieties induced by internationalized digitally networked racism and military missions. Thomas took on a journalism hustle as a Ph.D. student in an unfamiliar industry and disparaged Black Twitter's character to distance himself from being associated with its "foolishness." Russian hackers took advantage of the problem of digital blackface and cyber-minstrelsy by weaponizing conspiracy theories, Black solidarity (e.g., to support Black-owned business), and data illiteracy. Black feminists exposed how racist sexist web communities have been weaponizing information against Black Women years before the 2016 U.S. election. Their experiences foreshadowed the potential of an organization like the IRA to launch its comprehensive attack against U.S. internet users. Moderators of r/BlackPeopleTwitter deviated from web 1.0's most sacred values of anonymity and "free speech," creating their own rules for antiracist space that would offer users an opportunity to take pleasure in and celebrate the humor, beauty, and overall brilliance of Black culture.

Case Study: Black Twitter and the
Black Rhetorical Perspective

This chapter has explored some of the fascinating problems of studying Black Twitter: how is new media shifting relationships between bots and humans, researchers and journalists, cultural critics and activists, intelligence organizations and the public—all of whom rely and compete with one another to shape the terms of conversation about the subject? In this section, I'll shift from these macro-level issues and focus on some specific examples of Black Twitter communications, demonstrating an analysis that showcases a Black rhetorical perspective.

Web 2.0 technologies' advancement of ubiquitous surveillance remediates the historical relationship between surveillance and Black people. Within this scene, in which a proliferation of platforms exists for billions of internet users to share information about their personal lives and cultural affiliations, Black expression continues to be scrutinized. Black Twitter complicates post-racial narratives of a colorblind society because its primary speech acts revolve around the speech event of how to eloquently demonstrate (authentic) blackness. This network takes advantage of racialized surveillance politics to expose aspects of Black collective intelligence.

Black Twitter's politics of race and location are an extension of offline embodied blackness. Digital blackness can be recursively retrieved via Twitter and a search engine like Google if users are familiar with any of its codes, courtesy of a hashtag. Black Twitter's contestable classification tells a story about the racial politics of its very existence in a White-dominated cyberspot like Twitter. To be such an obviously raced phenomenon within the context of Trump's America signifies a straddling of American legacies—the persistence of segregationism through boutique multiculturalism on one hand and colorblindness as a consumer culture's pitiful vision of antiracism on the other. Clay and Evans describe this context in the chapter "#Blacknessbelike: White Racial Framing and Counter-Framing on Twitter's Digitally-Contested Cyberspace." They argue,

> Perceptions of race neutrality and colorblindness permeate mainstream thought and mask racial framing, discrimination, and experiences with oppression, and thus construct race inequality as the result of non-racial politics. This powerful ideology of colorblindness attempts to remove the significance of race and racism by framing race-related issues as resulting from a natural tendency to segregate, individualism, and the belief that things have greatly improved in the lives of black people. (217)

Indeed, the very existence of a Black Twitter illustrates how distributed networked users connect over rhetorical displays of blackness. Hashtags like #WhiteFeminism, #ThanksgivingwithBlackFamilies, #BlackHogwarts, #IfIdieinPoliceCustody, #BlackonCampus, and #HandsupDontShoot do not require a user to be part of Twitter to quickly recognize these assertions as "keeping it all the way real" about the fact of a racial narrative animating BIPOC lives. The critique may be a "call out" like Mikki Kendall's creation of #SolidarityisforWhiteWomen, which provides countless examples of how gender solidarity has long been compromised by racism. Being a so-called "woke White woman" doesn't mean that you will be capable of recognizing when your best interests don't serve non-White women or how all women's oppression ought to be acknowledged *as both raced and gendered* when oppression is theorized and discussed. (See Figures 5.2 and 5.3.)

Figure 5.2. Example of a popular Black Twitter user critiquing White feminism with a hashtag that she invented that spread to mass audiences and obtained global coverage.

Figure 5.3. Example of a Twitter user critiquing #whitefeminism in mainstream media coverage.

#IfIdieinPoliceCustody, #HandsupDontShoot, and #BlackonCampus are part of a stream of hashtags about the problematic relationship between police brutality and race. #BlackLivesMatter, which I analyzed in detail in the case study of Thomas and the *LA Times*, organizes the rhetorical purpose of these hashtags because they name the state as a causal force in the annihilation of Black people. Survival as an exigence of racialized talk moved these hashtags outside of the Twittersphere and into paperwork for 501(c)(3) organizations (e.g., the Black Lives Matter Global Network and #SayHerName).

However, the survival of Black culture depends on disputing the myth of a post-racial US. Although the popularity of #BlackLivesMatter associates Black Twitter with identifying anti-Black violence as an unfortunate consequence of being Black in the world, it is also defined by comedy (Sicha). #ThanksgivingwithBlackFamilies offers a self-deprecatingly humorous examination of Black life. These GIF-driven memes (the most popular ones show moving images, which is not conducive to a text-format essay), verify the idea of CPT (colored people time), the centrality of mac and cheese in the Thanksgiving Day menu in most Black households of various social class statuses, as well as how prone we are to mismatched Tupperware. (See Figures 5.4–5.6.)

Figure 5.4. Reference to Will Smith, known for his dramatic facial expressions and humorous personality, in the popular 1990s sitcom The Fresh Prince of Bel Air.

Figure 5.5. Reference to Tiffany "New York" Pollard, known for having an attitude and endlessly waiting on her unrequited lover Flavor Flav on the popular reality show Flavor of Love (2006).

Figure 5.6. How lots of Black folks' refrigerators be looking during the holidays.

Other hashtags that tap into a user's identification with Black culture include visualizing representations of Black people in predominantly White popular media. #BlackHogwarts eloquently re-imagines J.K. Rowling's Potterverse in ways that highlight the role of racial critique in Black cultural life. Harry Potter has its own raced narrative of wizardry through the battle between pure-bloods—natural born witches—and those who lack this ancestry—the muggles (or mudbloods if you want to be the most offensive about it). Most folks in this world are mixed blood, including Harry Potter, but pure-blood remains a sign of the elite in the HP world. An analogue to Nazis or the KKK, a not-so-secretive, but underground, organization of pure-blood supremacists called the Death Eaters inevitably chart HP's final battle to defeat Lord Voldemort. Of course, seeing HP readers weigh in on what a #BlackHogwarts would be like constitutes the kind of rhetorical action that defines #BlackTwitter as a site of Black cultural memory that is linked to but not segregated from the mainstream. (See Figures 5.7–5.9.)

Figure 5.7. Another Reference to Will Smith (See figure 5.4), known for his confidence and humor in the popular 1990s sitcom The Fresh Prince of Bel Air.

Figure 5.8. Images of globally impactful, and untimely (and unfortunately) deceased rappers Tupac Shakur (left) and Christopher George Latore Wallace, also known as Notorious B.I.G, Biggie, or Biggie Smalls. Screenshot.

Figure 5.9. Another reference to Tiffany "New York" Pollard (see figure 5.5). In this image, she's gratefully accepting a clock that will allow her to fight for love with Flavor Flav another day on the popular reality show Flavor of Love (2006). Screenshot.

Collectively, these iconic Black Twitter-associated hashtags function as a comprehensive archive of both Black cultural life, as well as the functions of digital blackness. In these contexts, and others like #IamJada and #IfTheyGunned MeDown, certain hashtags are testimony. In *Traces of a Stream*, Jacqueline Jones Royster points out that "Testimony, as it credits proximate experience, sets in motion the opportunity and obligation to actually give testimony, or as typically phrased, to bear witness" (67). The scaled documentation of Black people's lived experience with oppression is an affordance offered by Twitter that is part of a long tradition of Black media participation. In addition to slave narratives, Black people across the diaspora have been publishing about aspects of our experience since at least the founding of *Freedom's Journal* in 1827.

The explicitly political hashtag #SolidarityisforWhiteWomen enters a 19th century conversation about how White suffragists deliberately excluded Black Women from their movement. This hashtag testifies that Black Women continue to experience multiple oppressions, but our voices are frequently ignored and erased through language that defines racism and sexism as oppositional, either/or phenomena. Humor, fortunately, offers healing that helps us keep going. #ThanksgivingwithBlackFamilies is also testimony, and the deluge of user responses confirming certain kinds of Black cultural norms during the holidays offers a rich anthropological archive that also hosts a memory of influential pop cultural references almost exclusively of Black celebrities/shows.

As I pointed out earlier, memes are a powerful method of communication that can convey multiple meanings in a seemingly simple way. #ThanksgivingwithBlackFamilies pays homage to our shared traditions in ways that affirm our analog lived cultural experience. The memes show that Blackness has been remediating with popular culture media in ways that remix our family traditions with our favorite fictional "fam." Shows like *Fresh Prince of Bel Air* helped raise generations X and Y, and *Flavor of Love* was the genesis for many of the "ratchet" competition reality shows of today. Memes conjure the processes of reminiscing and passing this historical knowledge to young people in the community. Black identity reflects a complex construction of human and media discourses that are delivered through the meme's ability to provide multiple cross-generational references through a single image.

Through humor, Black Twitter enables us to observe the absurdity of being Black and flowing through online and offline worlds. It produces signs and symbols of blackness, which signify a cultural identity through linguistic performances. After all, Twitter users must construct an "authentic" representation of "being Black" beyond the use of a profile photograph or avatar of a person with melanated skin (Marwick and Boyd). However, as the moderators of r/BlackPeopleTwitter have discovered, verifying "real users" requires a tremendous amount of labor. Similar to offline, race must be made visible online through various acts of language. Demonstrating blackness relies on both Black English (BE), or African American Vernacular English (AAVE), and a myriad of speech acts that constitute BE. This insider knowledge empowers r/BlackPeopleTwitter and online Black feminists to detect fake accounts and posts that spread disinformation campaigns.

Public performances that illustrate the depth of eloquence of BE, such as #YourSlipisShowing, are worth examining, given the stigma associated with talkin' Black. As Keith Gilyard argues in his book *True to the Language Game*, "The very existence of African American Vernacular inscribes a significant rhetorical situation, and the prevailing functional character of African American artistic expression renders problematic any move to divorce its production and any criticism thereof from the realm of rhetorical inquiry" (209). Gilyard's critique aptly describes what is powerful about Black Twitter: we need to pay attention to how its users be talkin' and especially how they talk back. Rhetorical studies about Black Twitter and online racial identity must account for how BE contributes to its persuasive uses.

Ultimately, Black Twitter vividly rejects the colorblind society. Through naming and archiving (hashtagging), intertexting, and retweeting, some Twitter users expose how powerful racist ideologies continue to marginalize "race stuff." Black Twitter hosts a plethora of dynamic communication acts that focus on whiteness and specifically, White supremacy as "the problem." For example, when users claim the merits of Black culture, critique its appropriation, as well as inspire other members with happenings and objects that represent "insider" knowledge of cultural significance. Unfortunately, public Black cultural expression is not without its problems.

Analog blackness had different rules of secrecy. Being Black, especially talkin' Black and clapping back, has traditionally taken place away from the gaze of White folks. Clay and Evans further elaborate on this point, as follows: "In a society that remains physically and racially segregated, and where black communities remain hyper-surveilled, the technological advances of the internet have allowed global access to aspects of black culture without requiring that non-blacks have even superficial interactions with black people" (216). This observation is worth ongoing analysis because it raises questions about how digital environments scale the possible manifestations of Black cultural expression. In fact, as I discussed earlier in the case studies about r/Black-PeopleTwitter, 4Chan trolls, and the IRA's use of COINTELPRO infiltration tactics, some users engaging Black Twitter may not be Black at all. Or human, as in the case of bots.

Nevertheless, I contend that "#BlackTwitter is one of the most promising spaces for understanding the combinations and intersections at work in African-American digital rhetoric" (Gilyard and Banks 85). Similar to Gilyard and Banks, I have sought to demonstrate the persuasive potential of Black Twitter. They explain that "It is a space that is at once amorphous yet clearly discernible. It is public, counterpublic, and underground. It crosses the entire continuum between public address and deliberation for broad communal goals and the everyday and vernacular kinds of communication" (85). Gilyard and Banks' comprehensive taxonomy syncs many different studies that fail to acknowledge Black Twitter's rhetorical agency.

Whether we categorize Black Twitter as a site of Black rhetorical practice, the news, a counter-culture community, or as a sociopolitical movement, it warrants some degree of autoethnographic examination. Arguably, some personal and/or historical knowledge about Black cultural expression and folklore would be useful. In fact, many researchers struggle with articulating the dynamic history of Black cultural life in language. For example, Farhad Manjoo seems to struggle to understand the various kinds of cultural rituals that are being enacted by Black Twitter. With the assistance of Geneva Smitherman's

Talkin and Testifyin, he may have been able to document the dozens as part of a host of speech acts—*bragging, jiving, talking shit, one-upping, insulting,* and *affirming.*

Furthermore, researching race and Twitter requires a certain technical familiarity with the platform. I need to know what a hashtag is, how users interact, the role of retweeting, etc. I need to have heard about it through the grapevine to know how to search for a particular tweet. This kind of awareness stems from "insider knowledge," and there are a number of ways to use Black literacy to decipher the significance of #BlackTwitter happenings. I know about trending hashtags and their subsequent popularity because I am a (Black) Twitter user myself who has encountered the most widely retweeted material. Moreover, I have to rely on some journalists to cover trending topics emerging as #BlackTwitter. Both of these approaches could be historically problematic in academic space. Certainly, researchers are trained to be suspicious of bias, which has presented challenges to autoethnographic research. Furthermore, researchers aren't reporters, yet both researchers and journalists produce work that informs. To situate Black Twitter or #BlackTwitter within the interdependent categorical boundaries of a Black rhetorical object, digital media, and an archive offers researchers a wide range of ways to make meaning about this phenomenon.

Some reporters, such as Donovan Ramsey,[29] Stereo Williams,[30] and Jenna Wortham,[31] recognize that Black Twitter is a plurality of its own sub-communities. This mass-distributed nature of the entity contributes to the challenge of re-finding hashtags and threads; neither Black Twitter's history nor the total sum of its participants (and their identities) can be easily known. Moreover, scholars like Anjali Vats pay attention to Black Twitter as a particularized distributed expression of blackness within a novel social conflict about how blackness is, can, and ought to be performed online:

> Black Twitter does not reference a monolithic black voice; rather, it refers to **racialized content and practices**, often marked by "ambiguous racialized humour," which works to resist dominant narratives of race and disrupt Twitter's **usual whiteness**. It is also emblematic of a relatively new mode of activism through which politics and identity are negotiated via hashtag. (Vats, emphasis added)

---

29   See http://bit.ly/3vUOEBN.
30   See http://bit.ly/314c0Xi.
31   See https://bit.ly/37knNUL.

As Vats' definition shows, the hashtag serves as a call and response mechanism. Regardless of quantity, hashtags testify. Hashtags originate from narratives about Black survival via Twitter. Users wield the hashtag to assert a collective witnessing. The hashtag, both a declaration may also serve as a revelation. As revelation, if #BlackLivesMatter was true, we would not to be forced into a daily routine of bearing witness to seeing unarmed Black people being killed by the state and those claiming to be operating on its behalf (e.g., George Zimmerman). Reflecting on the absurdity of the constant need to confront threats to Black life, Cullors, Tometi, and Garza stated an assumption that has come to signify a conclusion that would only need to be said in a social scene that disproportionately devalues life: Black lives *matter*. They testified that what we were seeing was jacked up and unnecessary. Millions agreed.

The scaled recirculation of #BlackLivesMatter generated and amplified countless threads about violence against unarmed Black persons. In addition, the unanticipated virality of the hashtag became associated with activism and Black Twitter. Without network contagion, a hashtag could simply be part of some users' quasi-public conversation. However, when the hashtag scales enough to sustain its own life, users can't control who or what will be erased. Researchers bear the responsibility of attributing knowledge to its creators, but who (or what, if we give agency to bots and platforms) gets credit for appropriating Black Twitter or who should be trusted to understand it?

The categorical issues with Black Twitter coincide with the problem of authorship and attribution. When intellectual herstories are generated via Twitter, giving Black Twitter the agency of persons erases individual contributions to the space and absorbs the weight of their distinctive voice under the general banner of "activism," which makes the (uncopyrighted) expression part of a public domain that makes its reclamation fair game for any group or individual. How much money are Cullors, Tometi, and Garza making from that hashtag they generated? Hudson? I'm certain it wasn't as much as the White Australian Ian Mackay, or any of the countless sales of shirts, bags, pins, and posters. Will Hudson's or Crockett's organizing work ever be considered in their future hiring, promotion, or other types of financially valuable recognition?

In fact, the re-circulation of hashtags associated with Black Twitter does not necessarily benefit their authors. Stereo Williams insightfully critiques mainstream media outlets for thieving Black Twitter's content and not providing attribution to those sources that they re-publish on their own media. For example, April Reign (@reignofapril) composed #OscarsSoWhite, but CNN failed to credit her or hire her despite their shameless appropriation of her hashtag to cover the problem of diversity and Hollywood. Williams passionately argues that this kind of cultural theft leads to erasure:

What has happened with Black Twitter is another example
of how white marginalization leads to ingenuity in black
people; so many have been able to fortify black professionals
via networking and symposiums like Blogging While Brown,
or organized events like the Black Brunch. That has been
facilitated through relationships cultivated via the community of Black Twitter. And that in and of itself is a powerful
resource—but it doesn't change the fact that the platforms
that have the widest reach are still virtually ignoring a wealth
of black talent and creativity while pilfering from that very
same well.

Williams' quote applies to various contexts in which journalism shamelessly
appropriates from the Black counter-public (Graham and Smith; Hill).

CONCLUSION: RACE AND POSITIONALITY

As a cultural phenomenon, Black Twitter simulates the distinctive behavior of
Black intelligence by pushing the racialized linguistic territories that diminish
the visibility of creative Black cultural expression. Black Twitter is what happens
when knowledge-making is both distributed and visible. Thus, Black Twitter
refers to a declaration of Black intelligence which is being archived and tagged
through algorithms processing and assembling codes for blackness. On the other
hand, as with offline blackness, Black Twitter derives its meaning from those who
do not want to be associated with the media such as those who think it's silly or
"ignorant," and/or people who undermine its significance by not acknowledging
it at all. Black Twitter, then, generates a great deal of encomia.

As a storytelling place, Black Twitter's production will display the collective cultural intelligence of blackness. It shows how blackness moves through
the space as a familiar image and unfamiliar information, especially as it is
objectified as an topic of discussion. It is a memory of the analog world that
also constructed racial identities through its emerging technologies, and Black
engagement with cultural objects indicates "cool" stuff from the stuff that ain't.
"Cool performance," or the value of wit, drives rapid sharing within smaller
networks. As they delight in its exchange, the act of identifying with its "read"
on any kind of cultural exchange, whether intra or inter-racial, invites encomia.
This ritual of praising Black Twitter occurs during moments in which it captures
the "ether" and represents some meaningful take on something we all should be
looking at. And "we" usually ain't the majority of White people, but the "cool"
ones who know "what's really going on" rely on information from Black Twitter.
Network analysis enables us to measure Twitter traffic, which may offer a clue

about the reach. Regardless, as an archival tag, #BlackTwitter categorically exists as a retrievable subject that has been identified by somebody taking up space. Thus, any construction of Black Twitter must be invented by some user and recognized by another through that tag.

One of the most interesting aspects of discovering #BlackTwitter is that those who identify with this phenomenon have created a large archive of its intellectual history. In other words, you may find "traces" of Black Twitter by examining how it has been tagged and archived as part of a database that may be retrieved by an algorithm capable of "reading" all things explicitly referring to "Black Twitter." The users who recognize its power even create meta-tags like #GreatestMomentsinBlackTwitterHistory. Its recognition, ultimately, is all that matters, and we are uniquely positioned to study Black Twitter as a *discourse*, not a stable cultural group. The communication opened up by the performance is a causal gateway to one of the most important rhetorical canons—invention.

In sum, Black Twitter has an effect on language. To a large extent, this impact is recognized as a transhuman speaker. It is not uncommon to hear news reporters using expressions like "The internet says" and "Black Twitter thinks." To bestow networked media with the agency of "symbol-using animals" raises critical questions about the technological politics of race vis-a-vis social media (Burke). If researchers are not insiders/contributors to this vast, distributed assemblage of linguistic resistance, they will be unlikely to participate in effective research about it. Thus, Black Twitter is simultaneously personal and detached, fundamentally human and transhuman, elusively retrievable.

WORKS CITED

Abreu, Manuel Arturo. "Online Imagined Black English." *Arachne*, A Project by Dorothy Howard and André Fincato, 2015, bit.ly/3puOcWm.

Anderson, Monica, et al. "Activism in the Social Media Age." *Pew Research Center*, 11 July 2018, www.pewinternet.org/2018/07/11/activism-in-the-social-media-age/.

Arceneaux, Michael. "Black Twitter's 2013 All-Stars." *Complex*, 23 Dec. 2013, www.complex.com/pop-culture/2013/12/black-twitter-all-stars/.

Banks, Adam J. *Race, Rhetoric, and Technology: Searching for Higher Ground*. Lawrence Erlbaum, 2006.

Barlow, Jameta N. "#WhenIFellInLoveWithMyself: Disrupting the Gaze and Loving Our Black Womanist Self as an Act of Political Warfare." *Meridians: Feminism, Race, Transnationalism*, vol. 15, no. 1, 2016, pp. 205–17, doi:10.2979/meridians.15.1.11.

Barroso, Amanda. "Most Black Adults Say Race Is Central to Their Identity and Feel Connected to a Broader Black Community." *Pew Research Center*, 5 Feb. 2020, pewrsr.ch/3930UZS.

Bates, Karen Grigsby. "'Los Angeles Times' Recognizes Black Twitter's Relevance." *NPR*, 8 July 2015, n.pr/3sanLYb.

Bauman, Zygmunt. *Liquid Life*. Polity Press, 2005.

Benjamin, Ruha. *Race after Technology: Abolitionist Tools for the New Jim Code*. John Wiley & Sons, 2019.

Black Enterprise Editors. "LA Times Becomes First Newspaper to Cover 'Black Twitter.'" *Black Enterprise*, 10 July 2015, bit.ly/3twsLH9.

Blackstock, Nelson. *COINTELPRO: The FBI's Secret War on Political Freedom*. Vintage Books, 1976.

Blain, Keisha N. "Introduction to the #Blackpanthersyllabus." *AAIHS*, 20 Feb. 2016, www.aaihs.org/blackpanthersyllabus/.

Bonilla, Yarimar, and Jonathan Rosa. "#Ferguson: Digital Protest, Hashtag Ethnography, and the Racial Politics of Social Media in the United States." *American Ethnologist*, vol. 42, no. 1, 2015, pp. 4–17, bit.ly/3dn6VR2.

Brock, André. "Critical Technocultural Discourse Analysis." *New Media & Society*, vol. 20, no. 3, 2018, pp. 1012–1030, bit.ly/2ZpP2sJ.

———."From the Blackhand Side: Twitter as a Cultural Conversation." *Journal of Broadcasting & Electronic Media*, vol. 56, no. 4, 2012, pp. 529–49, b.gatech.edu /3auGlnn.

Broderick, Ryan. "Activists Are Outing Hundreds of Twitter Users Believed to Be 4chan Trolls Posing as Feminists." *BuzzFeed News*, 17 June 2014, bit.ly/3vNGefd.

Brown, Elaine. *A Taste of Power: A Black Woman's Story*. W. Ross MacDonald School Resource Services Library, 2009.

Burke, Kenneth. *Language As Symbolic Action: Essays on Life, Literature, and Method*. U of California P, 1966.

Byers, Dylan. "Pew: Twitter Unreliable for Public Opinion." *POLITICO*, 4 Nov. 2013, politi.co/390fsqo.

Cadwalladr, Carole, and Emma Graham-Harrison. "How Cambridge Analytica Turned Facebook 'Likes' into a Lucrative Political Tool." *The Guardian*, 17 Mar. 2018, bit.ly/3r3USvb.

Caldwell, Courtney. "#EndFathersDay: Using Hashtags as Retribution Against Women of Color." *Skepchick*, 17 June 2014, bit.ly/2QmETvz.

Carroll, Caitlin, and Rachel Cohen. "Senate Intel Committee Releases Bipartisan Report on Russia's Use of Social Media." *U.S. Senate Select Committee on Intelligence*, 8 Oct. 2019, bit.ly/3vOv9dJ.

Chatman, Dayna, et al. "Black Twitter Project." *Declara*, Media Impact Project/USC Annenberg Innovation Lab, 5 Sept. 2014, declara.com/content/d1qWQd59.

Chaudhry, I. "'Not So Black and White': Discussions of Race on Twitter in the Aftermath of #Ferguson and the Shooting Death of Mike Brown." *Cultural Studies <-> Critical Methodologies*, vol. 16, no.3, 2016, pp. 296–304. bit.ly/2N8tApQ.

Church Committee. *Intelligence Activities and the Rights of Americans. Book II, Final Report*, U.S. Government Printing Office, 1976.

Churchill, Ward, and James Jim Vander Wall. *Agents of Repression: The FBI's Secret Wars Against the Black Panther Party and the American Indian Movement*. Vol. 7. South End Press, 2002.

Clark, Meredith D. "Making the Case for Black with a Capital B. Again." *Poynter*, 23 Aug. 2015, bit.ly/3cONFu0.

———. "The 'Black Twitter' Beat Raises Questions of Cultural Competency and Audience Engagement for Newsrooms." *Poynter*, 8 July 2015, bit.ly/3tFj5ty.

———. To Tweet Our Own Cause: *A Mixed-methods Study of the Online Phenomenon "Black Twitter."* Chapel Hill, NC: University of North Carolina at Chapel Hill Graduate School, 2014. doi:10.17615/7bfs-rp55.

Clay, Charity, and Louwanda Evans. "#Blacknessbelike: White Racial Framing and Counter-Framing on Twitter's Digitally Contested Cyber-Space." *Systemic Racism*, edited by Ruth Thompson-Miller and Kimberley Ducey, Palgrave Macmillan, 2017, pp. 205–37.

Dadas, Caroline. "Hashtag Activism: The Promise and Risk of 'Attention.'" *Social Writing/Social Media: Publics, Presentations, Pedagogies*, edited by Douglas M. Walls and Stephanie Vie, The WAC Clearinghouse; UP of Colorado, 2017, doi:10.37514/PER-B.2017.0063.2.01.

Daniel, Florian, et al. "Bots Acting Like Humans: Understanding and Preventing Harm. *IEEE Internet Computing*, vol. 23, no. 2, 2019, pp. 40–49, bit.ly/3cY4u5A.

Davis, Angela Y. *Blues Legacies and Black Feminism: Gertrude Ma Rainey, Bessie Smith, and Billie Holiday*. Vintage, 2011.

Dickey, Megan Rose. "Thoughts on White People Using Dark-Skinned Emoji." *Tech-Crunch*, 1 Oct. 2017, tcrn.ch/3cY9s2k.

DiResta, Renee, et al. *The Tactics & Tropes of the Internet Research Agency*. New Knowledge, 2018, bit.ly/38ZqMmj.

Duggan, Maeve, et al. "Demographics of Key Social Networking Platforms." *Pew Research Center*, 9 Jan. 2015, http://pewrsr.ch/3vPVmbQ.

Durrani, Mariam. "AN News: 'Digital Counterpublics: Black Twitter in the Aftermath of Ferguson.'" *Society for Linguistic Anthropology*, 26 Mar. 2015, bit.ly/3tHb9If.

Edwards, Meridith, and Dakin Andone. "Ex-South Carolina Cop Michael Slager Gets 20 Years for Walter Scott Killing." CNN, Cable News Network, 7 Dec. 2017, cnn.it/3ae5D91.

Eromosele, Diana Ozemebhoya. "Black Twitter Defends Self from L.A. Times Columnist Who Says It's Not as Progressive, United as It Seems." *The Root*, 16 July 2015, bit.ly/3s8s9qp.

"Exposing Russia's Effort to Sow Discord Online: The Internet Research Agency and Advertisements." *U.S. House of Representatives Permanent Select Committee on Intelligence*, intelligence.house.gov/social-media-content/.

Federal Bureau of Investigation. "COINTELPRO Black Extremist [Part 01 of 23]." *FBI*, 5 May 2011, bit.ly/3f2NEWc.

Flock, Elizabeth, and Melissa Bell. "'Paula Brooks,' Editor of 'Lez Get Real,' Also a Man." *The Washington Post*, 13 June 2011, wapo.st/3u1lz6B.

Florini, S. "Tweets, Tweeps, and Signifyin': Communication and Cultural Performance on 'Black Twitter.'" *Television and New Media*, vol. 15, no. 3, 2013, pp. 223–37.

"Fred Hampton (August 30, 1948–December 4, 1969)." *National Archives and Records Administration*, National Archives and Records Administration, 25 Aug. 2020, bit .ly/3x42imx.

Freelon, Deen, et al. "Beyond the Hashtags: #Ferguson, #Blacklivesmatter, and the Online Struggle for Offline Justice." *Center for Media and Social Impact*, 29 Feb. 2016, http://bit.ly/3sahhsi.

Freelon, Deen, et al. *How Black Twitter and Other Social Media Communities Interact with Mainstream News*. Knight Foundation, 2018, https://bit.ly/2Qj9Xfl.

Friedberg, Brian, and Joan Donovan. "On the Internet, Nobody Knows You're a Bot: Pseudoanonymous Influence Operations and Networked Social Movements." *Journal of Design and Science*, vol. 1, no. 6, 2019, jods.mitpress.mit.edu/pub/2gnso48a/release/8.

Garcia, Megan. "Racist in the Machine: The Disturbing Implications of Algorithmic Bias." *World Policy Journal*, vol. 33, no. 4, 2016, pp. 111–117.

Gilyard, Keith. *True to the Language Game: African American Discourse, Cultural Politics, and Pedagogy*. Taylor and Francis, 2013.

Gilyard, Keith, and Adam J. Banks. *On African-American Rhetoric*. Routledge, 2018.

"Glossary." Twitter, help.twitter.com/en/glossary.

Gourarie, Chava. "Why the *LA Times* Chose Dexter Thomas to Cover Black Twitter." *Columbia Journalism Review*, Q and A: *The Journalism Crisis Project*. 10 July 2010, bit.ly/3aucECZ.

Gourley, L. E. "Capital B for Black." *American Psychologist*, vol. 30, no. 2, 1975, pp. 181, doi:10.1037/h0078439.

Graham, Roderick, and Shawn Smith. "The Content of Our #Characters: Black Twitter as Counterpublic." *Sociology of Race and Ethnicity*, vol. 2, no. 4, 2016, pp. 433–49.

Greenwood, Shannon, et al. "Social Media Update 2016." *Pew Research Center: Internet, Science & Tech*, 11 Nov. 2016, pewrsr.ch/2QmHHJ7.

Guo, Jeff. "What People Don't Get about 'Black Twitter.'" *The Washington Post*, 22 Oct. 2015, wapo.st/317dTlU.

Hampton, Rachelle. "The Black Feminists Who Saw the Alt-Right Threat Coming." *Slate*, 23 Apr. 2019, bit.ly/3s8WYeT.

Harmon, Amy. "Prove You're Not White: For an Article About Race-Verification on Reddit, I Had an Unusual Request." *The New York Times*, 10 Oct. 2019, nyti.ms/3vPfACE.

———. "Discussing Blackness on Reddit? Photograph Your Forearm First." *The New York Times*, The New York Times, 8 Oct. 2019, nyti.ms/2PiyNvF.

Harriot, Michael. "Mueller Report Reveals How Black Activists, White Tears and Racism Helped Trump Become President." *The Root*, 19 Apr. 2019, bit.ly/3lNOfwl.

Helsel, Phil. "Walter Scott Death: Bystander Who Recorded Cop Shooting Speaks Out." *NBCNews.com*, NBCUniversal News Group, 9 Apr. 2015, bit.ly/3c766Li.

Hesse, Monica. "'A Gay Girl in Damascus' Displays Ease of Fudging Authenticity Online." *The Washington Post*, 13 June 2011, wapo.st/3c1Y4Dl.

Hill, Marc Lamont. "'Thank You, Black Twitter': State Violence, Digital Counterpublics, and Pedagogies of Resistance." *Urban Education*, vol. 53, no. 2, 2018, pp. 286–302.

Horowitz, Juliana Menasce, et al. "Views on Race in America 2019." *Pew Research Center's Social and Demographic Trends Project*, 9 Apr. 2019, pewrsr.ch/3cULIMD.

Hughes, Adam. "A Small Group of Prolific Users Account for a Majority of Political Tweets Sent by U.S. Adults." *Pew Research Center*, 23 Oct. 2019, pewrsr.ch/3vMt4PI.

"Internet/Broadband Fact Sheet." *Pew Research Center*, 12 June 2019, pewrsr.ch/3d0k1lM.

"Is It OK to Use Black Emojis and Gifs?" *BBC News*, 14 Aug. 2017, bbc.in/3s8vfuH.

Jackson, Laur M. "Memes and Misogynoir." *The Awl*, 28 Aug. 2014, www.theawl.com/2014/08/memes-and-misogynoir/.

Jackson, Lauren Michele. "We Need to Talk About Digital Blackface in Reaction GIFs." *Teen Vogue*, 2 Aug. 2017, bit.ly/2NDOOvP.

Jones, Cassandra L. "The Data Thief, the Cyberflaneur, and Rhythm Science: Challenging Anti-Technological Blackness with the Metaphors of Afrofuturism." *CLA Journal*, vol. 61, no. 4, 2018, pp. 202–17, bit.ly/3lD3DLH.

Jones, Taylor. "Toward a Description of African American Vernacular English Dialect Regions Using 'Black Twitter.'" *American Speech*, vol. 90, no. 4, 2015, pp. 403–40, bit.ly/314i6a6.

Kenneally, Tim. "LA Times' First Black Twitter Story Slammed by Black Twitter." *The Wrap*, 6 July 2015, bit.ly/2QnX1oV.

King Jr., Martin Luther. *Where Do We go From Here: Chaos or Community?* Vol. 2, Beacon Press, 2010.

Langford, Catherine L., and Monté Speight. "#BlackLivesMatter: Epistemic Positioning, Challenges, and Possibilities." *Journal of Contemporary Rhetoric*, vol. 5, no.3/4, 2015, pp. 78–89, bit.ly/3jZ0qp0.

Lanham, David, and Amy Liu. "Not Just a Typographical Change: Why Brookings Is Capitalizing Black." *Brookings*, 23 Sept. 2019, www.brookings.edu/research/brookingscapitalizesblack/.

Lemieux, Jamilah. "When Black Twitter Sounds Like Something You Don't Understand." *EBONY*, 17 July 2015, bit.ly/3tIWPyU.

Lewis, Taylor. "The 23 Most Memorable Black Twitter Hashtags of 2015." *Essence*, 15 Dec. 2015, bit.ly/3c6pU1b.

Lockett, Alexandria. "Scaling Black Feminism: A Critical Discussion about the Digital Labor of Representation." *Humans at Work in the Digital Age: Forms of Digital Textual Labor*, edited by Shawna Ross and Andrew Pilsch, Routledge, 2020.

Lockhart, P. R. "The Largest Black Lives Matter Page on Facebook Was a Scam." *Vox*, 11 Apr. 2018, bit.ly/2OSqcQw.

Magee, Ny. "Let The Purge Begin, #BlackTwitter Comes for LA Times Reporter." *EURweb*, 17 July 2015, bit.ly/3tVhPCX.

Manjoo, Farhad. "How Black People Use Twitter." *Slate*, 10 Aug. 2010, bit.ly/2M13zYX.

Marwick, Alice E., and Danah Boyd. "I Tweet Honestly, I Tweet Passionately: Twitter Users, Context Collapse, and the Imagined Audience." *New Media & Society*, vol. 13, no. 1, 2011, pp. 114–33.

McDonald, Soraya. "Black Twitter: A Virtual Community Ready to Hashtag out a Response to Cultural Issues." *The Washington Post*, 20 Jan. 2014, wapo.st/3ub33si.

Meier, Florian, and David Elsweiler. "Other Times It's Just Strolling Back Through My Timeline: Investigating Re-finding Behaviour on Twitter and Its Motivations." *Proceedings of the 2018 Conference on Human Information Interaction & Retrieval*, ACM, 2018, pp. 130–39.

Mitchell, Amy, and Paul Hitlin. "Twitter Reaction to Events Often at Odds with Overall Public Opinion." *Pew Research Center*, 4 Mar. 2013, bit.ly/3scIgTS.

Mock, Brentin. "There's Something Familiar About the Russian 'Blacktivist' Campaign." *CityLab*, 29 Sept. 2017, bit.ly/3cSDpAU.

Molina, Brett. "Twitter Overcounted Active Users Since 2014, Shares Surge on Profit Hopes." *USA Today*, 26 Oct. 2017, bit.ly/2Pan8z8.

Monroe, Barbara Jean. *Crossing the Digital Divide: Race, Writing, and Technology in the Classroom*. Teachers College Press, 2004.

Moore, Dhoruba. "Strategies of Repression Against the Black Movement." *The Black Scholar*, vol. 12, no. 3, 1981, pp. 10–16, doi:10.1080/00064246.1981.11414179.

Mueller, Robert S. *Report on the Investigation into Russian Interference in the 2016 Presidential Election*. Vol. 1–2, U.S. Department of Justice, 2019.

Mueller, Robert S. *The United States v. Internet Research Agency*. The United States Department of Justice, 16 Feb. 2018, www.justice.gov/file/1035477.

Nakamura, Lisa. "Cyberrace." *PMLA*, vol. 123, no. 5, 2008, pp. 1673–1682.

"National Politics on Twitter: Small Share of U.S. Adults Produce Majority of Tweets." *Pew Research Center for the People and the Press*, 23 Oct. 2019, pewrsr.ch/2NEN7OT.

Noble, Safiya Umoja. *Algorithms of Oppression: How Search Engines Reinforce Racism*. New York UP, 2018.

OMG! Black People! 2009, omgblackpeople.wordpress.com/. Accessed 8 Apr. 2016.

Opam, Kwame. "Media Might Finally Start Giving Black Twitter the Recognition It Deserves." *The Verge*, 9 July 2015, bit.ly/316AmQ1.

O'Sullivan, Donie. "The Biggest Black Lives Matter Page on Facebook Is Fake." *CNN*, 9 Apr. 2018, cnn.it/3cYen3c.

Perez, Sarah. "Twitter Lite Expands to 21 More Countries, Adds Push Notifications." *TechCrunch*, 13 Aug. 2018, tcrn.ch/3r2ddJe.

Pluralist. "Anti-Racist Reddit Forum Asks Users to Send in Photos to Prove They're Not White." *Pluralist*, 10 Oct. 2019, pluralist.com/blackpeopletwitter-reddit-white/.

Powell, Ed. "Feiden Santana, Man Who Taped Walter Scott Murder Comes Forward." WERE-AM 1490, WERE-AM 1490, 9 Apr. 2015, bit.ly/2LKWg7p.

Prasad, Pritha. "Beyond Rights as Recognition: Black Twitter and Posthuman Coalitional Possibilities." *Prose Studies*, vol. 38, no. 1, 2016, pp. 50–73.

Prendergast, Catherine. "Before #blacklivesmatter." *Rhetorics of Whiteness: Postracial Hauntings in Popular Culture, Social Media, and Education,* edited by Tammie M. Kennedy et al., 2017, pp. 89–91.

Price, Anne. "Spell It with a Capital 'B.'" *Medium/Insight Center for Community Economic Development*, 1 Oct. 2019, bit.ly/3fa1ypc.

"r/BlackPeopleTwitter." *Reddit*, www.reddit.com/r/BlackPeopleTwitter/.

Raengo, Alessandra. "About Liquid Blackness." *Liquid Blackness*, 24 Jan. 2016, liquidblackness.com/home/.

Raengo, Alessandra. "Black Matters." *Discourse*, vol. 38, no. 2, 2016, pp. 246–64.

Raengo, Alessandra, editor. "What Is Liquid Blackness?", *Liquid Blackness: A Research Project on Blackness and Aesthetics*, Department of Communication, Georgia State University, 12 Feb. 2019, liquidblackness.com/what-is-liquid-blackness.

Ramsey, Donovan. "The Truth About Black Twitter." *The Atlantic*, 10 Apr. 2015, bit.ly/3fa1ypc.

Rashidian, Nushin, et al. "Friend and Foe: The Platform Press at the Heart of Journalism." *Academic Commons*, Tow Center for Digital Journalism, Columbia University, 27 Feb. 2019, bit.ly/3f0Aqcr.

Richardson, Allissa V. "Bearing Witness While Black: Theorizing African American Mobile Journalism after Ferguson." *Digital Journalism*, vol. 17, no. 4, 2016, pp. 398–414.

Richardson, Elaine B. *African American Literacies*. Routledge, 2003.

Richardson, Elaine, and Alice Ragland. "#StayWoke: The Language and Literacies of the #BlackLivesMatter Movement." *Community Literacy Journal*, vol. 12, no .2, 2018, pp. 27–56.

Romano, Aja. "Twitter Released 9 Million Tweets from One Russian Troll Farm. Here's What We Learned." *Vox*, 19 Oct. 2018, bit.ly/3f1S9Qx.

Royster, Jacqueline Jones. *Traces of a Stream: Literacy and Social Change among African American Women*. U of Pittsburgh P, 2000.

Sack, Jessica Van. "Twitter, News Media Should Finally Tie Knot." *Boston Herald*, 18 Nov. 2018, bit.ly/2ONhvHu.

Schiappa, Jacqueline. "#IfTheyGunnedMeDown: The Necessity of 'Black Twitter' and Hashtags in the Age of Ferguson." *ProudFlesh: New Afrikan Journal of Culture, Politics and Consciousness*, no. 10, 2014.

"Search Result FAQs." *Twitter*, Twitter, 2020, bit.ly/3rJGpFw.

Shakur, Assata. *Assata: An Autobiography*. Zed Books, 2016.

Shane, Scott, and Sheera Frenkel. "Russian 2016 Influence Operation Targeted African-Americans on Social Media." *The New York Times*, 17 Dec. 2018, nyti.ms/3s9HS8Q.

Sharma, Sanjay. "Black Twitter? Racial Hashtags, Networks and Contagion." *New Formations*, vol. 78, no. 78, 2013, pp. 46–64.

Shearer, Elisa. "Social Media Outpaces Print Newspapers in the U.S. as a News Source." *Pew Research Center*, 10 Dec. 2018, pewrsr.ch/3cSPvKu.

Shetty, Abhishek. "Throwback Thursday: Fifty-Year Anniversary of 'Bunchy' Carter, John Huggins Shooting." *Daily Bruin*, UCLA, 17 Jan. 2019, bit.ly/3lE6wM8.

Sicha, Choire. "What Were Black People Talking About on Twitter Last Night?" *The Awl*, 11 Nov. 2009, bit.ly/393yVGz.

Smith, Aaron. "Twitter Update 2011." *Pew Research Center: Internet, Science & Tech*, 1 June 2011, pewrsr.ch/3tFopgA.

Smith, Aaron, and Joanna Brenner. "Twitter Use 2012." *Pew Research Center: Internet, Science &; Tech*, 31 May 2012, pewrsr.ch/3tFopgA.

Smith, Aaron, and Monica Anderson. "Social Media Use in 2018." *Pew Research Center: Internet, Science & Tech*, 1 Mar. 2018, pewrsr.ch/3c5MV4n.

Smitherman, Geneva. *Talkin and Testifyin: The Language of Black America*. Houghton Mifflin, 1977.

———. *Talkin That Talk: Language, Culture, and Education in African America*. Routledge, 2000.

Sommer, Will. "Reddit's BlackPeopleTwitter Forum Wants to Know If Its Users Are Actually White." *The Daily Beast*, 8 May 2019, bit.ly/3c7WMHd.

Starr, Terrell Jermaine. "Russia's Recent Facebook Ads Prove the Kremlin Never Loved Black People." *The Root*, 28 Sept. 2017, bit.ly/393Du3y.

Stewart, Ian. "Now We Stronger than Ever: African-American English Syntax in Twitter." *Proceedings of the Student Research Workshop at the 14th Conference of the European Chapter of the Association for Computational Linguistics*, 2014.

Stocking, Galen, and Nami Sumida. "Social Media Bots Draw Public's Attention and Concern." *Pew Research Center's Journalism Project*, 15 Oct. 2018, pewrsr.ch/3lANXZi.

Szymanski, Katie. "Ferguson, Journalism, and Social Media: #UMichChat Recap." *#UMSocial*, UMSocial Office of the Vice President for Communications/University of Michigan, 22 June 2017, socialmedia.umich.edu/blog/socialjournalism/.

"The 66 Most Hilarious Posts In The History Of Black People Twitter." *Runt Of The Web*, 25 Mar. 2016, runt-of-the-web.com/black-people-twitter.

"The Reason #BlackTwitter Exists (And Is Totally Awesome)." *WGBH*, GBH 89.7/PBS, 3 June 2019, bit.ly/3s5bJPE.

Thomas, Dexter. "Is 'Black Twitter' Dead?" *The Daily Dot*, 12 Dec. 2015, bit.ly/3c4eiMh.

———. "When 'Black Twitter' Sounds Like 'White Twitter.'" *Los Angeles Times*, 15 July 2015, lat.ms/2OYH1cB.

Twitter Search Result FAQs. Twitter, bit.ly/3rJGpFw.

U.S. Senate Select Committee on Intelligence. *Report of the Select Committee on Intelligence United States Senate on Russian Active Measures Campaigns and Interference in the 2016 U.S. Election Volume 2: Russia's Use of Social Media with Additional Views*, 2019, pp. 1–85, bit.ly/312LfCH.

United States District Court. United States v. Internet Research Agency. 18 U.S.C. §§ 2, 371, 1349, 1028A. Department of Justice. February 16, 2018.

u/BPTMods. "r/BlackPeopleTwitter - /r/BlackPeopleTwitter Is Open to Everyone Again." *Reddit*, 2019, bit.ly/3skEUi1.

u/DubTeeDub. "r/BlackPeopleTwitter - BPT Country Club Threads." *Reddit*, 2019, bit.ly/3vPQkwj.

Vasilogambros, Matt, and National Journal. "Black Twitter in Capital Letters." *The Atlantic*, 7 Oct. 2015, bit.ly/3vVTaQv.

Vats, Anjali. "Cooking Up Hashtag Activism: #PaulasBestDishes and Counternarratives of Southern Food." *Communication and Critical/Cultural Studies*, vol. 12, no. 2, 2015, pp. 209–13.

Wajcman, Judy. *Technofeminism*. Polity, 2004.

Warschauer, Max L. *Technology and Social Inclusion: Rethinking the Digital Divide*. Massachusetts Institute of Technology, 2003.

Williams, Sherri. "Digital Defense: Black Feminists Resist Violence with Hashtag Activism." *Feminist Media Studies*, vol. 15, no. 2, 2015, pp. 341–44.

Williams, Stereo. "The Power of Black Twitter." *The Daily Beast*, 6 July 2015, www .thedailybeast.com/the-power-of-black-twitter.

Wojcik, Stefan, and Adam Hughes. "Sizing Up Twitter Users." *Pew Research Center: Internet, Science, and Tech*, 24 Apr. 2019, pewrsr.ch/314uOFQ.

Wojcik, Stefan, et al. "Bots in the Twittersphere." *Pew Research Center.*

Wortham, Jenna. "Black Tweets Matter." Smithsonian.com, Smithsonian Institution, 1 Sept. 2016, bit.ly/37knNUL.

Young, Kevin. "How to Hoax Yourself: The Case of a Gay Girl in Damascus." *The New Yorker*, 9 Nov. 2017, bit.ly/3pogm52.

Zuckerman, Ethan. "This Is So Much Bigger Than Facebook." *The Atlantic*, 23 Mar. 2018, bit.ly/3sb4S7c.

INTERCHAPTER DIALOGUE
FOR CHAPTER 5

Iris: I've learned so much from reading this chapter. We have a lot of different things going on here: digital expressions of Black English (BE) or African American vernacular English (AAVE), which intersects digital and cultural literacies (and rhetorics), as well as social movements. Alex, could you please expand a little bit upon how researching Black Twitter generates this thinking and how we should understand and navigate this rich form of online cultural expression?

Alex: Sure, I'll begin by saying that Black Twitter is a vexed rhetorical object because it's hard for outsiders to recognize and know it. It is also a public performance of Black cultural invention. The mainstream news, for example, often capitalizes on Black Twitter's knowledge, citing tweets without credit or casually referring to Black Twitter as an authority on cultural critique. Therefore, Black Twitter represents Black media and journalism. It also functions as a culture and community capable of organizing, promoting, and/or archiving social movements. Take, for instance, the popularity of #BlackLivesMatter, which is the most famous hashtag to be attributed to Black Twitter. Alicia Garza, Opal Tometi, and Patrice Cullors developed that expression when they were grieving over the death of Trayvon Martin and discussing their outrage about the acquittal of George Zimmerman. These events reverberated loudly against waves of anti-Black police brutality. Of course, Black Twitter does not represent "all Black people" using Twitter. We aren't a monolith, nor do we all know each other. But a long history of segregation is reflected in how we socialize online, as our associations appear to be tightly networked.

The phenomenon of Black Twitter shows that we are using social media to produce and preserve our culture. However, Twitter is a for-profit platform and publisher, and thus mediates our culture with the power to popularize or marginalize our rhetoric and knowledge, which becomes part of the flow of capital when it gets appropriated into the content of mainstream media. These are some of the reasons that it's difficult to make claims about the transformative or liberatory power of Black Twitter. Specifying when Black Twitter has something going on is challenging because unless you're an insider, you may not even know. Twitter moves so fast, as does Black culture. So that's the other component of the research: looking at Black Twitter as a digital enactment of race helps us understand the analog performances of race and the constructedness of those performances through our network interaction.

Overall, studying Black Twitter is important because it reflects the complex relationship between race and language, labor and culture.

Iris: You seem suspicious of cultural authenticity, which you connect to the problem of cultural appropriation. Could you speak more about the relationship between authenticity and Black Twitter?

Alex: Well, authenticity is an inextricable problem of race. Subsequently, trust and distrust drive the engines of racism.

An obvious example is the phenomenon of colorism and passing. The one-drop rule made it possible to categorize even the fairest skinned person as "Black." But skin color was hardly the only factor that played a role in whether a person could pass. Speech, body type, movement, educational attainment and affiliation, among other characteristics, would contribute to a persuasive performance of whiteness. Thus, the decision to live as White meant uprooting, migrating, and living one's life in secrecy. The cost of that extreme decision was Black cultural erasure and divisiveness within the community.

We could also consider 19th century Black writers and rhetors who were publicly representing their experiences in various ways. As Toni Morrison argues in *The Site of Memory,* slave narratives disrupted societal expectations of Black literacy. Taking advantage of mass media and making our knowledge visible is part of the Black literary and rhetorical tradition. Black Twitter follows this intellectual heritage, as it is commonly associated with Black cultural expression as a tool of resisting whiteness. But as I pointed out earlier and in my chapter, Black Twitter (and Black people) are not a monolith. Users will have varying opinions about Black Twitter's liberatory potential. Nevertheless, it can be interpreted as a counter-public that has generated one of the most successful social movements centered on race and civil rights since the 1960s.

Black Twitter unquestionably highlights the issue of race, especially in terms of explicit calls to end systemic racism and White supremacy (#BLM). This political communication is conveyed through Black English and digital rhetorical forms such as memes, hashtagging, etc. That distinctive expression of blackness that we're seeing online influences how other communities signify their identity. We can, for instance, observe seamless appropriations of what Black Twitter is doing because now there's Asian Twitter, Academic Twitter, Twitterstorians, Science Twitter, and so on. Arguably, Black Twitter made it possible for the invention and spread of all these additional "spaces" for people to represent their interests.

Perhaps it is the "realness" evoked by "authentic" Black discourse that is persuasive to outsiders—when they recognize persuasive uses of Black rhetorical forms that they can claim for their own discourse communities. Unfortunately, such appropriation often fails to cite or compensate the creators and literate users of these forms. In other words, when Black cultural production becomes popular, suddenly it is public domain. It's not even Black anymore: now the cultural contribution just belongs to everybody. In some cases, only a few people actually capitalize on it. The Kardashian sisters most quickly come to mind. They have profited from aesthetics that have traditionally caused Black women to be hypersexualized—plumped lips, large buttocks, etc.

Remember that controversial *Paper* photoshoot featuring Kim Kardashian posing as Saartje Baartman? Baartman, as many people may know, was a South African Khoikhoi woman who was enslaved and put on 19th century European exhibitions throughout her life. Also known as the Hottentot Venus, Baartman's body continued to be on display in France long after her death (until at least the 1970s). Given the horrific racist, sexist, and colonialist treatment of Baartman, it is appalling for Kardashian to continue to fetishize Baartman—and by extension Black Women—for the purposes of popularizing her brand as an ethnically ambiguous, fair-skinned bombshell socialite that picks and chooses which Black features she puts on and takes off without any of the stigma of actually being Black. Kardashian's wealth, fame, and influence make it impossible to ignore the destructive aspects of this type of appropriation.

Iris: Thank you. In your chapter, you mention that Black Twitter follows a long tradition of Black media such *Freedom's Journal* (the oldest Black newspaper), the *Chicago Defender*, *Ebony*, etc. These outlets rejected the racist mainstream press by centering Black life and excellence. Historically speaking, some argue that social justice movements have often been centered upon the Black experience and leadership. How does this perception relate to Black Twitter?

Alex: When we talk about the Black experience, I'll refer to Morrison again, who claims that our historical narratives have been veiled. The formerly enslaved, when composing slave narratives, for example, faced the inability to explore one's creative resources publicly. For Morrison, this is the charge of the Black writer. When we look at the fact that Alicia Garza, Opal Tometi, and Patrisse Cullors coined what is literally the most well-known hashtag associated with Black Twitter—Black Lives Matter—we see that Black Women originated and collaboratively organized this contemporary social movement, as Black Women so often do. When you think about feminist social movements in the US, Black Women made huge contributions by speaking publicly about race and gender. Maria W. Stewart, inspired by David Walker's *Appeal to Colored Citizens*, is considered to be the first Black Woman documented giving speeches (she kept a record of them) in about 1832.

Meanwhile, White American feminists tended to completely separate the issue of suffrage for White Women and Black people, favoring a platform that wouldn't be "distracted" by the "race problem." We have faced major solidarity challenges since, which were intensified by the fact that White Women could also be cruel slave mistresses and get any Black person (but especially men) punished at mere suggestion of them looking at her, talking to her "out of turn," and for no reason at all other than wielding White power. Clearly, Black and White Women continue to have racial issues because the outcomes of the 2016 election showed that White feminists failed to secure a more progressive vote from the vast majority of their demographic. Over 90 percent of Black Women voters, by contrast, showed up at the polls for Hillary Clinton even though she wasn't necessarily their most preferred candidate. Personally, I'm always having to deal with being caught between race and gender, which is accompanied by the problem of invisibility. Far too often, Black Women's intellectual and cultural production, as well as our political activism, fails to receive credit. Our work almost always gets absorbed in a patriarchal racial discourse. This erasure happens to other women of color as well.

This context needs to be acknowledged because it demonstrates some of the potential dangers of Black Twitter circulating in pop culture. A hashtag like #BLM generates more hashtags like #ICantBreathe and #NotJustUVA. To be sure, civil rights is no longer organized around a fixed, central body of leadership. In fact, this is why it is difficult to study and talk about. Rather, it's a digital, globally distributed social movement. That's what makes Black Lives Matter distinctive. It emerged from a historically continuous present. What emerged from a spontaneous but tirelessly ongoing and repetitive conversation about Black pain and suffering came from three women having a conversation. Their quasi-public deliberation about how crazy it was that Trayvon Martin, a teenager, could face sudden demise while he was simply walking home. "Enough," they said. And others agreed. Millions and millions of people agreed. So #BLM begins a new chapter in the long fight for Civil Rights. #BlackLivesMatter has been very effective at initiating and sustaining a national conversation about race and criminality. Coalitions have emerged like #SayHerName and #CiteBlackWomen. In sum, Black Women have always played a major role in the tradition of fighting for Civil Rights. Unfortunately, they aren't always given their proper due.

Chris: Considerations of race, gender, and intersectionality are always present in your work, Alex. I was fortunate enough to direct your Master's thesis "Hidden in the Backwaters: The Legacy of Blues Women." I also read your dissertation on leak culture. Both of these projects engage these issues with technology, media, and information systems.

In this most recent work, I noticed that you're engaging with Alessandra Raengo's idea of liquid blackness. The liquid metaphor runs continuously throughout your research. Could you comment on that? I'm interested in what you see as some of the through lines of your research and how they have led to your current work.

Alex: I have long been critical of the perspective that the internet would liberate us from social injustices like racism and sexism. In fact, this is one of those "dominant ideologies" that I'm resisting by using a Critical Technological Discourse Analysis throughout my chapter.

As a Web 1.0 user, and a teen, I recall the dilemmas I faced in chat rooms, discussion forums, and newsgroups as a Black Woman. I used to play with various avatars of different genders and races for profile images to see how it would affect my interactions. Then several years later, around 2007 or so, Facebook opened their platform to everyone outside of college networks, requiring its users to provide their real names. While there's a culture of say, Black Women users, who embed hacker names in their Facebook identities (e.g., LouiseBrownBabyDollSmith), most users blindly traded some of their protected personally identifying info for the ability to join the neatly organized interface that used to be exclusive to college students.

When social media became more global, it became more obviously political. Around 2008, I noticed entities like WikiLeaks emerging. WikiLeaks started affecting public discourses about government transparency, corruption, and the political role of hackers in the 21st century. Although Julian Assange is hardly a trustworthy messenger, as WikiLeaks' meddling in the 2016 U.S. presidential elections showed, his organization made it clear that Web 2.0 platforms scaled data production. Additionally, surveillance and leaks could be weaponized by everyday people, which used to be an affordance that was exclusive to government intelligence agencies. Now, Folks be spying back!

Equipped with mobile devices, cameras, and an internet connection, most people are capable of documenting any event they participate in or just happen upon. Consequently, surveillance has become more and more democratized. There's been a major increase in leaks because people are sharing information that they think needs to be shared. Secrets and cover-ups are more salacious in this context because internet users are drowning in data. Another aspect of this scene to consider is how we talk about progress and technology. For example, should we still be describing social media networks as "new?"

This language of novelty bothers me because we risk erasing histories of science and technology. With this in mind, I analyze technology while being aware of the fact that there's always a time "when old technologies were new"—which is the title of a book written by Carolyn Marvin. While reading Marvin's book, I was also reading Angela Davis's *Blues Legacies and Black Feminisms* for a grad seminar entitled "Jazz and Blues in American Literature." Her philosophical analysis and exhaustive transcription of Bessie Smith and Ma Rainey's work inspired me to consider how these women utilized emerging technologies of their day. After all, they utilized the phonograph and radio to communicate to mass audiences. They also performed Vaudeville shows, traveling with the Theatre Owner's Booking Association (TOBA), which involved (emerging new) transportation technologies like the railroad and trains. During the 1920s, these mass communication technologies made it possible for dozens and dozens of working-class Black Women, regardless of their ability to "read and write," to tell their story. This research on Blueswomen's use of Black rhetoric and new technologies made me develop a more nuanced way of theorizing composition. I became much more critical about assuming that the written word is the supreme marker of "civilization," or the ultimate measures of literacy and intelligence.

Blueswomen also taught me a lot about the taboo of disclosure, writ large and within the Black community. They were subjected to the politics of respectability. Blueswomen were shut out of Black Women's clubs by their educated, middle- to upper-class sisters for being "unladylike." Their racy lyrics covered topics like lesbianism and gender fluidity (Ma Rainey's "Prove it on Me"), domestic violence (Bessie Smith's "T'aint Nobody's Business if I Do" and "I've Been Mistreated and I Don't Like It"), alcoholism (Bessie Smith's "Me and My Gin"), trifling romantic partners (Bessie Smith's "Pinchbacks, Take Em' Away," and "Aggravatin' Papa (Don't You Try to Two-Time")), natural disasters (Bessie Smith's "Backwater Blues"), police brutality (Rosa Henderson's "Chicago Policeman Blues"), imprisonment (Bessie Smith's "Jailhouse Blues"), widespread illnesses (Victoria Spivey's "T.B. Blues"), promiscuity (Bessie Smith's "Need a Little Sugar in My Bowl"), superstitions (Bessie Smith's "Blue Spirit Blues"), and even scathing critiques of racism and sexism (Bessie Smith's "Poor Man's Blues" and "Washwoman Blues").[1] These narratives forced Blueswomen into an underground culture of the nightlife. They were pushed to the edges of Black culture at the turn of the 20th century, but they were also the first to record popular music in a genre designated "race records." Despite criticisms about their sinful "low-brow" lifestyles, artists like Bessie Smith sold hundreds of thousands of records to Black consumers struggling for mobility and self-definition in the (then) new century. These sales enabled Black people to be recognized as viable consumers as new forms of entertainment became part of a post-agrarian industrial economy.

I continued to be interested in the issue of disclosure and its relationship to technology. However, I turned my attention to leaks during my Ph.D. because I was concerned by the lack of scholarly attention to hate speech, online harassment, and the increase of leaks in all forms from Chelsea Manning's leaking of

---

1   See Appendix B. You can access these songs at http://bit.ly/YouTubePlaylistRRRM

the Iraq and Afghanistan war logs and the U.S. Embassy cables to large corporations like Target and Macy's leaking consumer data. Even the Pentagon couldn't seem to "protect" user information. Leaks seemed everywhere, but little analysis of them seemed to be happening anywhere, with exception of Glenn Greenwald and Amy Goodman of *Democracy Now!* I paid close attention to how the language of Watergate became part of the conversation about WikiLeaks. So I applied my inquiry about "when old technologies were new," which helped me come across William Burroughs' *The Electronic Revolution*, in which he forecasts the mass distribution of aural technologies. In this book, he talks specifically about tape recorders and the way they would create "the word virus." This concept will influence my research on Black Twitter beyond this project because I'm eager to start writing a racial theory of contagion.

Chris: Could you elaborate a little bit more on Burroughs's concept of "the word virus?" I'm fascinated that you are turning to Burroughs's work to make sense of Watergate. I don't want to move us too far away from Black Twitter, but I really want to know more how his theories might tell us more about the socio-political relationship between the Beats and the Black Power Movement.

Alex: Sure! I can address this concept, and I'll be sure to relate it to Black Twitter. But y'all got to bear with me, cuz it's a very long answer.

Burroughs's work made me think about leaks and the inevitability of Watergate. I've always been inspired by American counter-culture, whether Conjurefolk, Blueswomen, Transcendentalists, Beats, Hippies, Black Panthers, Psychedelic Researchers, Hip-Hop, Punk, etc. On one hand, you could say these identities have been commodified in commercials, t-shirt slogans, and all kinds of stuff. However, my research makes it clear that nearly all of these cultures are threatening to the government. Wherever the government is trying to shut down a certain kind of aesthetic or inclusive political agenda, they go after solidarity. They seek to destroy social contact among so-called radicals through a systemic mechanism like COINTELPRO. But activists and artists used their work to make it clear that the truth was that White supremacy and patriarchy were self-destructive, violent systems that would kill us all through their cruelty and incompetence. Sorry for the frankness, but I need us to understand the level of fear that I live with daily.

When researching leaks, I was asking categorical questions about Watergate that are similar to those I ask about Black Twitter. I wondered, "What the hell is Watergate?" I knew it was a literal place, but when most people refer to Watergate, they mean this sprawling, convoluted drama about criminality that goes to the highest level. In that case, the American public questioned whether our justice system was capable of delivering "justice for all" when presidential power can be used for immunity. Within that vastness that is Watergate—which was happening during the spread of the Black Power Movement, the birth of Black studies, and perpetual incidents of police brutality—I asked, "How is race operating in this narrative?" I then discovered that the man responsible for the entire Watergate affair was a Black security guard by the name of Frank Wills. And with that discovery, the names in the Watergate drama told as much of the story as the events themselves. Wills willed Watergate.

Watergate introduced all kinds of leaky language into the hemisphere; the signs came to life through the names of characters and places—how you gonna gate Water?—and organizations—the folks who funded the political sabotage were literally CREEPs, or Nixon's Committee to Re-Elect the President, and so on. It is important to note that the entire trial was a leak drama. It exemplified Burroughs's "word virus" or humans' inability to control the spread of data.

Burroughs defines a virus as "a very small unit of word and image . . . [that] can be biologically activated to act as communicable virus strains." He says that the virus "reminds you of its unwanted presence." This quote made me think long and hard about what information means in this century. What are the "unwanted presences" of information, how do they become visible?

From Blueswomen to Watergate to WikiLeaks to Black Twitter, each of these subjects revealed something about the rhetorical significance of disclosure.

Iris: Could you say more about Wills, or more about how you see Watergate as connected to race?

Alex: Absolutely. Wills noticed the tape on the door where the five men in suits, four Cubans and one ex-CIA officer, James McCord,[2] entered to retrieve some wiretapping equipment that was used to bug Nixon's democratic rivals. Wills called the police and the men were arrested. This one incident set in motion a lengthy trial that unraveled the vast scope of cover-up and control culture.

Watergate connects to race because this is the same culture that designed and authorized programs of mass surveillance against Black Americans. Watergate showed how expansive the government was when executing its militaristic destruction of progressive movements. I researched how the news covered Frank Wills. Once again, I became immersed in the fact of our history of segregation. The Black press had a very different depiction of Wills than the mainstream papers. Many outlets hailed him as the hero of Watergate. He even won an NAACP image award in the late seventies for his role in cracking open the scandal. However, he barely got a blip in the national press and rarely was his race mentioned. The differences in depictions sparked my interest in Black perspectives on the whole matter of "intelligence" and surveillance, just as it was

---

2 See https://en.wikipedia.org/wiki/James_W._McCord_Jr.

when I turned to the Black papers for knowledge about Blues women and how the phonograph, radio, and film were being received by the Black community.

Chris: Earlier, you mentioned counter-cultures and counter-publics. How is the idea of a counter-public useful in discussing Black Twitter, and what are its inadequacies?

Alex: Many researchers have labeled Black Twitter as a counter-public. I understand their reasoning. The #BlackLivesMatter hashtag evolved into both a social movement and target of law enforcement. Large-scale fraud has been committed in its name. Right-wing pundits accuse its supporters of being "anarchists" and "terrorists" to stoke national fear. Race is at the center of this reception. Folks don't want to talk about the state of race relations right now, but it's unavoidable. Trump has successfully energized white nationalists. Now, I don't know who you imagine, but these people aren't just everyday Billys and Joes from the Deep South. I'm talking about our congresspeople, political advisors, and billionaires. Their hate for poor and colored people is more transparent than ever, so any visibility of folks speaking out is ripe for spreading widely. Thus, Black Twitter is absolutely a counter-public in the Twitterverse. The very name signifies the ongoing racism that leads to systemic racism and segregation. It reflects and affects how knowledge spreads throughout ecologies. It is a traceable entity that offers a record of how everyday people respond to injustice, as well as how they sought to connect with other users over shared cultural experiences, or how they laughed or cried.

But as I discussed earlier in our dialogue, we must always keep in mind that Twitter is a company, a publisher, and a public. How it moves affects what Black Twitter is. At any time, its users can be impacted by who owns and controls Twitter. As we speak, Paul Singer—the Republican billionaire—just purchased a huge stake in Twitter. It's rumored that he's trying to oust Dorsey and change company policies like their recent ban on political advertising. We must be wary of interpreting any communication that takes place on a for-profit platform as "revolutionary" or "liberatory."

Chris: Do scholars need to rethink the idea of counter-publics, given those problems of commodification, and given the participation of sophisticated bots in online political discourse?

Alex: Yes, I think so. We aren't just dealing with human agents in the current media scene. We talkin' bout a fully realized post-nuclear age complete with automation and what seems to be the collapse of the US as a symbol of democracy and freedom. However, we ain't gonna see no sudden total collapse of our country's military power. But we will see how global access to the internet exposes the U.S. security vulnerabilities as more and more countries see how easy it is to hack our systems. For example, the Chinese hacking of Equifax is a clear case of the political complexity of now. Who are the politicians who actually center issues of internet freedom, cybersecurity, or algorithmic bias at the core of their campaigns? The lack of policies regarding our data infrastructures may lead people to spend so much of their time criticizing culture that they get caught up in a constant loop of social media sharing that doesn't transform offline action much. I'm not saying critique isn't a good thing, or that a social movement should be written off if people aren't marching in the streets. I also don't want to marginalize the effectiveness of local grassroots activism. But folks be doing a whole lot of talking and a whole lot of re-sharing other people's content while thinking they are meaningfully contributing to a movement like #MeToo or #BLM. Testifying is definitely a necessary part of the process of theorizing about social change, but telling stories without also seeking out strategies to solve problems weakens the meaning of movements.

Iris: Thank you for that detailed clarification! It worries me that the concept of social justice seems to be more and more watered down. Lots of people try to use rhetorical appeals to being "woke" as a way to appear ethical or to stake out research territory or drum up speaking gigs. Black Twitter doesn't seem to be seeking out popularity, so there's something authentic about some of the posts. I found the connections you draw between journalists and social media were interesting in that way. Black Twitter is making people reimagine how activism looks.

But I hope you will conclude this dialogue by talking more about how you use government data in your chapter. I was really caught by surprise by your inclusion of the Mueller report and COINTELPRO. I am also interested in this history. I include it in my ethnic studies courses, especially when we discuss the Black Panthers. My question is related to that section. Why did you feel it necessary to bring in this information and connection? How does it inform Black Twitter? Black cultural expression? Black identity?

Alex: Since my chapter focuses on the challenges of studying Black Twitter, I thought it was relevant to examine some of the political context that contributes to the issue of race, technology, and information. Plenty of studies have already been done about how Black Twitter is political—such as the impact of popular hashtags like #BlackLivesMatter. Few studies include considerations of how emerging technologies have always been weaponized to deploy disinformation strategies that rely on racism to divide people. Wherever we are examining performances of racial identity, such as the language acts that constitute Black Twitter, it is critical to think about how race affects the meaning of privacy. Historically, privacy is not something that can be afforded to anyone without property, let alone those who were legally defined as such. The matter of Black people as property marked their bodies as publicly available for sale, to be managed and disciplined under a system of surveillance that they managed to hack. Equipped with creative spiritual and linguistic resources representing various parts of the African continent, the enslaved took advantage of their oppressor's lack of this knowledge. They organized information systems through complex multimodal texts and codes for mapping under extreme duress while also facing the risk of punishment for reading and writing. Through this illegal communication, as well as song, quilt, and knowledge of star systems, for example, enslaved Black people could locate one another, provide directions towards freedom, and potentially preserve some aspects of their ancestral cultures.

Having lived in this world and the segregated one that would follow, Black people continue to struggle over the meaning of privacy as offline and online realities have merged and surveillance has become ubiquitous. Everyone with a mobile phone and internet access is a walking camera with instantaneous access to free mass publishing platforms. Whereas in the past, Black life could be more carefully coded and controlled within our local communities away from the gaze of White people, as well as through Black media like *Jet*, *Essence*, and *Ebony* magazines, which for decades represented only the "best" of our leaders, entrepreneurs, entertainers, etc., the internet distributes blackness in its variety and location. Access to Black cultural expression has scaled, which complicates how blackness is performed and recognized. The problem of how to determine who is *really* Black, similar to the question of who was *really* down with the Black Power Movement during the 60s and 70s and not an informant, is exposed by 4chan trolls and the IRA's expansive, expensive attempts to divide online Black social media communities. Of course, Black feminists like Hudson and Crockett, as well as the moderators of r/BlackPeopleTwitter, who actively battle disinformation, demonstrate that insider knowledge about Black cultural expression like Black English isn't as simple to replicate as outsiders may think. Online performances are just as multiple, just as complicated as offline, and in fact are affected by their manifestations in each social space.

James: What do you think about the coalitional possibilities of Black Twitter? More specifically, what do you think about other people of color participating in Black Twitter? Are there common threads where certain people of color should be invited in? Or should Black Twitter exist solely for Black folks?

Alex: I appreciate that question because it raises questions about what the BIPOC have in common, in terms of language and discourses. Twitter is one thing that users of any color have in common. Next, there are certain ways of communicating that signify particular discourses. The performative nature of race becomes much more visible online, then, because an avatar or profile image can hardly serve as an "authentication" of a person's race. Offline, skin is the first thing people see along with other racialized characteristics. Next, we are racially marked by the way we talk (e.g., *talking Black, talking Back, talking "proper," or sounding White, being articulate,* etc.).

Online, racial performance is even more dependent on linguistic expression. This is why critical technological discourse analysis is an appropriate method for studying Black Twitter. Black English, for example, is one of the social languages that you might find via Black Twitter. However, meme sharing is a major form of communication that drives posts, threads, re-tweets, etc. Meme sharing is a language practice employed by most internet users. It is not exclusive to Black Twitter. As I mentioned earlier, Black Twitter is not independent of Twitter, the company. No one is "invited" to Black Twitter. Lots of people flex with the hashtags and they either get liked and reshared or they don't. No one can control, say, Asian or Latinx participation, unless those users aren't adept enough with language to "fit in" with the rest of that crowd.

In fact, I did come across a study during my research about how Black Twitter influences the ways in which other marginalized groups engage on Twitter. Deen Freelon, Lori Lopez, Meredith D. Clark, and Sarah J. Jackson co-wrote a report for the Knight Foundation in 2018, entitled, "How Black Twitter and Other Social Media Communities Interact with Mainstream News." That report looks at how #BlackTwitter, #AsianTwitter, and #FeministTwitter are increasingly replacing the mainstream news as some users' main source of information. Their report looks at some popular hashtags like #Asians4BlackLives to demonstrate how these "subcultures" (note: their term not mine, I definitely prefer counter-public or to refer to them as discourses since they are symbolic communications) build on and overlap with each other and #BlackTwitter.

The issue regarding POC's engagement with Black Twitter that concerns me is whether they show up when Black lives are really at stake. Anti-blackness is too real and frequently happens unconsciously—both within and outside of the Black community. Digital Blackface and cultural tourism are a problem, but Black people have resisted stereotyping and racial fraud in mass media since the minstrel show (and obviously before that as evidenced by slave narratives).

Black Twitter provides some relief from the pressure to hide one's blackness from the stifling White gaze. But I have to constantly question whether users are having a shared experience. Are me and the Asian woman looking at the bougie aunt meme and laughing for the same reasons? The reason for the laughter matters to me. I worry that negative stereotypes of Black people permeate how other POC engage us as a community. To be sure, some POC are cool, but some ain't, and definitely not the culture vultures that are looking to appropriate Black English and culture for social and monetary gains. Luckily, identity performance online tends to follow the same rules as speech acts happening offline. Basically, the crowd will determine if a POC user is "down" by the way they respond to their participation.

This concern brings me back to Iris' questions about authenticity. It matters how blackness appears to outsiders, and who ultimately battles over and controls that image. Violent, racialized surveillance has always played a role in the fight for literacy, the battle over Blackness as a commodity vs. cultural identity, and how the Black community hacks anti-Blackness through spontaneous interactions that rely on a certain shared knowledge of form, historical references, pop culture happenings.

Overall, this issue is mediated by the politics of state-sponsored surveillance and how social media platforms simultaneously empower the spread of misinformation tactics while also providing a space for the marginalized to "clap back," so to speak. In sum, the phenomenon of Black Twitter and how it is valued and how it will be studied must take into account how complex Black culture and its language practices are, as well as the history of data warfare that I've discussed throughout this dialogue.

WORKS CITED

Burroughs, William S. *Electronic Revolution*. Originally published in 1970 by Expanded Media Editions and republished by Ubuclassics 2005, katab.asia/wp-content/uploads/2015/04/Burroughs-electronic_revolution.pdf.

Davis, Angela Y. *Blues Legacies and Black Feminism: Gertrude Ma Rainey, Bessie Smith, and Billie Holiday*. Vintage, 2011.

Freelon, Deen, et al. "How Black Twitter and Other Social Media Communities Interact with Mainstream News." *Knight Foundation*, 27 Feb. 2018, knightfoundation.org/features/twittermedia/.

"Image Award Presentations Bring Out Top Show Stars." *Jet Magazine*, 7 Feb. 1974, bit.ly/3dkJisn.

Marvin, Carolyn. *When Old Technologies Were New: Thinking about Electric Communication in the Late Nineteenth Century*. Oxford UP, 1988.

Morrison, Toni. "The Site of Memory." *Inventing the Truth: The Art and Craft of Memoir*, edited by William Zinsser. 1987.

POSTSCRIPT

The title of this book was inspired by two works that, for us, define an emerging tradition in RCWS research that attempts to theorize race—*Race, Rhetoric, and Composition*, edited by Keith Gilyard, and *Race, Rhetoric, and Technology* by Adam Banks. We owe a great debt to these two texts, which offer philosophical lines of inquiry that have led to a significant body of works about race and racism in the field (see Chapter 1). In the introduction of this book, we review some of this research, noting that such work identifies the absence of race in RCWS research, interrogates negative characterizations of BIPOC, and/or resists the marginalization of minoritized people via linguistic dominance. We envision our book as part of current transformations in "critical" knowledge making in the discipline that takes seriously the need to address how structural racism affects our scholarship. Focusing on this problem motivated us to create work that could open up even more space for research that is guided by antiracism as a critical methodology. Whether you work on historical or contemporary subjects, we sincerely hope that our various approaches represent and/or stimulate your research interests, as well as your willingness to talk about race.

One way that our book differs from Gilyard's collection (an edited collection) and Banks' work (a single-author text) is that *Race, Rhetoric, and Research Methods* is a co-authored work. Four authors developing a book as one voice that could showcase multiple voices embedded into a coherent work required us to work differently than any of us were trained during our academic studies. The process requires negotiation, flexibility, and trust. Nevertheless, we crafted this book as a cross-cultural effort in overcoming these composition challenges.

Collaborative authorship has the potential to serve as a major characteristic of antiracism research. More people need to write together about how politics, especially structural oppression and violence, affects our everyday lives. In our case, it increased critical engagement with one another's work, as well as presented us with a long-term writing group that could support the development of our research writing and enrich our race-consciousness. Collaboration may also provide a way to have very difficult conversations about race and improve one's understanding about how to learn how to talk about it. We also believe that collaborative race-centered research will enable us to create new knowledge about high-stakes political issues and improve the generosity of idea exchange, overall.

Since we aim to produce ethical work, we must concede that composing this work has not been a seamlessly harmonious enterprise. We definitely encountered plenty of conflict along the way. Miscommunication occurred via long email chains, and commitment to the project was tested by various constraints such as the professional demands of directing writing programs, teaching in a Trump-era, negotiating multiple research projects, communicating with editors, succeeding on the academic job market, organizing comprehensive tenure and promotion portfolios, as well as grappling with extreme personal issues such as deaths in the family, parents' medical problems, poverty, incarceration, relationship break-ups, and so much more. Admittedly, we did not all enter the project with strong interpersonal relationships, which affected our ability to show care for one another. At any given time, two of us knew each other prior to the project, whereas the other two were strangers albeit colleagues. Some of us thought the best of each other or the worst of others. We cried, laughed, made meetings, missed meetings, provoked, relented, retracted, apologized, and forgave. Emotions ran too high to ever forget the experience. Some feelings were hurt, other feelings were good, passion and commitment were tested, and synergy was sometimes achieved.

Despite our struggles, the project continued. Our relationships strengthened as much as our desire to develop and finish this work. Working on our communication was a critical part of the creative process that yielded dramatic insights that prevailed over any obstacles we experienced along the way. We were better together, we had to trust each other, and absolute respect was necessary to inspire each other to create their best contributions to the work. But we aren't perfect. We aren't ashamed to discuss our difficulties because, as we often preach to our students and acknowledge in composition research, writing ain't easy. Our cycles of creation and resistance simply emulate this thing called "life." We know that we may not recognize lessons of this collaboration—its joys, traumas, etc.—for many years to come.

For graduate students and faculty seeking to innovate their methods and locate opportunities for eradicating racism, we hope that our book will serve as a critical resource that models a range of ways to make meaningful antiracist research. As we discussed in our introduction and throughout the text, antiracism informs the selection of methods capable of investigating culture, difference, and knowledge as concepts that are embedded in conflicts over the meaning of justice. Our book has attempted to shift the social justice turn in RCWS away from shallow conversations that briefly acknowledge that structural inequality exists towards deeper contemplations about how such observations ought to affect the field's research practices. Certainly, RCWS has a strong tradition of critical inquiry, as well as recovering texts that enable us to construct diverse disciplinary herstories. Our scholarship about injustice includes the problem of equitable assessment, lack of engagement between Minority-Serving Institutions (MSIs) and writing programs, linguistic imperialism, institutional racism, "remedial" program design, inadequate working conditions, unequal pay, insufficient racial diversity across all ranks, and sexual harassment, among several other issues. We build upon this work by focusing on some of the episte-mological implications of studying race and racism.

All our chapters, collectively, culminate in a series of strategic questions that could help guide future work that draws on antiracism as a research methodology:

1. Why am I interested in studying race and racism?
2. What sources of knowledge affect my understanding of race and racism?
3. What are my most memorable personal experiences with race and racism? Have I adequately considered the role of these experiences in how I think about knowledge, who produces it, who owns it, and what we ought to be studying?
4. How am I responding to national and global events involving race, class, gender, and sexuality? To what extent should this context be addressed in my scholarship? Why or why not?
5. When and how do I talk about race? For what purposes? What do I learn from these conversations?
6. How do conversations about race and racism, or oppression in general, tend to make me feel? What makes me uncomfortable, passionate, disin-terested, etc.?
7. Have I disclosed my personal interest in studying race and racism? Did I discuss how I feel affected by these subjects? Have I been explicit about the challenges that affect my ability to do this kind of scholarship?
8. Do my research questions about race reflect an attempt to eradicate racism?
9. Do I consult and engage (e.g., cite) research written by women, under-represented minorities, and other marginalized writers?
10. Does my research clarify specifically what it contributes to our knowledge about race and racism?

This line of inquiry, by no means exhaustive, informs methods that we already practice in the field: critical historiography, autoethnography, filmmak-ing, visual rhetorical analysis, and critical technological discourse analysis. These methods benefit studies about race and racism because they bring researchers into contact with their own habits of seeing and their relationship to their own racial identit(ies). This methodology invites researchers to build their confidence about how to responsibly talk about and study race. When more people engage antiracism as methodology, we will be capable of having much richer dialogues about race without alienating each other. We recognize that people are afraid to talk about race because they don't want to get it wrong, offend, and face harsh penalties for "ignorance." However, we strongly believe that the nature of this work is emotional because it requires grappling with absurdity, pain, violence, and (how we ought to share) responsibility.

As we conclude this book, we must draw your attention to the great catastrophes of 2020. We are currently living in a global pandemic where the US has failed to control the virus. Over 100,000 Americans have died from COVID-19, and we have millions of cases compared to numerous developed countries who are flattening their curves down to only a few hundred cases or less. Black, American Indian, and Latinx people disproportionately make up over half of COVID-19's victims (Wood). The U.S. president refuses to listen to leading scientists and doctors and implement nationwide measures that would enable us to reduce our scaled suffering. Instead, he has left states to fend for themselves while he hosts large rallies where people don't have to be socially distanced or wear masks. He weaponized the virus, racializing it by calling it the "Kung Flu" and the "China Virus," at the glee of his white supremacist base of voters. He compared peaceful protesters to Antifa, Fascists, Terrorists, Thugs, and Scum, deploying the national guard in D.C., who then used rubber bullets and teargas against the demonstrators.

Meanwhile, the entire nation has experienced a major awakening regarding racism and police violence. Millions of people all over the world are still staying home. Our attempt to combat the virus plus the mass unemployment rate (likely over 11 percent nationwide), as well as the cancellation of sports, slowed us down and made us focus on three heinous murders (Iacurci). Ahmaud Arbery, a Black man on a jog, was hunted and gunned down by three white supremacists in Brunswick, Georgia. Breonna Taylor, a Black woman EMT was asleep with her boyfriend, Kenneth Walker, when police conducted a no-knock warrant in Louisville, Kentucky. Walker, thinking it was a home invasion, grabbed his licensed firearm and confronted the police. Police immediately opened fire into the home, brutally killing Taylor in her sleep. They were at the wrong house. The police involved have not been charged. These two incidents were amplified by the cruel murder of George Floyd, a tall Black man in Minneapolis, MN. Bystander Darnella Frazier recorded officer Derek Chauvin placing his knee on Floyd's neck for eight minutes and forty-six seconds. Three other officers actively participated and/or passively watched. The reception of this video sparked global outcry unlike any other film footage before it.

Of course, Floyd's suffering is part of an ocean of human pain. So many hashtags preceded #JusticeforGeorgeFloyd, like #BlackLivesMatter, #ICantBreathe, #HandsupDontShoot, and #SayHerName. Yet, the citizen videography of Floyd rhetorically appealed to the masses. Like Emmett Till, the four little girls in Birmingham, MLK Jr., Malcolm X, Fred Hampton, Medgar Evers, and countless others, Floyd's unnecessary death signifies a clear and present danger to any claims to American Democracy.

During his eulogy of George Floyd, Reverend Al Sharpton declared that Floyd's literal death symbolized the current human condition under violent, corrupt, inhumane systems:

> What happened to Floyd happens every day in this country—in education, in health services, and in every area of American life. It's time for us to stand up in George's name and say, "Get yo' knee off our necks!" (See Appendix B: YouTubePlaylist)

And suddenly, people were putting on their masks by the millions, protesting police brutality and cruelty against humans during a pandemic. Books on antiracism are on bestseller lists. Monuments of racists and colonists are falling. The state of Mississippi finally signed a law to remove the confederacy symbol from their state flag—they are the last state in the US to do so. Suddenly, every major corporation is using the slogan #BlackLivesMatter. NFL Commissioner, Roger Goodall, apologized for not listening to players (whom he did not name) peacefully protesting the national anthem. Even Mitt Romney showed up to a protest and actually said that he believes that #BlackLivesMatter.

Indeed, it is worth dwelling on the fact that publicly talking about race and racism has always been extremely taboo. These concepts are highly emotional subjects that we all experience differently. Take race, for instance. It is absurd. It is a riddle. It is everywhere and nowhere. It is something that we may not see and we can't get out of. More specifically, it is hard to talk about race and racism because it is nearly impossible to tell the truth about what we see. Nowhere feels all that safe, and the precarity of safety leads to fear, suspicion, and shame. Regardless of who you are, or how "objective" and "professional" you attempt to be, we have to choose our words carefully when it comes to race. We make meaning about it as we go along, relying on a complex mapping of visual signs and linguistic codes that signal whether we should or shouldn't say certain things to certain audiences.

However, structural racism has created so many catastrophic consequences that it manifests quickly as a matter of life and death. The parallels between the behavior of COVID-19 and racism are increasingly striking enough to expose that the world has become so hostile and inhabitable for human beings, in general, that everyone's lives are at stake. Under this crushing reality, we are grateful that it is making conversations about antiracism more urgent and culturally relevant to the mainstream. Seeing #BlackLivesMatter and discussions about the possibility of defunding the police taken seriously by journalists and everyday people is something we could not have anticipated when we began this project in 2015.

Nevertheless, there is still so much work to do.

The preservation of human life and its overall quality literally depends on the eradication of practicing racial hierarchies in sign and deed. The "lives" in the Black Lives Matter (#BLM) movement vividly illustrate that unchecked, unexamined acts of racism disproportionately kill people. In fact, #BlackLivesMatter inspired us to wonder about the rhetorical power of the word "life" and how it presents an opportunity for literary and rhetorical investigation. Antiracism encourages us to consider how racism is unsustainable in the most literal sense. How does it systematically destroy and fail to sustain life? To consider antiracism as a methodology means acknowledging that everything we do—even research—has real implications for human survival and quality of life. Thus, we must choose research methods that are capable of generating knowledge about what it means to live and survive in a colonial, capitalist, patriarchal, white supremacist global society. How many risks are we willing to take in our research to fight for truth and justice? If our goal is to make knowledge about language and culture, how are we limited by the extent to which we can be honest about what we do and don't see?

The energy of this moment is anxious, frustrated, and unstable. The US has failed so miserably at responding to the rapid spread of COVID-19 that the EU has banned travel from this country. Some colleges and universities are laying off thousands of contingent laborers and demanding that faculty return to in-person teaching in fall 2020. Almost every single state is surging in COVID-19 cases, as experts estimate over 350,000 deaths as of January 2021. November feels like ages away. We anticipate that during these intense times, navigating graduate education will be the most difficult that it has ever been. The academic job market was already terrible, and it is destined to get worse and worse if U.S. leaders continue to ineffectively balance public health with "the economy." However, education is a public good that will never lose value as long as people seek excellence and a better life for us all. With these rhetorical considerations and opportunities in mind, antiracism is a profound and necessary course of epistemic action.

WORKS CITED

Iacurci, Greg. "Why the Real Unemployment Rate Is Likely over 11 Percent." *CNBC*, 8 Sep. 2020, www.cnbc.com/2020/09/08/why-the-real-unemployment-rate-is-likely -over-11percent.html.

Wood, Graeme. "What's behind the COVID-19 Racial Disparity?" *The Atlantic*, 27 May 2020, www.theatlantic.com/ideas/archive/2020/05/we-dont-know-whats -behind-covid-19-racial-disparity/612106/.

A BRIEF LIST OF KEY TERMS AND CONCEPTS FOR ENGAGING ANTIRACISM AS A RESEARCH METHODOLOGY

These terms are not inclusive of the full scope of the concepts that are operating in our text by any means. However, for the purposes of making our work even more accessible to readers, we have provided this glossary for quick reference. In the examples below, we have tried our best to clearly show how certain key terms that we introduced in the book's introduction and chapters are operating in our collaborative text.

Antiracism (as a methodology)

As a methodology, antiracism aims to destabilize the assumption that research (or the researcher) can be neutral, objective, and unbiased. Rather, it assumes that research is socially situated and its processes of knowledge production (such as citation) are always political. Antiracism refers to critical interventions that acknowledge how race and racism affect everyday life, in terms of the various epistemologies, discourses, environments, and ecologies where these concepts unfold. This methodology may inform research methods that seek to make knowledge from lived experience such as autoethnography, critical discourse analysis, and critical historiography.

Antiracism (as a theory)

As a theory, antiracism refers to the most desirable forms of human arrangements and interactions that enable us to vividly articulate that racism is viral, destructive, illogical, and unsustainable. In a white supremacist and/or colonial society, violence is used variously to broker and preserve power. Antiracism constitutes a logical and emotional response to the violent methods of preserving white and/or colonial supremacy.

Countervisuality

The denaturalization of culturally dominant optics by dissident or historically suppressed ways of seeing. The term has particular prominence in the work of Nicholas Mirzoeff, who frames visuality not as the neutral process of viewing or spectatorship, but rather as a set of preoccupations that condition what people notice and ignore. Put in conversation with Kenneth Burke's rhetorical theories, countervisuality at once challenges hegemonic varieties of the "terministic screen" and articulates contrary frameworks.

Book Applications: Carter relates this idea to citizen videography. Sanchez goes further, however, by helping produce a documentary film about antiracist protest and its reception in Grand Saline, Texas. Whereas Carter attempts to describe countervisuality and its relation to policing, Sanchez enacts the idea through collaborative, multimodal practice.

Decolonial Historiography

A critical research method that refers to the practice of reading histories, especially those composed in English, with an awareness of the colonial perspective. This perspective may be detected if the historian fails to disclose their position in relation to their subject (e.g., as a Western European or Occidental writing about an indigenous cultural group, or a White American writing about Black or Latinx populations) or writes about historically colonized groups as subjects to be studied and analyzed rather than as agents of their history. Composition, rhetoric, and literacy studies scholarship features many scholars who utilize this method to fill major gaps in the field's historical knowledge about the contributions of marginalized groups. These scholars often represent the groups they study and utilize this method as a way to demonstrate the field's lack of diversity. Examples of this work include Damian Baca and Victor Villanueva's *Rhetorics of the Americas: 3114 BCE to 2012 CE*, Shirley Wilson Logan's *We Are Coming: The Persuasive Discourse of Nineteenth-Century Black Women*, Jacqueline Jones Royster's *Traces of a Stream: Literacy and Social Change Among African American Women*, and Iris Ruiz's *Reclaiming Composition for Chicano/as and Other Ethnic Minorities: A Critical History and Pedagogy*.

Book Applications: Ruiz employs this approach in Chapter 2. It is also modeled in Chapter 1.

Epistemic Mediation

The production, or influencing, of epistemology through varied technologies of communication—whether as elemental as words, sounds, and pictures or as multiform as virtual reality and artificial intelligence. Carter's chapter utilizes this method to investigate how phone and body cameras mediate public deliberation about race and police brutality. For example, Carter observed that the news and television media have a long history of representing non-White subjects as latent or explicit threats to social order, thus, exerting a significant influence on law enforcement, judicial procedures, and the larger array of discursive norms that reproduce dominant ideas of authority and justice. The phrase "epistemic mediation" also entails a different meaning which inverts the previous emphasis, shifting from how media inform epistemologies to how those epistemologies work to generate media platforms. Lockett's chapter on Black Twitter's relationship to Black culture and language provides a key example, as does Ruiz's analysis of knowledge-making via decolonial storytelling such as how Curanderisma infuses Latinx writing.

Essentialism

Essentialism, within the context of critical race theory, suggests that certain groups of people, especially racial and ethnic groups, can be defined by certain immutable qualities. Historically, people have used the concept of essentialism to propagate racist ideologies that establish and perpetuate stereotypes. These include, for example, negative stereotypes like the idea that Black people have lower IQs or are more violent, or that Latinx people are lazier or quick to anger ("spicy"), as well as positive (but still harmful) stereotypes such as Asians are good at Math, Blacks are good at sports, etc. Examples of work that discuss essentialism include Harris' "Race and Essentialism in Feminist Legal Theory," Hanson-Easy, Augoustinos, and Moloney's "They're All Tribals": Essentialism, Context and the Discursive Representation of Sudanese Refugees," Williams' "Dissolving the Sameness/Difference Debate: A Post-Modern Path beyond Essentialism in Feminist and Critical Race Theory," and Phillips' "What's Wrong with Essentialism?"

Book Applications: In Sanchez's chapter (Chapter 3), he analyzes the relationship between essentialism and autoethnography. For Sanchez, this term can offer routes to self-reflection that are necessary for studying our personal relationship to racial epistemologies when doing autoethnographic work. He focuses on this term to consider how he handles his subjects in the inquiry, as follows: do our stories about literacy and culture essentialize peoples or communities? Are there ways we should ethically combat or acknowledge this?

Geography/Territory

This term may refer to both physical and symbolic space. In decolonial discourses, the issue of geography or territories is at the center of inquiry. For example, the United States gained territory through the notion of "Manifest Destiny," which was both the name of its colonialist pursuits, as well as the slogan for propaganda campaigns that legitimized those aims. Topography and cartography also represent colonialist practices of genocide and theft. For example, the creation of maps that increase the actual size of the US out of proportion with the rest of the world, or the British renaming of Gaelic land in Ireland. For further elaboration, see Kiran Asher's "Latin American Decolonial Thought, or Making the Subaltern Speak," Eve Tuck and K. Wayne Yang's "Decolonization is Not a Metaphor," Brian Friel's *Translations*, Walter Mignolo's "The Geopolitics of Knowledge and the Colonial Difference," and Ruiz and Sanchez's *Decolonizing Rhetoric and Composition: New Latinx Keywords for Theory and Practice.*

Book Applications: Each author—Ruiz, Sanchez, Carter, and Lockett—focuses their investigation of race and racism on specific places and spaces. Whether they were investigating digital media, a small town, sites of state-sponsored violence, and/or institutional/disciplinary boundaries, geography is emphasized in every chapter.

Nahui Ollin

Aztec/Mexica sun stone symbol signifying the number four (Nahui) and movement (Ollin; see Chapter 2 by Ruiz), also known as the fourth movement or four movements, four philosophies or principles of movement, four directions, four corners of the earth, and four seasons, all of which generalize into an understanding of cosmological, symbiotic, and universal harmony. There are four basic movements imprinted on the sunstone that represent four different philosophical worldviews that are interdependent and cyclical.

The first is hidden in the subconscious—Tezcatlipoca is the black obsidian mirror, also known as smoky mirror of the subconscious, self-reflection, and the creations of dreams and memory. The second is Quetzalcoatl, or "precious and beautiful knowledge." Once one gains the ability to self-reflect and gain a notion of self, one can then apply the faculties to gain knowledge and experience around them with the understanding that knowledge of the self, the family, the community, the land, and the cosmos are all interconnected and can provide sources of environmental, familial, societal, scientific, and intimate comfort that are a reflection of the higher spirit that is within all of us.

The third is Huitzilopochtli, which is part of the cycle of the Nahui Ollin that means to take action, or exercise the will to act. With the ability to self-reflect, as well as gain and develop knowledge, comes the challenge of being able to act upon the world in harmony with the intent of continuing on with self-realization regarding one's actions while also realizing that these actions will have material consequences on the physical world. With a conscious will to act, one must also be open to the consequences of their actions. If there is a lesson to be learned, that lesson would lead into the fourth concept: Xipec Totec, or transformation and renewal.

These four philosophies represent the Nahui Ollin and can be applied to the present day, in terms of indigenous reclamation of the epistemic and the spiritual—both present in the Aztec sun stone. When performing decolonial, antiracist research, this indigenous paradigm offers a more comprehensive framework for visualizing and actualizing possibilities than what we commonly refer to as "self-reflexivity" and "ethical research practices."

Book Applications: Ruiz employs this approach in Chapter 2.

Parrhesia

An Ancient Greek trope for determined resistance under conditions of inequality—in short, speaking truth to power. Vorris Nunley sees this blunt communication as necessary to "deep democracy," which presumes uneven agency among social demographics while noting how race permeates politics on the transnational scale and at the micro-level (164). Deep democratic praxis does not retreat from rhetorical agonism, which necessarily arises when antiracist actors contest structures of bodily privilege. Parrhesia inhabits antiracist practice in prose and in public demonstrations, in pedagogy as well as research design.

Book Applications: Carter employs this approach in Chapter 4.

People of Color

A term that is commonly used to refer to marginalized groups that represent a plurality of historically underrepresented, marginalized, or disadvantaged cultural identities. Many people utilize this term as a method of demonstrating their identification with and/or recognition of the collective suffering of Black, Brown, and colonized populations. However, it is not without controversy. Being a person of color (POC) may essentialize skin color in ways that continue to reify White supremacy because the notion of "White people" continues to be omitted from racial categorization. Furthermore, it erases the distinctive experiences of Black people, in regards to colorism. Access to White privilege, especially the ability to be identified as "White," is most limited to Black people unless they are fair-skinned enough to pass. However, being recognized as a White person depends on a combination of skin color, religion, educational background, linguistic dexterity, and economic class.

The demographic categories "People of color" and "White people" are socially constructed subject positions that indicate a historical, economic, and legal relationship to colorism, which is at the center of anti-Black racism and colonialism as structural practices. The distinction between "White" or "non-White" status, when at the center of the identity and social life of cultural groups, is enforced by genocide, theft, and exploitation of lands, resources, and people, which effectively serves to increase Western European and New World (American) economic power.

We propose that there needs to be an expansion of Alternative terms for POC. This would constitute antiracist praxis and enable us to re-imagine our relationship to race, in terms of the possibilities of livelihood, as well as our survival chances—both historically and present. This more comprehensive terminology might include: White/non-White, marginalized groups, minoritized populations,(historically) underserved populations, (historically) underrepresented groups, (historically) dehumanized peoples, (historically) terrorized cultures, and so on.

Note: We are not including "minorities" as a designation for POC even though some literature continues to do so. The term "minority" is factually inaccurate. White people are clearly the minority when considering the relationship between race and geography (see our definition of Geography/Territories) from a global vantage point.

See also M. Omi and H. Winant's *Racial Formation in the United States* and the other texts referenced as part of the "race" and "racism" definitions.

Book Applications: Some authors prefer the term "people of color," whereas other authors do not. We hope readers will pay attention to the specific contexts in which that term appears, as well as the specific authors who choose to use it to decide how the term's contestability is negotiated.

Race

Race is a cultural invention that emerged from certain scientific, technological, religious, and economic arrangements of human beings over time. It is comprised of a set of codes that assign certain values to the skin color of individuals and groups, as well as the style and performance of linguistic and cultural practices.

Race refers to a method of taxonomy that assigns value to an expansive categorical system that color-codes and geographically situates signs and symbols of dominance, entitlement, submission, and suffering. This system, when practiced, constitutes racism. Hardly "natural" or scientific, race is a human invention. It is both a socially constructed phenomenon and a ubiquitous feature of Western culture. Thus, race and racism are learned concepts and behavior, which means one's understanding is capable of being transformed.

Countless scholars across disciplines have attempted to define race. Some of the most widely circulated texts include Michelle Alexander's *The New Jim Crow: Mass Incarceration in the Age of Colorblindness*, Karen Brodkin's *How Jews Became White Folks and What that Says about Race in America*, John F. Dovidio and Samuel L. Gaertner's "Aversive Racism and Selection Decisions: 1989 and 1999,*"* Michael Omi and Howard Winant's *Racial Formation in the United States*, and Beverly Daniel Tatum's *Why Are All the Black Kids Sitting Together at the Cafeteria?: And Other Conversations About Race*.

Book Applications: Race, as a construct, is at the center of this text's critical framework. We envision research about this term's relationship to epistemology, as it offers a key site of investigation for examining how knowledge is produced, managed, and circulated.

Racial Literacy

Typically, literacy is defined as the individual's ability to read and write in a specific language, but in literacy studies, and in the context of a racial literacy, the term "literacy" would be better defined as the comprehension of specific cultural and social contexts. Thus, a racial literacy looks at how the researcher understands their own race—in relationship to time, space, location, and other social and cultural factors—or the race of others. In other words, a racial literacy focuses on how to "read" race. Racial literacies have been utilized in RCWS and other fields (such as education studies and cultural studies) and are typically employed to better understand the structure, dynamics, and realities of race and how race impacts education (Victor Villanueva's *Bootstraps*), language practices (Keith Gilyard's *Voices of the Self*), and other subjects. Most racial literacies take an autoethnographic approach and emphasize how the individual found something about their self through various cultural factors. Examples of work that discuss racial literacies (or embody the form) include Yolanda Sealy-Ruiz's "Building Racial Literacy in First-Year Composition," Elaine Richardson's *PHD to Ph.D.: How Education Saved my Life*, Ta-Nehisi Coates's *Between the World and Me*, and Mara Grayson's "Race Talk in the Composition Classroom: Narrative Song Lyrics as Texts for Racial Literacy."

Racism

The conscious or unconscious act of erasing another human being's life force to some degree or another. At its most extreme, racism is targeted murder that leads to the literal erasure of a human life. It is also more or less practiced as a matter of enforcing "normal" behavior in any community setting that measures and values performances of whiteness/coloniality as superior to other kinds of cultural expression. For example, the act of making a statement that claims someone else is cognitively deficient because they don't speak or write in Standard White English (SWE) or refusing to comment on the witnessing of police brutality against unarmed persons.

Racism is not a matter of personal opinion and prejudice. As scholar Beverly Daniel Tatum argues, racism is "prejudice plus power" because it maintains and perpetuates a system of advantage based on race (10). A systemic phenomenon, racism is a practice that allocates social, political, and economic advantages based on fair skin and European facial characteristics; it creates and maintains White supremacy, regardless of intent or intensity of manifestation.

Racism may be overt, as in the use of racial slurs, racist symbols and hate crimes, or aversive. Pearson, Dovidio, and Gaertner make this point in their article "The Nature of Contemporary Prejudice": "Aversive racists sympathize with victims of past injustice, support the principle of racial equality, and regard themselves as non-prejudiced, but at the same time, possess negative feelings and beliefs about [marginalized groups such as] Blacks, which may be unconscious" (316). Indeed, unconscious racial bias significantly contributes to systemic discrimination during jury selection and hiring processes, as well as miscommunication and distrust during interracial interaction, which affects whether relationships will form and how (Dovidio and Gaertner 322–325). For more information on this sense of the word racism, see J. F. Dovidio and S. L. Gaertner's "Aversive Racism and Selection Decisions: 1989 and 1999" for more information about unconscious, or subtle acts, of racism. This foundational work maintained the word "racism" in its definition of certain racial practices, unlike the term "microaggressions," which we have omitted because it removes the language of race from its categorization of racist phenomena.

Countless scholars across disciplines have attempted to explicitly define racism. Some of the foundational texts in this area of scholarship include D. A. Bell's *Faces at the Bottom of the Well: The Permanence of Racism*, E. Bonilla-Silva's "Rethinking Racism: Toward a Structural Interpretation," and J. F. Dovidio and S. L. Gaertner's *The Aversive Form of Racism*, as well as M. Wetherell and J. Potter's *Mapping the Language of Racism: Discourse and the Legitimation of Exploitation*.

Many scholars have also acknowledged the intersection of gender, ethnicity, and race in their formulations of the definition. This inclusive scholarship includes work such as Lauren Berlant's *The Queen of America Goes to Washington City: Essays on Sex and Citizenship*, Philomena Essed's *Understanding Everyday Racism: An Interdisciplinary Theory*, and Patricia Hill-Collins' *Black Sexual Politics: African Americans, Gender, and the New Racism*.

The most marginalized scholarship about racism is research on environmental racism. Widely cited research in this area includes Robert D. Bullard's *Confronting Environmental Racism: Voices from the Grassroots*, Robert D. Bullard and Beverly Wright's *The Wrong Complexion for Protection: How the Government Response to Disaster Endangers African American Communities*, and Steven Gregory's *Black Corona: Race and the Politics of Place in an Urban Community*.

Book Applications: In the introduction, Chapter 1, we argue that racism is a consequence of researchers failing to take race into account when they conduct and publish research.

Reconciliation

The act of reconciliation is typically understood to be a two-party process, in which the "wrongdoer" attempts to make amends with the person or party who is wronged. In academia, we typically use this term to think of larger atrocities (such as the Truth and Reconciliation Commission that attempts to "reconcile" post-apartheid South Africa). However, the term can be employed to study other forms of transgression too, ones that might be more personal or might be between community and individual. More importantly, we can use reconciliation to better understand the relationship between researcher and subjects when the subjects have a personal interest for the researcher.

For the field of RCWS, reconciliation can be an important theme to help the researcher position themselves in relation to their subject and to navigate how to make the personal scholarly. Examples of work that discuss reconciliation include John B. Hatch's "Reconciliation: Building a Bridge from Complicity to Coherence" and "The Hope of Reconciliation: Continuing the Conversation," Erik Doxtader's "Reconciliation—A Rhetorical Concept/ion," and Erik Doxtader's *With Faith in the Works of Words*.

Book Applications: This concept is further explored in Chapter 3.

Sustainability

An ecological practice and symbiotic ideal in which human activity is directed towards preserving and generating biological and cultural life throughout all levels of the biosphere. This includes resisting the further contamination of air, water, and soil, promoting the healthy function of human bodies, as well as increasing linguistic and genetic diversity among humans.

This book utilizes the term to argue that sustainability should be the ultimate goal of antiracism. When race and racism are defined as ecological (e.g., structural and material) phenomena, they should be embedded in discourses of sustainability. Our book's theoretical framework merges several disciplinary perspectives on race and racism that fail to articulate the glaring assumptions about the purpose of talking about race and resisting racism: to reduce human suffering and increase peace—two goals that are compatible with a less toxic physical environment.

Some recent scholarship in interdisciplinary fields like public health and environmental studies acknowledging the relationship between appeals to life and the purposes of antiracism include Jennifer Jee-Lyn García and Mienah Zulfacar Sharif's "Black Lives Matter: A Commentary on Racism and Public Health," Phoebe Godfrey and Denise Torres' "Systemic Crises of Global Climate Change: Intersections of Race, Class, and Gender," and David Pellow's *Toward a Critical Environmental Justice Studies: Black Lives Matter as an Environmental Justice Challenge-Corrigendum*.

Book Applications: Sustainability ought to be the goal of any human activity, especially antiracism. Antiracism that contributes to sustainability seeks to value and preserve human life and the biosphere.

Whiteness

Racial performance that is marked by its users' ability to conceal race as a visible construct operating in the space. For example, the terms man and woman without racial modification (e.g., Black man) will likely be imagined as Caucasians, which normalizes and, thus, privileges whiteness. In other words, it is a benefit to be identified as someone who is "beyond" race precisely because of the vast number of negative consequences of being considered a raced or "colored body." The color of our bodies bears the mark of the degree to which one is likely to own property, inherit wealth, have documented lineage via news coverage, tax record, or cemetery visibility, as well as be subject to mob violence, imprisonment, homelessness, and general poverty.

Book Applications: All chapters address the concept of whiteness. Ch. 2 illustrates how whiteness is perpetuated through the racialized politics of citation. Ch. 3 describes whiteness as a cultural identity rooted in place and anti-Black regional traditions. Ch. 4 demonstrates how whiteness is protected by institutions, especially law enforcement. Ch. 5 analyzes whiteness, citizenship, and online identity performances.

WORKS CITED

Alexander, Michelle. *The New Jim Crow: Mass Incarceration in the Age of Colorblindness.* New Press, 2020.

Asher, Kiran. "Latin American Decolonial Thought, or Making the Subaltern Speak." *Wiley Online Library*, John Wiley & Sons, Ltd, 3 Dec. 2013, onlinelibrary. wiley.com/doi/10.1111/gec3.12102.

Baca, Damián, and Victor Villanueva. *Rhetorics of the Americas: 3114 BCE to 2012 CE.* Palgrave Macmillan, 2010.

Bell, Derrick. *Faces at the Bottom of the Well: the Permanence of Racism.* Basic Books, 2018.

Berlant, Lauren. *The Queen of America Goes to Washington City Essays on Sex and Citizenship.* Duke UP, 2012.

Bonilla-Silva, Eduardo. "Rethinking Racism: Toward a Structural Interpretation." *American Sociological Review*, vol. 62, no. 3, June 1997, pp. 465–480. doi:10.2307/2657316.

Brodkin, Karen. *How Jews Became White Folks: and What That Says about Race in America.* Rutgers UP, 2010.

Bullard, Robert D. *Confronting Environmental Racism: Voices from the Grassroots.* South End Press, 1993.

Bullard, Robert D., and Beverly Wright. *The Wrong Complexion for Protection: How the Government Response to Disaster Endangers African American Communities.* New York UP, 2012.

Burke, Kenneth. *A Grammar of Motives, and A Rhetoric of Motives*. Meridian, 1962.

Coates, Ta-Nehisi. *Between the World and Me*. Random House Publishing Group, 2015.

Collins, Patricia Hill. *Black Sexual Politics: African Americans, Gender, and the New Racism*. Routledge, 2006.

Dovidio, John F., and Samuel L. Gaertner. "Aversive Racism and Selection Decisions: 1989 and 1999." *Psychological Science*, vol. 11, no. 4, 2000, pp. 315–319.

———."The Aversive Form of Racism." *Stereotypes and Prejudice: Essential Readings*, Psychology Press, 2000, pp. 289–304.

Doxtader, Erik. "Reconciliation—a Rhetorical Concept/ion." *Quarterly Journal of Speech*, vol. 89, no. 4, 2003, pp. 267–292.

Doxtader, Erik. *With Faith in the Works of Words: the Beginnings of Reconciliation in South Africa, 1985–1995*. Michigan State UP, 2009.

Essed, Philomena. *Understanding Everyday Racism: an Interdisciplinary Theory*. SAGE Publications, 1994.

Friel, Brian. *Translations: A Play*. Samuel French, 1981.

García, Jennifer Jee-Lyn and Mienah Zulfacar Sharif. "Black Lives Matter: A Commentary on Racism and Public Health." *American Journal of Public Health*, vol. 105, no. 8, 2015, pp. e27-e30. doi:10.2105/AJPH.2015.302706.

Gilyard, Keith. *Voices of the Self: a Study of Language Competence*. Wayne State UP, 1991.

Godfrey, Phoebe, and Denise Torres. *Systemic Crises of Global Climate Change: Intersections of Race, Class and Gender*. Routledge, 2018.

Grayson, Mara Lee. "Race Talk in the Composition Classroom: Narrative Song Lyrics as Texts for Racial Literacy." *Teaching English in the Two Year College*, vol. 45, no. 2, 2017, pp. 143–167.

Gregory, Steven. *Black Corona Race and the Politics of Place in an Urban Community*. Princeton UP, 2011.

Hanson-Easey, Scott, Martha Augoustinos, and Gail Moloney. "'They're all Tribals': Essentialism, Context and the Discursive Representation of Sudanese Refugees." *Discourse & Society*, vol. 25, no. 3, 2014, pp. 362–382.

Harris, Angela P. "Race and Essentialism in Feminist Legal Theory." *Stanford Law Review*, vol. 42, no. 3, 1990, pp. 581–616.

Hatch, John B. "Reconciliation: Building a Bridge from Complicity to Coherence in the Rhetoric of Race Relations." *Rhetoric & Public Affairs*, vol. 6, no. 4, 2003, pp. 737–764.

Hatch, John B. "The Hope of Reconciliation: Continuing the Conversation." *Rhetoric & Public Affairs*, vol. 9, no. 2, 2006, pp. 259–277.

Logan, Shirley W. *We Are Coming: the Persuasive Discourse of Nineteenth-Century Black Women*. Southern Illinois UP, 1999.

Mignolo, Walter. "The Geopolitics of Knowledge and the Colonial Difference." *The South Atlantic Quarterly*, vol. 101, no. 1, 2002, pp. 57–96.

Mirzoeff, Nicholas. *The Visual Culture Reader*. Routledge, 2013.

Nunley, Vorris L. *Keepin' It Hushed: the Barbershop and African American Hush Harbor Rhetoric*. Wayne State UP, 2011.

Omi, Michael, and Howard Winant. *Racial Formation in the United States*. Routledge, 2015.

Pearson, Adam R., John F. Dovidio, and Samuel L. Gaertner. "The Nature of Contemporary Prejudice: Insights from Aversive Racism." *Social and Personality Psychology Compass*, vol. 3, no. 3, 2009, pp. 314–338, bit.ly/3s00dVm.

Pellow, David N. "Toward A Critical Environmental Justice Studies: Black Lives Matter as an Environmental Justice Challenge." *Du Bois Review: Social Science Research on Race*, vol. 13, no. 2, 2016, pp. 221–236. doi:10.1017/S1742058X1600014X.

Phillips, Anne. "What's Wrong with Essentialism?." *Distinktion: Scandinavian Journal of Social Theory*, vol. 11, no. 1, 2010, pp. 47–60.

Potter, Jonathan, and Margaret Wetherell. *Mapping the Language of Racism: Discourse and the Legitimation of Exploitation*. Harvester Wheatsheaf, 1993.

Richardson, Elaine B. *PHD to Ph. D: How Education Saved My Life*. New City Community, 2013.

Royster, Jacqueline Jones. *Traces of a Stream: Literacy and Social Change among African American Women*. U of Pittsburgh P, 2000.

Ruiz, Iris D. *Reclaiming Composition for Chicano/as and Other Ethnic Minorities: a Critical History and Pedagogy*. Palgrave Macmillan, 2016.

Ruiz, Iris D., and Raúl Sánchez, eds. *Decolonizing Rhetoric and Composition Studies: New Latinx Keywords for Theory and Pedagogy*. Springer, 2016.

Sealey-Ruiz, Yolanda. "Building Racial Literacy in First-Year Composition." *Teaching English in the Two-Year College*, vol. 40, no 4, 2013, pp. 384–398.

Tatum, Beverly Daniel. *Why Are All the Black Kids Sitting Together in the Cafeteria? and Other Conversations about Race*. BasicBooks, 1997.

Tuck, Eve, and K. Wayne Yang. "Decolonization is not a Metaphor." Decolonization: Indigeneity, *Education & Society*, vol. 1, no.1, 2012, pp. 1–40.

Villanueva, Victor. *Bootstraps: from an American Academic of Color*. National Council of Teachers of English, 1993.

Williams, Joan C. "Dissolving the Sameness/difference Debate: A Post-Modern Path Beyond Essentialism in Feminist and Critical Race Theory." *Duke Law Journal*, vol. 1991, no. 2, pp. 296–323. doi:10.2307/1372729.

APPENDIX B.
YOUTUBE PLAYLIST FOR RACE, RHETORIC, AND RESEARCH METHODS

This playlist is comprised of multimedia materials we have referenced in this book. We created this comprehensive YouTube Playlist to provide another way to access our work. Instructors, for example, may find it to be a useful addition to their teaching of the text. Other readers may find it convenient not to have to chase dead links, and others may find it easier to consume some of our references via video.

View the playlist at bit.ly/YouTubePlaylistRRRM.

ABOUT THE AUTHORS

Alexandria L. Lockett is Assistant Professor of English at Spelman College. She is one of the co-editors of the book *Learning from the Lived Experiences of Graduate Student Writers* (Utah State University Press). She also publishes about the technological politics of race, surveillance, and access in articles that have appeared in *Composition Studies, Enculturation,* and *Praxis,* as well as chapters featured in *Wikipedia@20: An Incomplete Revolution* (MIT Press), *Humans at Work in the Digital Age* (Routledge), *Out in the Center* (Utah State University Press), and *Black Perspectives on Writing Program Administration: From the Margins to the Center* (SWR Press). As a first-generation college student, she is deeply concerned about knowledge equity. For as long as she has been teaching college writing, she has integrated Wikipedia editing and centered marginalized writers in the curriculum. She is committed to building and expanding institutional cultures that practice digital humanities, antiracism, womanism, and critical digital literacy. An extended biography is available via her portfolio at www. alexandrialockett.com.

Iris D. Ruiz is Continuing Lecturer for Merritt Writing Program and Lecturer in Ethnic Studies at California State University, Stanislaus. Her current publications are her monograph, *Reclaiming Composition for Chicano/as and other Ethnic Minorities: A Critical History and Pedagogy*, winner of the honorable mention CCCC Outstanding Book Award, and *Decolonizing Rhetoric and Composition Studies: New Latinx Keywords for Theory and Pedagogy*, which she co-edited in addition to contributing a chapter on the keyword "Race." Her work on race and writing program administration (WPA) was published as an article in the *WPA: Writing Program Administration*. Finally, her current research focuses upon Chicanx history, decolonial theory, methods, intersectional and cross-generational trauma, and the politics of critical imperial scholarship and citation practices. Her work is also featured in the NCTE/CCCC Latinx Caucus history book with Parlor Press, *Viva Nuestra Caucus*, and in the Series for Writing and Rhetoric co-edited collection, *Rhetorics Elsewhere and Otherwise*. She aims to continue to work toward transformative and antiracist leadership, scholarship and pedagogical practice.

James Chase Sanchez is Assistant Professor of Writing and Rhetoric at Middlebury College in Vermont. His research interests are in cultural and racial rhetorics, public memory, and methodology, and his research has appeared in *College Composition and Communication, Pedagogy, Journal of Contemporary Rhetoric, Present Tense,* and *Writing Program Administration*. Sanchez has a single-authored monograph, titled *Salt of the Earth: Rhetoric, Preservation, and White Supremacy*, that will be published with NCTE in 2021. He also produced a documentary about racism in his hometown of Grand Saline, TX in 2017. The film, *Man on Fire*, won numerous awards, including an International Documentary Association award in 2017, and premiered on PBS in 2018 as a part of *Independent Lens*. He is currently in production of his second documentary, *In Loco Parentis*, that investigates the history of sexual abuse and rape at New England boarding schools.

Christopher Carter is Professor of English and Divisional Dean of Humanities at the University of Cincinnati. He teaches courses in writing theory, activist rhetoric, and visual culture. His books include *Rhetoric and Resistance in the Corporate Academy* (Hampton Press, 2008), *Rhetorical Exposures: Confrontation and Contradiction in US Social Documentary Photography* (University of Alabama Press, 2015), *Metafilm: Materialist Rhetoric and Reflexive Cinema* (Ohio State University Press, 2018), and *The Corruption of Ethos in Fortress America: Billionaires, Bureaucrats, and Body Slams* (Lexington Books, 2020). Metafilm was nominated for the Rhetoric Society of America Book Award in 2019. His essays have appeared in *Works and Days, JAC, College English*, and *Rhetoric Review*, and he has written chapters for *Tenured Bosses and Disposable Teachers* as well as *Narrative Acts: Rhetoric, Race and Identity, Knowledge*. He is a White critic committed to critical Whiteness studies, and since Hurricane Katrina made landfall in 2005, his work has consistently featured antiracist analyses of social space, popular imagery, and their overlap.

INDEX